This is an excellent book and surely comes in due time as more and more language testing and assessment demands the development of local solutions. Starting from their own experience with the development of tests in their own contexts, the authors manage to cover all the important issues to be taken into account, from construct definition to score reporting.

Gladys Quevedo-Camargo, University of Brasília

Local Language Testing: Design, Implementation, and Development captures the authors' collective years of local test development wisdom in reader-friendly language that helps to demystify the often-vexing test development process. Professors Slobodanka Dimova, Xun Yan, and April Ginther offer sage advice to a broad audience including language program directors and classroom teachers who seek to create tests locally for purposes such as placement and diagnosis. Chapters such as Scaling and Data Collection and Management serve as roadmaps to lead local test developers to an understanding of the steps in the process of test creation. *Local Language Testing* should be on the reading list of anyone seeking know-how for the creation of fair and usable assessments.

Deborah Crusan, Wright State University

A lucid and accessible account of the art of developing language tests for use in local contexts. Teachers and program directors who may have thought language testing was beyond them should think again. Three seasoned testing practitioners (Dimova, Yan and Ginther) characterize language testing as a problem-solving activity best tackled by those with an understanding of the context of concern. Reflecting on their own practical experience in diverse teaching environments, the authors outline the processes and likely challenges involved in developing and delivering custom-built tests designed for particular local needs. This book is a welcome addition to a field dominated thus far by research on large-scale commercial language tests.

Catherine Elder, University of Melbourne

D1447128

LOCAL LANGUAGE TESTING

Local Language Testing: Design, Implementation, and Development describes the language testing practice that exists in the intermediate space between large-scale standardized testing and classroom assessment, an area that is rarely addressed in the language testing and assessment literature. Covering both theory and practice, the book focuses on the advantages of local tests, fosters and encourages their use, and provides suggested ideas for their development and maintenance. The authors include examples of operational tests with well-proven track records and discuss:

- the ability of local tests to represent local contexts and values, explicitly and purposefully embed test results within instructional practice, and provide data for program evaluation and research;
- local testing practices grounded in the theoretical principles of language testing, drawing from experiences with local testing and providing practical examples of local language tests, illustrating how they can be designed to effectively function within and across different institutional contexts;
- examples of how local language tests and assessments are developed for use within a specific context and how they serve a variety of purposes (e.g., entry-level proficiency testing, placement testing, international teaching assistant testing, writing assessment, and program evaluation).

Aimed at language program directors, graduate students, and researchers involved in language program development and evaluation, this is a timely book in that it focuses on the advantages of local tests, fosters and encourages their use, and outlines their development and maintenance. It constitutes essential reading for language program directors, graduate students, and researchers involved in language program development and evaluation.

Slobodanka Dimova is an associate professor in Language Testing and the coordinator of the Test of Oral English Proficiency for Academic Staff (TOEPAS) at the University of Copenhagen, Denmark. She currently serves as the book review editor for the journal *Language Testing*, a member of the Executive Committee of the European Association of Language Testing and Assessment (EALTA), and the Chair of the Danish Network for Language Testing and Assessment (DASTEN). She has also been a language testing consultant for the Danish Ministry of Education regarding the foreign language tests administered at the end of obligatory education. Her current research interests include rater training and rater behavior for oral proficiency tests, the development and validation of scales for performance-based tests, the use of technology in language testing and assessment, and the policies and practices related to the implementation of English-medium instruction (EMI) programs at non-Anglophone universities.

Xun Yan is an assistant professor of Linguistics, Second Language Acquisition and Teacher Education (SLATE) and Educational Psychology at the University of Illinois at Urbana-Champaign (UIUC). At UIUC, he also supervises the university-level English Placement Test (EPT), designed to assess international students' writing and speaking skills. His research interests include speaking and writing assessment, scale development and validation, psycholinguistic approaches to language testing, rater behavior and cognition, and language assessment literacy. His work has been published in *Language Testing*, *Assessing Writing*, *TESOL Quarterly*, and *Journal of Second Language Writing*.

April Ginther is a professor of English at Purdue University and teaches graduate classes in language testing and quantitative research. During her tenure at Purdue, she has advised more than 20 graduate student dissertations. She is also the director of Purdue's two primary English language support programs: The Oral English Proficiency Program, the support program for international teaching assistants, and The Purdue Language and Cultural Exchange, the support program for incoming international undergraduate students. As director of both programs, she is responsible for the development, maintenance, and administration of the local tests used to evaluate the English language skills of 1,000 incoming students each academic year. She is a founding member of MwALT, the Midwest Association of Language Testers, and is a well-respected member of the international language testing community. She served as the co-editor of the journal *Language Testing* from 2012 to 2017.

LOCAL LANGUAGE TESTING

Design, Implementation, and Development

Slobodanka Dimova, Xun Yan, and April Ginther

Routledge
Taylor & Francis Group

LONDON AND NEW YORK

First published 2020
by Routledge
2 Park Square, Milton Park, Abingdon, Oxon, OX14 4RN

and by Routledge
52 Vanderbilt Avenue, New York, NY 10017

Routledge is an imprint of the Taylor & Francis Group, an informa business

© 2020 Slobodanka Dimova, Xun Yan and April Ginther

British Library Cataloguing-in-Publication Data
A catalogue record for this book is available from the British Library

Library of Congress Cataloging-in-Publication Data
Names: Dimova, Slobodanka, author. | Ginther, April, author. | Yan,
Xun, author.
Title: Local language testing : design, implementation, and development /
Slobodanka Dimova, Xun Yan and April Ginther.
Identifiers: LCCN 2019046125 (print) | LCCN 2019046126 (ebook)
Subjects: LCSH: Second language acquisition–Ability testing. |
Educational tests and measurements. | Examinations.
Classification: LCC P118.75 .D56 2020 (print) | LCC P118.75 (ebook) |
DDC 418.0076–dc23
LC record available at https://lccn.loc.gov/2019046125
LC ebook record available at https://lccn.loc.gov/2019046126

ISBN: 978-1-138-58848-6 (hbk)
ISBN: 978-1-138-58849-3 (pbk)
ISBN: 978-0-429-49224-2 (ebk)

Typeset in Bembo
by Swales & Willis, Exeter, Devon, UK

CONTENTS

8   Data collection, management, and score reporting   **158**

9   Reflections   **181**

FIGURES

TABLES

PREFACE

Directors of language programs, level coordinators within first-, second-, and foreign-language programs, and grade-level teachers in public schools often find themselves in situations where they would like to develop language tests for their programs but consider the task beyond their abilities and expertise. While they may have been exposed to testing and assessment principles in their programs of study, they typically do not consider themselves *language testers*. It's true: the specialized content knowledge associated with language testing is of considerable benefit to those who may be considering the development of a test; however, we believe that the requisite knowledge is not beyond the abilities that program directors and classroom teachers already possess. Practitioners within programs are not only well positioned for the development of local tests; they are indispensable to the process, as representing the local instructional context is what local tests are designed to do. Thus, local practitioners are the most suitable stakeholders to delineate the purpose of the tests they design.

Local Language Testing: Design, Implementation, and Development is designed for language instructors, level coordinators, and program directors – an audience we refer to as prospective language testing practitioners. Our intention is not to suggest that anyone and everyone can make a good test but rather that prospective language testing practitioners have the wherewithal to develop tests that are more than sufficient. We will argue that prospective language testing practitioners have specialized knowledge that allows them to develop assessments that are better than commercially-available alternatives, which are not explicitly linked to the contexts in which they will be employed. The information provided in this volume should allow prospective test developers to engage in the process more efficiently, effectively, and with a reduction of the uncertainty and anxiety that inevitably accompanies undertakings associated with considerable responsibility. *Local Language Testing* provides information that will allow prospective local language testers to make informed decisions as they work through the development efforts that are certain to transform, enhance, and complicate their work.

Each of us has had the advantage of studying language testing in graduate school but, more importantly, we have each developed and maintained a local test that has been embedded in and directly related to an instructional language program. These tests share the broad academic context of higher education, but we contend that the development efforts described in this book are applicable to other contexts as well.

The value of on-the-job training has enhanced the benefits of our exposure to the history and theoretical foundations of language testing. Because we have benefitted so greatly from the information provided by language testers, we have provided an annotated bibliography of selected articles on assessment at the end of each chapter for those who would like more information. In the chapters that follow, we will introduce core assessment principles and discuss them in relation to the actual development, administration, management, and revision of local tests. Our focus is on practice and purpose. We will highlight examples from operational tests with proven track records and link key concepts to practical, real-world concerns: the benefits and opportunities, the challenges and hazards, our accomplishments, and, while not exactly failures, those times when we missed the mark. Our tests have been adapted and have changed over time.

Our intention is to provide both encouragement and the means for prospective language testing practitioners to make the leap into actual practice.

ACKNOWLEDGEMENTS

We would like to express our gratitude to Catherine Elder for her constructive feedback and creative suggestions, to Kyle McIntosh for his careful edits and useful comments, and to Shareh T. Vahed and Ji-young Shin for their assistance with the further readings.

1

INTRODUCTION

Why *local* tests?

This chapter introduces the terms "local test" and "local context", offering definitions of these terms and discussing the differences between local tests and large-scale standardized tests. Local test is defined as one whose development is designed to represent the values and priorities within a local instructional program and designed to address problems that emerge out of a need within the local context in which the test will be used. "Local context" is operationalized first as the specific language curriculum with which the local test is associated and secondly as the broader target language use domain, i.e., the "situation or context in which the test-taker will be using the language outside of the test itself" (Bachman & Palmer, 1996, p. 18). The chapter also discusses the advantages and disadvantages of local tests and presents the three local tests that will be referred to throughout the book and the contexts in which they are embedded.

Introduction

Tests and assessments that are developed for use within a local context serve a variety of purposes that cannot be addressed effectively using either large-scale, commercial tests or classroom assessments. This volume, *Local Language Testing: Design, Implementation, and Development*, describes language testing practices that exist in the intermediate space between the two. We define a "local test" as one whose development is designed to represent the values and priorities within a local instructional program and designed to address problems that emerge out of a need within the context in which the test will be used. That is, local tests do not stand alone; they are embedded. We operationalize "local context" first as the specific language curriculum with which the local test is associated and second as the broader target language use domain, i.e., the "situation or context in which the test-taker will be using the language outside of the test itself" (Bachman & Palmer, 1996, p. 18).

Another key feature that distinguishes a local test from a large-scale, commercial test is that the development of a local test must, both of necessity and choice, rely on local expertise. Such expertise may be embodied in teachers, students, researchers, and program administrators who practice/work in the local context. Local test development requires the participation of each of these critical actors; however, within local test development teams, the contributions of instructors because of their representation of and familiarity with the local instructional context, are central to test development efforts.

The advantages of local tests include their design as representations of local contexts and values, the potential to link scores and performances to instructional practice, and the provision of data for program evaluation and research. While large-scale standardized tests provide scores, local tests generate both scores and data. Unfettered access to test data, item-level, raw score data, and actual performance data, is only possible when a test is locally developed.

In addition, local tests can be developed not only to provide test users with information about a test-taker's language abilities but also to provide test-takers with information about the language use characteristic of the broader context in which they will be required to perform. In other words, local tests have the potential to function as instructional devices that offer information about the performance expectations associated with the local context.

The development of local tests and their representation of local contexts and values creates the conditions for the emergence of a community of practice (Lave, 1991). Fostering this community through continued and iterative test development efforts and the use of test results to examine the success of the instructional program can lead to improvements in both the test and the program it is designed to serve. Evaluation of the test will include analyses of the fit between the test and the instructional program, and for the potential contributions of a local test to be fully realized, test development, program development, and test and program evaluation should be understood as ongoing processes, with ample time and resources devoted to these complementary efforts.

In our discussions of defining characteristics of local tests, we realized that our description requires, at least, two qualifications. Both qualifications arose in discussions of assumptions that we believe logically accompany the notion of local tests. First, because local tests are embedded in local instructional programs, it might be assumed that local tests are always small-scale. However, the local values and instructional emphases associated with the development of a local test may align with district, provincial, state, and/or national instructional standards. In this sense, even a large, national test could be considered a local test when the values represented by the test reflect distinctive features of a broader instructional context. However, the directionality of the development of a local test is a critical distinguishing feature of a local test; that is, because local tests are grounded in the local context, development and implementation is as much a bottom-up as a top-down process, allowing for not only typically top-down adoption but also bottom-up adaptation of district, provincial, state, and/or national instructional standards. At the same time, the qualification presented above is largely theoretical. Most local tests do involve relatively small populations of test-takers. (In our cases, we test between 25 and 2000 test-takers annually.)

The second qualification involves test content. Given their orientation towards local instructional values and emphases, it might be expected that local tests will not or should not resemble their large-scale counterparts; however, if the purpose of a local program is to prepare students for a standardized test at a subsequent stage of their educational programs, local tests and instructional programs may reasonably be designed to mirror and prepare students for the characteristics of the large-scale test that awaits.

In summary, unlike large-scale tests, a local language test is intentionally embedded in and designed to represent a local instructional context. The local test's relationship to the context is a central characteristic of the development of a local test and an advantage that the development and use of a local test provides. The motivation for the development of a local test typically arises out of a desire to address a problem that the use of a large-scale or a classroom assessment procedure cannot adequately address. Once a local test has been developed, the results of the test (particularly in relation to analyses of the data the test generates) can be linked and extended to the instructional purposes of the instructional program. The relationship between a local test and its context is one of the reasons that local test scores and data lend themselves to multiple and complementary local purposes, such as placement, achievement, and, most importantly, diagnosis. Program evaluation should be conducted on an ongoing and iterative manner which can lead to improvements in the test and the program it is designed to serve.

Our tests

Because local tests are the products of the contexts in which they are embedded and because we will be referring to our experiences with local test development, administration, and maintenance throughout the book, we will take the opportunity to introduce our tests and contexts at this point.

The OEPT, Purdue University

The Oral English Proficiency Test (OEPT, the Oral English Proficiency Program, 2015, 2019) is a semi-direct, computer-administered oral English proficiency test used for screening the oral English proficiency of prospective international graduate teaching assistants (ITAs) at Purdue University. Administration of the OEPT is one of the responsibilities of the Oral English Proficiency Program (OEPP), which also offers instruction for those who fail the test. The instructional side of the program consists of small-sized language classes (eight students) for prospective ITAs that emphasize individualized instruction in four hours of class time and one hour thirty minutes of individual tutoring each week.

Purdue University is a large public institution (33,000 undergraduate and 10,000 graduate students) of higher education in the state of Indiana in the United States (US). Like most large public universities in the US, Purdue has large populations of international undergraduate (15%) and graduate (50%) students. In the US, graduate students, particularly doctoral students, are funded through graduate research and teaching assistantships that cover tuition and provide living expenses. International students who want to receive teaching assistantships must demonstrate satisfactory English language proficiency before they can be offered teaching assistantships by their departments. There are many opportunities for teaching assistantships because, particularly at large public US institutions, introductory undergraduate classes are often taught by graduate teaching assistants (TAs). Science, technology, engineering, and mathematics (STEM) programs are highly populated by international graduate students, and the OEPP diagnoses and/or prepares the population of international TAs to communicate effectively in English with undergraduate students in classroom contexts.

The considerable increase in the international graduate student population in the 1980s led many US universities to require English language proficiency screening for prospective TAs (see Ginther, 2003). In 27 of the 50 states, English language proficiency is required or mandated by state legislation. From 1987 to 2001, the OEPP used the Speaking Proficiency Assessment Kit (SPEAK), retired versions of the Test of Spoken English (TSE), which had been administered as an additional component of the Test of English as a Foreign Language (TOEFL) until the introduction of its Internet version, TOEFL iBT. The OEPT was developed to replace the SPEAK in 2001 and has been revised three times since. The test is now part of a much larger testing and instructional system, which includes the OEPT itself, the OEPT Practice Test and Tutorial, the OEPT Rater Training Application, the OEPT Rater Interface, and the OEPT research database. The OEPT is administered to more than 500 prospective ITAs each academic year. Each test is rated by at least two trained raters. Approximately half of OEPT administrations are conducted, and scores reported, the week before school starts in August.

TOEPAS, the University of Copenhagen

The Test of Oral English Proficiency for Academic Staff (TOEPAS, Centre for Internationalisation and Parallel Language Use, 2009) is an oral English language proficiency test designed for non-native-speaking university lecturers who teach in English-medium instruction (EMI) degree programs. The overall purpose of the test is to certify lecturers' English language skills by assessing whether they have an adequate level of oral proficiency for lecturing and interacting with students in an EMI university setting. The TOEPAS is based on a 20-minute simulated lecture in which the test-takers present new material, give instructions, and interact with students. The lecturers/test-takers are provided with a score, a video recording, personalized written feedback, and a one-on-one, individualized feedback session/conference with a test administrator.

TOEPAS was developed and is administered by The Centre for Internationalization and Parallel Language Use (CIP), established in 2008 to augment the University's efforts to implement a language policy based on the principles of parallel language use, which is an important aspect of the internationalization process at the University of Copenhagen. The implementation of the parallel language use policy ensures consistently high standards of language use in Danish, as well as in English.

CIP functions both as a research and training center; its principal aim is to develop a research-based strategy for the enhancement of Danish and English language skills among various groups at the University. The objective of this strategy is to contribute to the strengthening of the University's international profile by supporting employees and students in meeting language-related challenges.

CIP offers language courses to a range of different groups at the University, including teachers, researchers, administrative staff, and students at all educational levels, both domestic and international. One of CIP's most important tasks is to develop and offer tailor-made language courses for employees and students at the University. Danish courses are available to employees who are non-native speakers of Danish, and English courses are available for employees and students who wish to improve their English language skills. Two important features characterize CIP's language courses: (1) they are shaped by the CIP's research findings, and (2) they are tailor-made to meet each participant's professional requirements, existing language skills, career development goals and, where relevant, teaching and preferred modes of academic publication.

The EPT, the University of Illinois at Urbana-Champaign

The English Placement Test (EPT, Linguistics Department, UIUC, 2015) is used for screening the oral and written proficiency of incoming undergraduates and graduate students at the University of Illinois at Urbana-Champaign (UIUC). Like Purdue, UIUC is a large public institution of higher learning in the US with substantial populations of international undergraduate and graduate students. The EPT is administered by the Linguistics Department and is linked to the writing and speaking courses for international students offered by the English as a Second Language (ESL) service program within the Linguistics Department. The EPT is administered to both undergraduate and graduate students and is used to place students into appropriate writing and/or oral pronunciation courses in the ESL Program. The EPT assesses English ability of newly admitted international students as validated against the English language demands of the campus. Students who are placed in one or more ESL courses must complete all their required ESL courses before graduation.

The EPT has a long history that dates back to the 1970s, but the current version was first developed in 2001. The EPT has both on-campus and online versions. While the on-campus EPT is administered mostly to graduate students, the online EPT is only administered to undergraduate students. The EPT has traditionally been administered on the UIUC campus before the first week of instruction each fall and spring semester. However, the large increase in the number of international undergraduate students at UIUC in 2008 led to the development of an online EPT to satisfy the growing need of undergraduate academic advisors for timely advising for incoming international undergraduate students. The online EPT is administered in summer only to undergraduate students via Moodle.

The EPT consists of two parts. The first part is a written test, and the second part is an oral test. The written test requires students to produce an academic essay based on the information obtained from a series of short reading passages and a short lecture. For the oral test, students are asked to complete a series of speaking tasks related to the same topic as in the writing section. If students speak intelligibly and coherently, they will be exempted from further oral testing. The EPT is administered to close to 2,000 students each academic year, the majority of whom complete the online version before arriving on campus. Although these students have been admitted, the EPT is used to place students into different levels of first-year composition classes. Each test is rated by two trained raters and the results determine whether test-takers will need to complete one or two composition courses and additional instruction in speaking.

The Ace-IN, Purdue University

The Assessment of College English, International (Ace-IN, Purdue Language and Cultural Exchange, 2015), is used for screening the general language proficiency of incoming undergraduates at Purdue University. The Ace-IN was developed as part of the Purdue Language and Cultural Exchange (PLaCE), a two-semester language support program for incoming international undergraduate students who have been admitted but will benefit from additional instruction. Enrollment in PLaCE courses does not substitute for any other general English language requirements; that is, PLaCE students must still complete the two English courses required of all undergraduate students: a first-year composition course and a communication course.

The Ace-IN consists of three modules: an elicited imitation and cloze-elide module, a free-response speaking module, and a writing module. The elicited imitation items, semi-direct speaking tasks, and the essay require human scoring. While scales have been developed for all rated sections, at present only EI is operationally scored for all students as a pre-test and post-test. Results are used primarily to track students' progress in oral fluency across the semesters they are enrolled in the program.

Originally developed as a placement test for all incoming students, the purpose changed when Purdue decided to require all incoming students who score 100 or below on the TOEFL iBT (or a comparable score on the IELTS) to enroll in the PLaCE sequence. However, students may be exempted from the second semester by meeting PLaCE exemption requirements, which include satisfactory completion of the first course, an instructor recommendation, and a passing score on all sections of the Ace-IN. Modules of the Ace-IN are scored as needed (e.g., for additional information contributing to exemption decisions).

PLaCE existed in pilot form for four years before the program was provided recurring funding in 2018. Because students must still complete additional writing and communication courses, PLaCE has focused its instructional efforts on helping students adapt to Purdue's academic environment, develop intercultural competence, and improve their speaking skills. We are still evaluating how information provided by the Ace-IN can be used most effectively within the instructional program.

Contexts and problem solving

Each test introduced above was designed to address particular problems in specific contexts. While all three universities share the context of higher education, their purposes and target test-taker populations differ. Both the OEPT and TOEPAS address the need for quality instruction, but while OEPT test-takers are ITAs, TOEPAS test-takers are primarily foreign language (L2) speakers of English who are professors, not teaching assistants. The EPT is administered to both undergraduate and graduate students and functions primarily for placement purposes into writing and speaking courses. The Ace-IN functions only within an undergraduate language support program to track student progress and to provide information for exemption from the second semester of the program course sequence. However, this summary of the tests' different purposes does not allow for appreciation of the multiple problems that developing our local tests helped each of us address. An example about the development of OEPT follows (Example 1.1).

EXAMPLE 1.1 DEVELOPMENT OF OEPT

The Oral English Proficiency Test (OEPT)

When we began development of the OEPT at Purdue, we were trying to solve a problem related to the administration of the instrument in use at that time. Since the establishment of the program in 1987 and until the development of the OEPT began in 1999, the OEPP used the SPEAK, retired versions of the Test of Spoken English (Educational Testing Service, 1980, 1982) for ITA oral English proficiency testing. The SPEAK is still used by some ITA programs today, although the test is no longer supported by the Educational Testing Service (ETS).

The administration of the SPEAK at Purdue was time-consuming and inefficient, especially with the growing influx of international graduate students. It was conducted one-on-one by test administrators who presented the prompts, recorded responses on cassette tapes, and then rated the cassette recordings later. Two language testing administrators/raters were needed for the SPEAK administration and to rate approximately 500 prospective international teaching assistants each academic year. In 1999, we began the development of the OEPT and decided to adopt a semi-direct, computer-administered testing format, primarily to ease the administrative burdens associated with our administration of the SPEAK. The adoption of the semi-direct, computer-delivered testing format allowed for group administration of the new test and reduced the time needed for administration and rating by 50%.

The development of this new test also afforded the opportunities associated with local test development that were alluded to above. Because the SPEAK was a general language proficiency test, it was not linked in any way to the ITA context, and the development of a new test created an opportunity to represent the local context. However, our initial OEPT test development efforts can be considered a failure because our first pass resulted in items that were, for the most part, simply replications of SPEAK items. The influence of our long use of and familiarity with the SPEAK was considerable. Had we stopped there, we would have simply had an old test on a new platform.

Instead, we shifted development efforts in order to represent the kinds of tasks and activities that ITAs perform in instructional contexts at Purdue. Test prompts were designed to introduce aspects of the context (*When you are a teaching assistant, you will have occasion to ...*) along with instructions for successful completion of the test task. Representing the local ITA instructional context became a central part of our revised test development efforts. These efforts were successful and, in response to our pilot, one test-taker commented, "Taking the test gave me an idea about what teaching assistants actually have to do." In addition, when we developed the scale for the OEPT, scores were directly related to the test-taker's readiness to perform duties as a classroom instructor. It is important to note that for some incoming graduate students, the OEPT serves as one of the few – perhaps only – introductions to ITA duties and responsibilities provided before the first day of class.

At the same time, we decided to train all OEPP classroom instructors as OEPT raters. OEPP instructors are well versed in the characteristics of the test; indeed, because instructors are raters, they are responsible for placement into and out of the instructional side of the program. This dual role as instructor and rater sets the stage for our instructional interventions. Those test-takers who do not pass the OEPT can enroll in the instructional side of the ITA program, which includes 4 hours of class time, a 30-minute individual session with the instructor, and a 50-minute tutorial with a tutor. OEPP class size is limited to eight students, and the generous support that students receive allows us to individualize instruction. One of the first instructional encounters that enrolled students have with their instructors and tutors, referred to as the OEPT Review, focuses on each test-taker's OEPT score and recorded item responses. After one student completed this OEPT Review, he commented, "This is the first time I have fully understood why I got the score that I got on a language test."

The development of the OEPT allowed us to address not only the initial, motivating problem of test administration, but also construct representation, instructors' understandings and uses of test scores, and test-takers' understandings of test scores. Over time, the OEPT scale was extended to provide the foundation for the self-evaluations, volunteer audience evaluations, and instructor evaluations associated with the four presentations that students in the program complete each semester. We consider the OEPT a good example of a local test that is fully integrated within the instructional context it was developed to serve and of the opportunities that local test development offers.

Large-scale language tests and academic language testing

Our discussion of the OEPT above illustrates not only the potential of local testing but also some of the differences between general language proficiency testing and the development and use of a test linked to and embedded in an instructional program. It is interesting to wonder, given the potential benefits of local language testing, why more attention has not been given to the development of local tests. Large-scale language tests like the Test of English as a Foreign Language (TOEFL) and the International English Language Test System (IELTS) cast a long shadow, and so it makes sense in this introduction to take a moment to consider the origins and preoccupations of large-scale test developers, the field of academic language testing, and academic language testers.

The origins and growth of language testing as a recognized subfield in applied linguistics is associated with the development of large-scale tests of English language proficiency that are used for admission to institutions of higher education. Because large-scale standardized tests must address the proficiency of test-takers without reference to any particular context, descriptions of performance at different levels of the scale are necessarily general, e.g., descriptors used for performance on TOEFL subscales are *high, intermediate, low* or *good, fair, weak* (see TOEFL iBT scale descriptors, Educational Testing Service, 2019). These scale descriptors are indeed useful, especially in terms of restricting admission at the lowest levels; however, general descriptors cannot provide information on the finer characteristics of performance of a student from China as compared to a student at the same level from Denmark or from India, all of whom can be assumed to have arrived at their level of proficiency in different instructional contexts with different instructional emphases. The stakes are high for both the test developer and the test-taker because a high-stakes test developer must deliver an instrument that produces a score that is an accurate and valid estimation of the test-taker's ability regardless of who that student is, where the student is from, or what the student has experienced, so establishing a test's technical qualities and developing arguments for the test's representation of underlying and necessarily abstract language constructs take center stage.

Language testers attend to the measurement linguistic characteristics of tests, and the field of language testing has been described as a hybrid of these fields (Davies, 1984). As a result, language testing is often perceived as esoteric – beyond the reach and interest of many program directors and language instructors. Language testers contribute to this impression by emphasizing the difficulty and complexity of language testing, along with reported deficiencies in the assessment literacy of teachers and practitioners. However, many appropriate test development and analysis procedures are well within teachers' and program directors' abilities. Indeed, the tenets of good language testing practice are familiar to instructors and program directors and will be recognized in the following section.

In 1961, John Carroll laid the foundation for the development of language testing as an academic sub-specialty in applied linguistics with his paper "Fundamental Considerations in Testing for English Language Proficiency of Foreign Students", presented at a conference organized to address the need for and development of a test of English language proficiency for university admissions purposes. As Ginther and McIntosh (2018) explain, "Carroll contrasted the discrete-structuralist approach, represented by Lado (1961), with his own integrative approach that emphasized productive and receptive modes, 'real world' settings, and communicative purposes" (p. 848). Carroll's approach is familiar to language teachers and program directors because his arguments were foundational to the development of communicative language teaching.

Of Carroll's presentation, Spolsky (1995) noted, "This may have well been the first call for testing communicative effect" (p. 224), providing impetus for the rich and varied theoretical and practical discussions of language testing and assessment that followed, including Canale and Swain's (1980) "Theoretical Bases of Communicative Approaches to Second Language Teaching and Testing", along with Bachman's (1990) and Bachman and Palmer's (1996) extended models of communicative competence. Furthermore, Carroll's (1961) paper heralded not only the development of the TOEFL, but also anticipated its transformations across versions: from the TOEFL Paper-based test (PBT), with its decidedly discrete/structuralist orientation, to the TOEFL Computer-based test (CBT), with its then innovative adaptive listening and structure subsections but more traditional, linear, multiple-choice reading subsection, and finally to the introduction of the TOEFL Internet-based test (TOEFL iBT) in 2005, which now includes subsections that incorporate and integrate writing and speaking skills (Ginther & McIntosh, 2018).

An important point for the purposes of our examination of local tests is that Carroll's (1961) discussions of testing tasks and methods, from discrete items focusing on points of grammar to integrated items and performance tasks, all remain viable options for the local test developer with a particular purpose in mind (see Chapter 4, Test Tasks). The selection of items, formats, and methods will depend on the instructional values and purposes of the language program in which a local test is embedded. While the assessment of the productive skills of speaking and writing is now part of TOEFL's standard test administration, in sharp contrast to the absence of speaking and the indirect measurement of writing with multiple-choice structure/vocabulary items that characterized the earliest versions of the TOEFL PBT, we believe that the fullest realization of Carroll's vision (i.e., productive and receptive modes, "real world" settings, and communicative purposes) can be more fully achieved when tests are linked to local instructional contexts in which communicative purposes are emphasized.

The shift toward functional, communicative tests led to considerations of interactivity and a focus on performance (McNamara, 1996) and was accompanied by the development and popularity of the American Council on the Teaching of Foreign Languages (ACTFL, 1986, 2004) proficiency guidelines and the Common European Framework of Reference (CEFR, Council of Europe, 2001), both of which are now part and parcel of the communicative language teaching and testing movement. Few would deny the intuitive appeal of language proficiency guidelines that easily lend themselves to the development of classroom activities and provide a common understanding of an assumed, if not empirically demonstrated, developmental progression (see Hawkins & Filipovic, 2012 on the relation of selected linguistic features and their relation to CEFR levels; Leahy & Wiliam, 2011 on developing learner progressions; and Baten & Cornillie, 2019 on elicited imitation and proficiency levels). Both teachers and program directors are well versed in the communicative movement, and local language tests linked to an instructional program can function as laboratories where links between testing, assessment, and instruction can be forged and examined.

Local language tests begin where large-scale tests end. As briefly discussed above, the primary purpose of large-scale tests (e.g., TOEFL and IELTS) is general language proficiency testing for admission/selection into institutions of higher education, and they serve that purpose well. However, their use is limited for placement, diagnosis, and achievement. The scope of a local test often involves a closer look at a limited range of proficiency, and the restriction of range results in the challenge and the benefit of focus or a shift in grain size – like changing optics to get a more detailed look at a microscopic specimen on a slide. A local test isolates a segment of a scale, expands the segment, and then, provides a new and revised scale through which relevant qualities of performance are highlighted.

Local language tests also provide the opportunity to shed light on and examine the utility of language proficiency guidelines. While the authors of guidelines are careful to state that guidelines may or may not actually represent developmental progressions, guidelines provide a resource for the development of instructional objectives and goals, classroom activities, and local test tasks within selected levels. Some activities, items, and tasks will work better than others. The development of local language tests provides an opportunity to examine what works in relation to instructional programs.

In the very short overview we provided above, we hope that we have highlighted some of the common values that large-scale and local tests share but also how language testing literature can serve as a valuable resource for local test development efforts. At the end of each chapter, we also provide briefly annotated suggestions for further reading that may be of particular interest to prospective local language test developers.

We have argued that the advantage of local language tests is that they can be used to inform teaching, curriculum, and ongoing development of language support programs. This chapter has discussed the potential for local language tests to become an integral part of language teaching programs by providing baseline information about test-takers' entry proficiency levels, information about students' progress over time, and information that can be used for program evaluation. The remainder of this volume focuses on the information that prospective local language test developers need to consider in order to realize these goals. The volume is organized into the following chapters, in which we consider, following both Carroll and Bachman, fundamental considerations in the development of local language tests.

Organization of the rest of this volume

Chapter 2: Local tests, local contexts

As we have argued throughout the introduction, a benefit of the development of local language tests is that they can be linked to and embedded in local instructional contexts. In this chapter we extend our discussion of context. We begin with a discussion of how the status of English as a lingua franca has influenced the development of national, state, and institutional educational policies and has affected the development of local language tests and instructional programs. We continue with a discussion of test purpose and functionality.

Chapter 3: Local test development

This chapter covers a broad array of considerations that need to be taken into account during the development of a local language test. It addresses the importance of clearly articulating the test's purpose in the specification design and of the roles that needs analysis and test developers' experience play in the process of item type selection and context representation.

Chapter 4: Test tasks

This chapter presents a variety of tasks that can be used to assess different skills. We argue that there is no single best method and that awareness of a variety of methods enhances test development options.

Chapter 5: Local test delivery

There are a number of issues related to the selection of a test delivery platform (paper-based, digital, online). This chapter examines the advantages of technology in improving test administration efficiency, while also outlining the difficulties test developers may encounter in the process of digital platform design, especially regarding cost-effectiveness, communication with software developers, and maintenance of the system over time.

Chapter 6: Scaling

This chapter focuses on different types of language test scoring systems, with particular attention to scale design for performance-based tests in speaking and writing. Alongside the presentation of different types of scales (analytic, holistic, primary-trait), this chapter includes discussions of different scale design methods (data-driven, theory-driven) and benchmarking, i.e., finding representative performances of each scalar level.

Chapter 7: Raters and rater training

This chapter describes the processes of rater selection, initial training, and continuous norming. It addresses different methods of rater training and the importance of rater agreement for the reliability of test results, as well as different instruments and methods that can be employed for the analysis of rater behavior and inter- and intra-rater reliability.

Chapter 8: Data collection, management, and reporting

While the chapters "Local test development" and "Local test delivery" deal with the front-end of test development, this chapter examines the back-end, i.e., data collection and management. More specifically, it looks at the kinds of test-taker data that can be beneficial to collect (e.g., background bio data) and how the data can be stored, organized, and retrieved (e.g., relational databases). Database design and security are at the center of these discussions. We argue that appropriate data collection and management need to be explicitly incorporated into the test design in the earliest stages of development because they are essential for the ongoing analyses of test reliability, validity, and extended research.

Chapter 9: Reflections

In this final chapter, we discuss the lessons learned through the development, administration, and maintenance of the four tests that we have developed and used as examples throughout the book.

Further reading

Bachman, L. F. (1990). *Fundamental considerations in language testing*. Oxford: Oxford University Press.

Bachman's *Fundamental considerations* provides an introduction of issues that must be addressed when developing language tests and an analysis of some of the challenges that a language test developer may encounter during the development and the use of an instrument used for measurement. The book provides a thorough explanation of classical measurement theory, generalizability theory, and item response theory. However, the reader of this book must keep in mind that the book is more concerned with "considerations" rather than "applications" of these concepts. The discussion of validity is also one of the salient features of this book as he describes validity as a unitary concept that requires evidence to support the various inferences we make on the basis of test scores.

Bachman, L. F., & Palmer, A. S. (1996). *Language testing in practice: Designing and developing useful language tests* (Vol. 1). Oxford: Oxford University Press.

Bachman and Palmer's (1996) main objective is to develop readers' competency in language test development and use. The book consists of three parts. Part one explores the concepts of test usefulness, test task characteristics, and characteristics of language use and language test performance. The second part, "language test development", discusses the practice of test development and use, from planning for a test to its administration and scoring. Some of the topics discussed in this section of the book include the design of a test (i.e., test purpose description, TLU domain analysis, construct definition, evaluation of usefulness, and allocation of resources), operationalization (i.e., development of test tasks and a blueprint, writing instructions, and choosing a scoring method), and test administration (i.e., collecting feedback, analyzing test scores, and archiving). The last part of the book provides ten sample test development projects, which include good examples of activities language test developers can use in their own test development endeavors.

Elder, C. (2017). Language assessment in higher education. In E. Shohamy, I. G. Or, & S. May (Eds.), *Language testing and assessment* (3rd Ed, pp. 271–286). New York: Springer.

Elder (2017) critically reviews validity issues concerning English language assessment in higher education, focusing on entry, post-entry, and exit tests. The author begins the review by discussing early developments in language testing led by two large-scale English language admission tests and the theoretical foundations of language proficiency. The author connects large-scale admission tests to alternative pathways such as preparatory courses or/and post-entry local tests and emphasizes the importance of not only identifying language needs of linguistically at-risk students but also providing appropriate intervention throughout their learning trajectories. She calls for attention to refining construct representation of English proficiency in the context of English as a lingua franca in higher education and establishing institutional policies to incorporate language assessment and examination of student growth over time.

Fulcher, G. (2010). *Practical language testing.* London, UK: Hodder Education.

Fulcher (2010) discusses test design, development, and administration. As stated by the author, the book is *practical* in that it focuses on both the *knowledge* and the *skills* necessary in developing a language test. The final chapter addresses issues related to teaching to a test. Because teachers often need to respond to the students' and parents' concerns with passing high-stakes tests, "teaching to the test" is an important consideration. A useful chapter in the book is Chapter 8, titled "Aligning Tests to Standards". This chapter discusses what standards are, why a test developer might need to use these standards, and what unintended consequences of the use these standards could be. Overall, this introductory yet all-inclusive book is perfect for providing a good overview of the language testing topics necessary for any novice language tester.

References

ACTFL. (1986). ACTFL proficiency guidelines (Revised). Hastings-on-Hudson, NY: American Council on the Teaching of Foreign Languages.

ACTFL. (2004). ACTFL proficiency guidelines (Revised). Hastings-on-Hudson, NY: American Council on the Teaching of Foreign Languages. Retrieved January 1, 2004, World Wide Web www.sil.org/lingualinks/LANGUAGELEARNING/OtherResources/ACTFLProficiencyGuidelines/ACTFLProficiencyGuidelines.htm

Bachman, L. S. (1990). *Fundamental considerations in language testing.* Oxford: Oxford University Press.

Bachman, L. S., & Palmer, A. S. (1996). *Language testing in practice: Designing and developing useful language tests.* Oxford: Oxford University Press.

Baten, K., & Cornillie, F. (2019). Elicited imitation as a window into developmental stages. *Journal of the European Second Language Association, 3*(1), 23–34.

Canale, M., & Swain, M. (1980). Theoretical bases of communicative approaches to second language teaching and testing. *Applied Linguistics, 1*(1), 1–47.

Carroll, J. B. (1961). Fundamental considerations in testing for English language proficiency of foreign students. In H. B. Allen & R. N. Campbell (Eds.), (1972), *Teaching English as a second language: A book of readings.* New York: McGraw Hill 313–321.

Centre for Internationalisation and Parallel Language Use. (2009). *Test of Oral English Proficiency for Academic Staff ((TOEPAS).* Copenhagen: The University of Copenhagen.

Council of Europe. (2001). *Common European framework of reference for languages: Learning, teaching, assessment.* Cambridge: Cambridge University Press.

Davies, A. (1984). Validating three tests of language proficiency. *Language Testing, 1*(1), 50–69.

Educational Testing Service.. (1980). *Test of spoken English.* Princeton, NJ: Educational Testing Service.

Educational Testing Service. (1982). *Guide to SPEAK.* Princeton, NJ: Educational Testing Service.

Educational Testing Service (2019). Performance Descriptors for the TOEFL iBT Test. Princeton, NJ: Educational Testing Service. https://www.ets.org/s/toefl/pdf/pd-toefl-ibt.pdf

Ginther, A. (2003). International teaching assistant testing: Policies and methods. In D. Douglas (Ed.), *English language testing in US colleges and universities* (pp. 57–84).

Ginther, A., & McIntosh, K. (2018). Language testing and assessment. In A. Phakiti, P. De Costa, L. Plonsky, & S. Starfield (Eds.), *The Palgrave handbook of applied linguistics research methodology* (pp. 845–867). New York: Palgrave.

Hawkins, J. M., & Filipovic, L. (2012). *Criterial features in L2 english: Specifying the reference levels of the common European framework.* Cambridge: Cambridge University Press.

Lado, R. (1961). *Language testing: The construction and use of foreign language tests.* London: Longman.

Purdue Language and Cultural Exchange. (2015). *The Assessment of College English, International (Ace-IN).* West Lafayette, IN: Purdue University.

Lave, J. (1991). Situating learning in communities of practice. *Perspectives on Socially Shared Cognition, 2,* 63–82.

Leahy, S., & Wiliam, D. (2011, April). Devising learning progressions. Paper presented at the annual meeting of the American Educational Research Association: Symposium on How to Build Learning Progressions, New Orleans, LA.

Linguistics Department, University of Illinois, Urbana-Champaign. (2015). *The English Proficiency Test (EPT).* Champaign-Urbana, IL: The University of Illinois.

McNamara, T. (1996). *Measuring second language performance.* London, England: Longman.

Oral English Proficiency Program. (2015). *The Oral English Proficiency Test.3 (OEPT.3).* West Lafayette, IN: Purdue University.

Oral English Proficiency Program. (2019). *OEPT technical manual.* West Lafayette, IN: Purdue University.

Spolsky, B. (1995). *Measured words: The development of objective language testing.* Oxford: Oxford University Press.

2
LOCAL TESTS, LOCAL CONTEXTS

This chapter begins by discussing the variety of contexts that need to be considered when developing a local test. For example, it presents variations of the contexts in which English is used as a lingua franca and the various contexts of language instruction. Then, test purpose and instructional goals and objectives are considered. The chapter argues that within local programs, the original purpose of a local test may be extended, from summative to formative purposes; the data generated by a local test has the potential to serve as the basis for diagnosis and feedback. Local tests can de designed to contribute to a larger assessment system when the test aligns with and is embedded in the local instructional context.

Introduction

As we argued in Chapter 1, the local context is central to the design, implementation, and maintenance of local tests. This relationship with the local context may, in fact, be the most important distinguishing feature of a local test. Because large-scale tests must reasonably focus on commonalities across a broad spectrum of language use, they may exclude specific characteristics of language use associated with particular contexts. Local tests can address the gap between large-scale and local representations of language use by targeting the domain that lies between the general and specific.

Influential characteristics of context can be represented in many ways because educational endeavors are influenced by the broad sociocultural, economic, and political contexts in which they are embedded, as well as the personal values, practical needs, and available resources of the stakeholders who interact within these broader contexts. In this chapter, we discuss the different levels of context that have influenced the development of our local English language tests and how the needs of stakeholders within these contexts were addressed, in part, through the development of local language tests. We begin with a discussion of the ever-increasing demand for developing proficiency in English in differing educational contexts around the world.

The status and influence of English in a global society

English is now widely recognized as the world's primary lingua franca. As Pennington and Hoekje (2010) remark:

> The fact that so much of human knowledge and the world's information in the present day is transmitted and developed in English means that at higher levels of learning, a knowledge of English is a virtual necessity. To be competitive in an increasingly international academic marketplace and to keep on top of developments in most fields requires a high level of knowledge in English, and this fact has contributed significantly to the accelerated and continuing spread of the language.
>
> *(pp. 4–5)*

Because of the importance of English in the development and transmission of knowledge across a wide range of disciplines and professions, institutions of higher education located in Anglophone countries where English is the primary language (e.g., the United States, the United Kingdom, Canada, Australia) have been – and remain – attractive destinations for international students.

Increasing enrollment of international students in the United States (US) and other Anglophone countries began most noticeably in the late 1980s. International student enrollment was encouraged, particularly at the graduate levels in science, technology, engineering, and mathematics (STEM), because of the institutional need to fill graduate classes, provide staff to support research, and provide staff for undergraduate teaching (Ginther, 2003). Concerns with preparedness, particularly with respect to instructional duties, led to requirements for screening the English language proficiency of prospective international teaching assistants (ITAs) and the development of many local language tests. The OEPT at Purdue, introduced in Chapter 1 and referred to throughout this volume, was developed to address this need.

Universities and colleges in Anglophone countries facilitated another shift in the early 2000s when international student enrollment, formerly associated primarily with international graduate admissions, extended to undergraduate admissions as well. Many institutions of higher education now welcome international undergrads in order to promote internationalization on campus and increase tuition revenue. Worries about maintaining high enrollments of Chinese undergraduate and graduate students led the University of Illinois to take out an insurance policy to protect against the loss of revenue that a decline in Chinese student enrollment would precipitate.

Competition among educational institutions within and between Anglophone countries to maintain and increase international enrollments has led to relatively liberal admission policies and has revealed problems with the use and interpretation of standardized language proficiency test scores for admission purposes (Ginther & Elder, 2014; Ginther & Yan, 2017). The importance of score use and interpretation increases as institutions compete to meet enrollment targets. Selectivity competes with enrollment, and increasing enrollment has led to the need to develop high-quality post-entry tests, assessments, and instructional support (Read, 2016).

Anglophone countries also remain attractive destinations for pre-entry university intensive English language instruction. These residential programs, which are required to provide at least 20 hours of English language instruction a week, are usually associated with an institution of higher education where entry may be facilitated upon program completion. Enrollment in intensive language institutes is linked to the economic strength and political conditions of the countries from which the students come, as evidenced by marked shifts in Iranian, Kuwaiti, Saudi Arabian, Japanese, Korean, Indian, and Chinese student enrollments in Anglophone countries since the 1980s. The survival of intensive language institutes depends largely on their ability to anticipate and meet the instructional needs of rapidly changing student populations. Information provided by local tests for placement, promotion, and exit is useful in these contexts and can fulfill a variety of purposes.

For example, local tests could be utilized in the US at the elementary and secondary level to provide appropriate social services and instructional support for language learners. Increased mobility of families and children throughout the world has resulted in increased pressure on elementary and secondary schools to provide appropriate social services and instructional support for language learners. Historically, in the United States, language learners might have been enrolled in a variety of instructional programs, such as bilingual maintenance or transitional. However, since the turn of the 21st century, and partly in response to the emphasis placed on English in national policies associated with No Child Left Behind (NCLB), instructional programs for language learners are now primarily English-only.

Nevertheless, US educators are currently optimistic about the possibilities presented by the 2015 passage of the Every Student Succeeds Act (ESSA), which has replaced No Child Left Behind (NCLB). Federal reauthorizations of funding for K-12 education often introduce shifts in priorities, and the shifts signaled by ESSA are substantial. Funds are provided to districts and schools to streamline testing procedures, reduce redundancies, and improve the use of assessments and to develop pilot programs that highlight the development of assessments focused on teaching and learning (Brown, Boser, Sargrad, & Marchitello, 2016). Positive aspects of the current reforms include a focus on teaching and learning rather than accountability, on growth rather than proficiency, and on the use of multiple assessments embedded in classroom practice rather than on standardized tests. These reforms have increased the need and opportunities for teachers to develop expertise in the development of local tests and classroom assessments.

National standards and English language proficiency in non-Anglophone contexts

Given the status of English as a lingua franca, the opportunities and stakes for language learners in non-Anglophone countries have also increased. The ascendance of the Common European Framework of Reference (CEFR) (North, 2014) reflects the increasing importance of language learning in multilingual contexts. The CEFR was developed with reference to any and all languages, and particularly with the intent to develop and protect minority languages in Europe. The influence of the CEFR has been "widespread and deep, impacting on curricula, syllabuses, teaching materials, tests and assessment systems and the development of scales of language proficiency geared to the six main levels [A1, A2, B1, B2, C1, C2] of the CEFR" (Alderson, 2002, p. 8). Obtaining B2 in English language proficiency is the expected outcome of secondary instruction in European contexts where English language learning is introduced in early primary grades and then emphasized throughout students' primary and secondary educational careers.

The influence of the CEFR, particularly with reference to English, has extended far beyond the boundaries of the European Union. For example, many countries in South America, including Argentina, Brazil, Chile, Colombia, Costa Rica, Ecuador, Mexico, Panama, and Uruguay, now require that students enrolled in national tertiary institutions demonstrate proficiency, not at the intermediate level in English, but at the B2 level of the CEFR *as a graduation requirement* (Cronquist & Fiszbein, 2017). Policies requiring B2 in English upon graduation are explicitly stated in the national language policies of each of the countries mentioned above. B2 is also commonly required for admission of international students in European tertiary institutions with medium of instruction other than English (Deygers, Zeidler, Vilcu, & Carlsen, 2018).

In China, the development of a national counterpart to the CEFR, the China Standards of English (CSE), has been underway since the early 2000s. Capstone results include national Chinese standards for English that are linked to the instructional goals and objectives outlined in China's College English Curriculum Requirements (CECR) (Ministry of Education, 2007). Much like the CEFR, the CSE standards and level descriptors will serve as guidelines for English teaching, learning, and assessment.

To address the growing need for students to develop proficiency in English at home and abroad, English language instruction consumes increasing amounts of instructional time and is being provided at ever earlier levels of instruction. Indeed, English language instruction has become a staple of primary, secondary, and tertiary education around the world. Language education in non-Anglophone countries may employ Content and Language Integrated Learning (CLIL) approaches, especially in elementary and secondary education. While CLIL is an instructional approach that may be applied to learning any language through disciplinary content, English-medium instruction (EMI) in tertiary institutions is implemented primarily for content learning and may not have a language learning component. The growing implementation of EMI at non-Anglophone universities has been associated with these universities' internationalization strategies, i.e., recruitment of international students and teachers and development of international curricula. Traditionally, in EMI courses, content (e.g., science, math, history) is taught and learnt in English; however, considering the linguistic diversity of students and professors, some universities present content instruction in other languages as well. The contexts and nomenclature associated with CLIL and EMI are legion and have yet to be sorted (Dimova & Kling, forthcoming), but there is no doubt that these programs are increasingly popular throughout the world, particularly in Europe.

EMI programs are distinctive because they typically involve professors and students who are users of English as an additional language in non-Anglophone contexts. For example, TOEPAS (introduced in Chapter 1) was developed as a screening device to ensure adequate English language proficiency of professors at the University of Copenhagen who teach in EMI programs. These professors are primarily Danish, and students are typically Danish who have learned English in their secondary education. However, the population of professors and students also includes first language speakers of languages besides Danish. These international students and scholars may need and want to develop proficiency in both English and Danish, and they are given opportunities to develop proficiency in both. Ideally, by supporting the development of English *and* the primary language(s) of the home/host country, students and scholars will be able to participate more fully in the disciplinary developments of their fields internationally while enhancing and extending disciplinary-specific developments at home.

The growth of EMI reflects non-Anglophone universities' desire to support domestic students in the development of both language skills and disciplinary knowledge in English, but not English alone. At the University of Copenhagen, for example, students are encouraged to develop skills in additional languages besides English and Danish. In essence, the guiding principle is more students, more languages (Holmen, 2015). The need for domestic students to maintain and develop academic language proficiency in Danish, English, and additional languages is largely supported. Providing EMI graduate programs increases the University's prospects for maintaining its population of domestic students and also attracts international students who might have otherwise gone to an Anglophone country for their graduate study.

The concomitant growth in the number of Anglophone university branches in host countries (particularly US universities' joint ventures in China and the Middle East) can be viewed, in part, as a response to the viability of EMI in non-Anglophone countries. The growth of these branch campuses reflects a desire on the part of Anglophone universities to protect their market share of "international" students by providing those students with the option to remain at home. In short, the spread of English as a truly global lingua franca has resulted in a situation where traveling to an Anglophone country in order to participate in programs that offer intensive or advanced English language instruction is becoming less necessary as non-Anglophone countries develop viable, home-grown options of their own.

The same adaptability in the development of language programs that is associated with the status and spread of English as a global lingua franca can also be a part of the development of local tests. The development and use of local language tests allow relatively easy adaption to local instructional needs. The specificities of the constructs in English as a Lingua Franca (ELF) contexts – the complexity of the multilingual contexts – can be represented in local tests designed to reflect characteristics of the local context. As Dimova and Kling (forthcoming) point out,

> … the one-size-fits-all fallacy becomes evident, as what could be considered an appropriate course of action for one context may not be relevant for another. However, we can also see commonalities that we can draw on and learn from, given our needs and contexts.

However, the potential contributions of local tests to instruction requires a shift on the part of both prospective test developers and test score users in order to bring the test from its traditional position outside of instruction to an inside position that contributes more fully to instruction.

As a test developer of a local language test, you should seek out opportunities to ground the test within the local language program by linking it to instructional goals, learning outcomes, and instructional practices, as well as by involving different stakeholders (instructors, students, parents, administrators) in the testing process. Before we proceed with the principles and considerations in the actual test development process, however, we need to explore first the possibilities for embedding the test within the local context, beginning with a discussion of test purpose.

Local contexts and test purpose – decisions about test-takers

Decisions about test development and subsequent use are governed by the intended test purpose. When identifying the test purpose, it is important to establish which language abilities, or which aspects of the language ability, will be targeted on the test and how that reflects the values and goals of the instructional program. The selected abilities are referred to as the *construct* in language testing. Since large-scale standardized tests must address the proficiency of test-takers across a broad range of proficiency and without reference to any particular context, descriptions of performance at different levels of the scale are necessarily general (Educational Testing Service, 2019). These scale descriptors are associated with a rich research tradition and provide an excellent representation of proficiency across levels (all linked to the CEFR); however, general descriptors provide limited information about the finer characteristics of level performance or how a particular score might relate to a test-taker's performance on critical tasks within an instructional context. A local test typically amplifies a given level on a scale (e.g., most OEPT test-takers score 20–24, or B2, on the TOEFL iBT speaking subsection). Thus, the data that local tests produce can be used to take a closer look at the characteristics of performance within a level that is only generally represented on a large-scale test.

Developing a test may help prospective language testing practitioners address a variety of problems. In broad terms, language tests can be categorized as attempts to address four kinds of problems: proficiency, placement, achievement, and diagnosis.

Although a student may initially be placed within an instructional level, the proficiency of test-takers often requires a closer look. Two students, both having completed four years of foreign language instruction, may obtain different levels of proficiency and may be placed into beginning, intermediate, or advanced language classes. Although a test-taker's proficiency may be considered sufficient for entry into a domain of use (such as the minimum needed for admission), it may be insufficient for advanced or specialized purposes (such as teaching an introductory class within a program). Given different proficiency levels at entry, test-takers may benefit from support. Once support is indicated, both students and instructors want to make the most efficient use of the time available for instruction. Appropriate placement into instructional levels is the primary purpose of placement testing.

When students are found to be in need of additional support, instructors may want to get a better idea of test-takers' strengths and weaknesses. Students with varying educational opportunities and experiences often have different sets of skills. Test-takers may have sub-scores that add up to the same total score but represent very different skills. A score user, such as an advisor or instructor, may infer that a student's strengths are consistent across skills, particularly when basing the assessment on face-to-face encounters with a student whose speaking abilities are high, but a closer look may reveal lower abilities in other skills (e.g., reading, writing). Even within a given skill (e.g., speaking), the sub-skills (e.g., intelligibility, fluency of delivery, coherence of message) may differ when examined in different ways. Uncovering students' strengths and weaknesses across and within skills is the primary purpose of diagnostic testing.

When instructors and program directors want – or are required – to provide evidence that students have met instructional goals and objectives, they need to be able to demonstrate how a curriculum provides opportunities to meet intended program outcomes. The importance of evidence has grown with the expectation that programs, institutions, school districts, states, and even nations can and should demonstrate the effectiveness of their programs (known as the "accountability movement" in the United States). Appropriate and accurate estimates of success or failure in a program of study is the primary purpose of achievement testing.

The broad purposes of proficiency, placement, diagnosis, and achievement are complementary and often overlap. Language testers regularly caution test users and developers that a test designed for one purpose should not be used for another purpose unless it is validated for both. While we agree in principle, local language tests often serve multiple purposes. Local language tests produce more than a score; they provide accessible data. For example, a local test designed for placement that provides both item-level scores and records of actual speaking and/or writing performances may also be used for diagnosis. In addition, since the purpose of local language tests is embedded in instructional goals and outcomes, a test that serves well for placement (a pre-test) may also serve well for achievement, examination of gain scores, and/or program evaluation (post-test). Therefore, developing multiple forms of a single test and adopting it for different uses within a single local context makes sense. A final important purpose served by local testing and assessment is research. Local language tests produce a wealth of data that can be adapted to address program and research purposes simultaneously.

While the decision to embark on the development of a test is often associated with the broad purposes introduced above, the actual trigger for test development is often something far more practical, such as the desire to improve administrative efficiency or to reduce expenses. Fortunately, technology like audio capture and playback, which was once available only to large-scale test developers or the technologically savvy, now lies within the reach of the average computer users. It is likely, as a growing number of digital instructional and administrative platforms (e.g., Blackboard, Bright Space, Moodle, GoSignMeUp) become more accessible and begin to offer additional functions, that language program administrators and classroom instructors will take full advantage of these resources to aid in their test development efforts. Perhaps the next stage in the development of language testing as a field (Spolsky, 1995) will be the era of local language tests.

In summary, the purpose of a test, in addition to addressing the construct of interest, must also take into account the decisions that will be made based on test scores. The initial purpose of a local test is to make a decision about test-takers (e.g., screening, placement, and/or diagnosis). These purposes are complementary. The screening purpose of tests helps select individuals who possess the necessary language requirements associated with an educational program of study or a job. When screening is the initial purpose of a local test, results are often extended to placement. If the language programs in educational institutions offer courses that include different proficiency levels or that focus on different language skills, then these programs may extend the use of scores to place incoming students into an appropriate level of the language course. For example, some high schools in Denmark offer Danish courses for Danish as a second language students at three different proficiency levels, and so they need a test that assists in placement. Similarly, results from the OEPT are used to place students into two instructional levels. The use of a local test first for screening, then for placement, anticipates and may then support subsequent instruction.

More than a score – maximizing test functionality by extending test purpose to diagnosis

In most local contexts, a single test may easily lend itself to functionality beyond the test's initial purpose. Increasing the potential for the use of a test beyond its initial purpose requires that test developers and program coordinators anticipate the extended, viable functions that test results might serve, such as placement. However, the more interesting and potentially beneficial extension of test purpose lies with diagnosis. The diagnostic purpose extends test use to the identification of the language-related strengths and weaknesses that test-takers possess so that they can obtain the relevant language instruction that will allow them to meet program outcomes. Extensions of test use to diagnosis are possible because local tests produce a vast wealth of performance data in addition to the provision of a score. The following are examples that illustrate the extended purpose of language tests (Examples 2.1 and 2.2).

EXAMPLE 2.1 THE EXTENDED PURPOSE OF TOEPAS HERE

The dual purpose of TOEPAS

The purpose of the TOEPAS was two-fold from the beginning: (1) to screen university lecturers for adequate oral English proficiency needed to teach in English-medium instruction (EMI) programs; and (2) to diagnose the strengths and weaknesses of their oral English skills so that lecturers could obtain relevant instructional support. Based on the test results, department heads or program coordinators not only make decisions about whether the lecturers should be assigned to teach EMI courses, but also what type of support they need to become ready or to improve their language skills in order to teach in EMI.

Results from the TOEPAS are used as the basis for individual written feedback reports, followed by oral feedback with an examiner. The feedback focuses on the strengths and weaknesses of the test-taker's performance and provides the basis for subsequent one-on-one tutorial instruction.

Approaches to definition of language abilities

Local language program coordinators and test developers often identify the language abilities of interest, or define the construct, in terms of test-takers' successful performances on tasks targeted within the instructional program and/or tasks performed in broader real-world contexts outside of the classroom. The National Research Council (2011) notes that "test development is less challenging when the construct is more concrete and discrete, such as specific subject-matter or job knowledge" (p. 95). Because curriculum and assessment developers may draw on existing curriculum, needs analyses, and language and learning frameworks as resources for the development of outcomes, local language test developers will want to also address these in the construct definition.

For instance, you may be required to employ descriptors or outcomes from language frameworks and standards that exist at the local, national, or international level when defining the construct. Examples of commonly used standards include: the CEFR; the ACTFL Guidelines, developed by the American Council on Teaching Foreign Languages (ACTFL, 2004); and the WIDA Guidelines (WIDA, 2018), developed by a consortium of US states to establish standards for early childhood and K–12 multilingual learners.

In local language test development, you may also want to consider other standards not directly associated with language teaching and learning. In the US tertiary education, for example, there is growing interest in students' development of the set of skills referred to as "21st century skills". The National Research Council (2011) explains:

> The modern workplace requires workers to have broad cognitive and affective skills … these skills include being able to solve complex problems, to think critically about tasks, to effectively communicate with people from a variety of different cultures and using a variety of different techniques, to work in collaboration with others, to adapt to rapidly changing environments and conditions for performing tasks, to effectively manage one's work, and to acquire new skills and information on one's own.
>
> *(p. 1)*

21st century skills clearly interact with language development and easily lend themselves for inclusion in language program curricula. These skills have been categorized by the National Research Council (2011) as follows:

> **Cognitive skills**: nonroutine problem solving, critical thinking, systems thinking;
> **Interpersonal skills**: complex communication, social skills, teamwork, cultural sensitivity, dealing with diversity;
> **Intrapersonal skills**: self-management, time management, self-development, self-regulation, adaptability, executive functioning.
>
> *(p. 2)*

Most 21st century skills are dependent on the concomitant development of language abilities, which include observing and listening, eliciting critical information, interpreting the information, and conveying the interpretation to others (Levy & Murnane, 2004). For example, the National Council operationalizes *Active Listening* as: "Paying close attention to what is being said, asking the other party to explain exactly what he or she means, and requesting that ambiguous ideas or statements are repeated" (p. 43); this demonstrates that these skills are largely language dependent. Indeed, if we expect language learners to effectively use 21st century skills, they must develop not only the foundational language skills associated with the commencement of a program, but also the sophisticated language abilities required throughout the course of study.

Different programs have different emphases, values, and contexts. As mentioned above, one size does not fit all; each program will likely identify and address the test construct, purpose, and instructional outcomes differently. Because the construct of language ability is foundational to the demonstration of other, wide-ranging abilities (e.g., interpersonal communication), curriculum developers, and language instructors in a given context have options in terms of what they want to emphasize within their instructional programs. Likewise, language testers have options in terms of how to represent those abilities in local tests. Example 2.2 presents an approach that was taken to address the construct in the development of OEPT.

EXAMPLE 2.2 APPROACH TO THE CONSTRUCT DESCRIPTION OF OEPT

The focused construct of OEPT

When the OEPT was developed, test developers adopted a semi-direct, computer-administered format that led to increased administrative efficiency and cost savings. We also had the opportunity to better represent the local context. All items are introduced with a short statement that links the test task to a communicative task in the university context. All prospective test-takers are encouraged to visit the OEPP Program website where they can complete the OEPT practice test and the OEPT Orientation Video (OEPP, 2019), which further describes the University's professional and instructional contexts in which test-takers will soon be embedded. More than 2,000 prospective test-takers visit the site each year, many of whom matriculate at Purdue. The practice tests and orientation videos provide one of the first introductions to life at the University for international students.

OEPT test developers, most of whom were graduate teaching assistants in introductory undergraduate courses, first relied on their own understanding of and familiarity with the local context in the development of OEPT items/tasks. Most of these items have survived close scrutiny and continue to function well. Test tasks highlight common communicative activities (e.g., introduce, describe, explain, summarize). More explicit operationalizations of the language abilities associated with graduate students' communicative activities have also been developed over time and have been accompanied by evaluation/revision of the curriculum.

At Purdue, students who do not pass the OEPT are required to complete at least one semester of English language instruction. The instructional side of the program supports graduate students' performance, not only as instructors but also as members of research seminars and collaborative laboratories and as participants at professional academic conferences and job interviews. International students are well aware that their degrees may

> get them a job interview, but it is the ability to effectively communicate that is essential for securing a job offer.
>
> When instructors shifted the instructional focus toward professional development with an emphasis on presentation skills, students could see the relevance to their goals after obtaining their degrees. The skills emphasized in the OEPP lend themselves easily to both undergraduate instructional contexts and professional graduate contexts at the University.

Gathering evidence for language ability (construct) in local tests

The approach that we are advocating in this book emphasizes the experience and expertise of instructors and test developers in the local context as a starting point for the identification of the construct, i.e., the language abilities of greatest interest in the local context. However, it is important to recognize that intuitive/experiential approaches to test development have been criticized for lacking an appropriate empirical foundation and for being circular; that is, the construct is what is taught; what is taught is what is assessed (Brindley, 1991; Fulcher, 1996). To address these criticisms, Brindley (1998) has suggested:

> The only way to break this circle is to try to build up a body of independent evidence on language ability and use through investigation of samples of actual task performance. As Messick (1994) notes: "We need to move beyond traditional professional judgement of content to accrue construct-related evidence that the ostensibly sampled processes are actually engaged by respondents in task performance."
>
> *(p. 19)*

The strength of local instructional programs is that they provide optimal environments in which to accrue construct-related evidence about how local tests function in the local context because of the opportunity to collect and analyze data as an ongoing process (Angoff, 1988). You can gather different types of independent construct-related evidence for local tests, ranging from analysis of test content and test performances, to evaluation of needs for local test implementation and use.

If you want to collect evidence about the relevance of the test content, you may take the opportunity to obtain subject specialists', instructors', and students' evaluation of the test content. Fulcher's (1997) discussion on the development and validation of a local language test used for placement at the University of Surrey is an example of test content evaluation. You can also gather construct-related evidence through analysis of the test performance characteristics. For example, Ginther, Dimova, and Yang (2010) looked at temporal measures of fluency and their relation to the OEPT holistic scale and argued that information provided by examination of the skills that underlie holistic scores can be used not only as supporting evidence for the validity of inferences associated with performance tests but also as a way to improve the scoring rubrics, descriptors, and benchmarks associated with scoring scales.

(p. 379)

Chapelle, Chung, Hegelheimer, Pendar, and Xu (2010) examined the characteristics of test-takers' performance on a local test of productive grammatical ability in relation to task/item specifications derived from studies of second language acquisition. This article also provides an excellent example of the construction of a validity argument (Kane, 2001, 2006). Test-takers can also provide important information about the content and administration of a test. Yan, Thirakunkovit, Kauper, and Ginther (2016) discuss the use of test-taker feedback for quality control of a local language test.

The examples of construct-related evidence above focus primarily on the validation of tests themselves and present valuable information and procedures for how the quality and functionality of placement tests may be evaluated. The usefulness of these tests can be extended when the results are linked to instructional outcomes.

Linking test purpose to instructional outcomes

As mentioned in the previous section regarding maximizing test functionality, the use of test results can gain extended functionality by being used for diagnostic purposes in language instruction. In order to further embed the test in the local instructional context, as well as gather information for instructional program evaluation, language test developers should consider outcome-based assessment. Linking test purpose to instructional outcomes makes sense, especially when considering opportunities that local contexts offer for learning throughout the course of a student's program of study. The importance of associating performance to explicitly-stated, transparent instructional outcomes is highlighted in the following quote:

> In the first place, the fact that outcomes are described in performance terms means that learners are focused on language as a tool for communication rather than on language knowledge as an end in itself. They are also able to obtain diagnostic feedback on the success of their learning since explicit performance criteria are provided against which they can judge their progress. Second, since there is a direct link between attainment targets, course objectives and learning activities, assessment is closely integrated with instruction: what is taught is directly related to what is assessed and (in theory at least) what is assessed is, in turn, linked to the outcomes that are reported. Third, instructors, by comparing students' progress and achievement with the standards statements, are able to make better-informed judgements about what individual learners need.
>
> *(Brindley, 1998, p. 52)*

It is important that the outcome statements are described in terms of performance (what the student can and should be able to do with language in broader educational and professional contexts). The focus on performance leads to a series of associated instructional and administrative opportunities. Here is Brindley's list of purposes for which outcome statements can be designed:

- to establish expected standards of achievement;
- to provide system-wide reference points to assist instructors in assessing individual progress;
- to provide a common framework for curriculum development;
- to provide more comprehensive information for reporting to interested parties outside the classroom, such as parents, employers, and educational authorities;
- to clarify the kinds of performance that lead to academic success;
- to support instructors in their implementation of curriculum objectives;
- to provide a basis for identifying needs and targeting resource allocation;
- to provide a resource for teacher professional development.

(Brindley, 1998, p. 50)

The local stakeholders (teachers, administration, management) in your context need to consider long-term institutional policy planning that takes into account the possibilities for ongoing language assessment in the instructional context(s). Language programs in higher education have many opportunities to expand their repertoires of post-admission language support. Elder (2017) argues:

the key to more valid and useful English assessment in higher education lies in effective long-term institutional policy-making which puts language tests in their rightful place as part of an integrated teaching and learning program which makes explicit not only the content objectives of courses and the standards of achievement expected but also the nature and level of English proficiency expected at various points in students' study trajectory. Effective policymaking, if concerns for language development are to be anything more than tokenistic, must stipulate not only the mechanism for ensuring adequate proficiency at entry but also the means of identifying learning needs and monitoring language development throughout students' courses and on graduation.

(p. 282)

Linking outcomes, performance, and classroom assessment is characteristic of the shift from an emphasis on the results of standardized tests to an emphasis on learning. The development of local language tests is part and parcel of these larger, positive developments, the potential of which is just beginning to be realized. The following are examples of outcome-based assessment. Example 2.3 provides information about the development of learning outcomes for a language program that are reflected on the test, while Example 2.4 discusses a language test designed on the basis of curricular learning outcomes.

EXAMPLE 2.3 DEVELOPING LEARNING OUTCOMES FOR A LOCAL LANGUAGE PROGRAM

Purdue Language and Cultural Exchange (PLaCE): performance objectives

In the establishment of the Purdue Language and Cultural Exchange (PLaCE), the program's performance objectives emphasized the development of students' core language skills as well as their interpersonal and intrapersonal skills. Performance objectives have evolved over time (PLaCE was established in 2014) as program outcomes are periodically evaluated and revised. What has remained constant from the beginning is the program's focus on students' development of language *ability for use* (Hymes, 1972) in the areas of oral and written communication, reading, group work, and intercultural knowledge and competence. Following is a list of some major learning outcomes of the instructional program:

- Increase fluency in reading, speaking, listening, and writing
- Communicate in English with increased clarity and accuracy in speech
- Develop strategies and skills for collaborating with peers and participating in active learning classes
- Present academic topics to an audience clearly and confidently
- Understand principles and practices for using sources in academic texts

---

These objectives are situated in a two-semester course sequence for first-year students. In the first course, students begin by working on tasks related to their personal learning spaces, such as setting goals for the semester, and end with a reflection-based project in which they create a digital storytelling project that relates their personal story of development. In the second semester, the curriculum takes a more outward and other-ward turn, as students complete research projects on diverse aspects of American society and language. At the end of the year, students create a digital portfolio to document their work, and participate in a showcase presentation with their peers.

EXAMPLE 2.4 LANGUAGE TESTS THAT REFLECT LEARNING OUTCOMES

Foreign language national tests in Danish elementary and lower secondary schools

In Denmark, primary school education is based on the development of individual student plans, and so diagnostic tests are implemented to identify the areas on which the students need to focus in the instructional period that follows. What is tested is linked to the goal and objectives of the foreign language curricula, and students are given the opportunity to develop the tested skills and abilities within an instructional program. Embedding a test within an instructional program creates program coherence; program coherence is further enhanced by continuing to assess targeted skills once students are placed within instructional levels.

The role of local tests in classroom assessment systems

Although we do not conceptualize local language tests as a classroom assessment method, local language tests can certainly contribute to classroom assessment systems. Assessment systems, which can take various forms, comprise a range of assessments designed to support teaching and learning and the ongoing monitoring of progress (Wiliam, 2004). Effective implementations of classroom assessment systems address three components of learner performance: the current state of the learner, the desired outcomes for the learner, and the provision of methods and activities designed to close the gap between current state and desired outcome (Black & William, 1998). The success of the system starts by finding out where to begin with the learner, and the results of a local test help to address this critical piece of the puzzle. The system functions at its fullest when the information gleaned from assessment activities is used to address and close the gap between the initial state of the learner and the desired outcomes.

Despite the possibility to use both large-scale and local tests for identifying learners' starting points, local tests have the advantage of allowing access to performance data for further analysis and detailed feedback. In other words, an instrument devised for summative purposes can also be used for formative purposes (Wiliam, 2004). Summative assessment refers to tests evaluating whether learning has occurred, and thus they are administered after instruction. Formative assessment, on the other hand, describes assessments conducted during instruction in order to support student learning (Black, Harrison, Lee, Marshall, & Wiliam, 2002). The provision of feedback extends the function of the test's original summative purpose (e.g., placement) to formative purposes such as explanation, diagnosis, and support of instructional activities. In order to ensure the formative function of feedback, "students must see the purpose of feedback as helping them improve, rather than simply judging their worth [...]"

(Wiliam & Thompson, 2013, p. 57). Timely provision of feedback is essential, but more importantly, the results of assessment activities should serve to enhance the instructional benefits to the student:

> An assessment activity can help learning if it provides information to be used as feedback, by instructors, and by their pupils, in assessing themselves and each other, to modify the teaching and learning activities in which they are engaged. Such assessment becomes 'formative assessment' when the evidence is actually used to adapt the teaching work to meet learning needs.
>
> *(Wiliam & Thompson, 2013, p. 57)*

The OEPT Review (Example 2.5) is a good example of how the summative use of an instrument can be extended for formative purposes.

EXAMPLE 2.5 THE OEPT REVIEW AND INSTRUCTIONAL OUTCOMES

Using a summative instrument for formative purposes

The Oral English Proficiency Program is first responsible for screening the oral English proficiency of prospective international teaching assistants, and then responsible for providing instruction for those who are identified by the instrument as likely to benefit from instruction. Instruction begins with the instructor's review of each student's OEPT item responses. The sound files are available within the OEPT testing platform. The instructor makes notes on the student's performance and the actual responses are then reviewed by the instructor with the student. This process can help students understand the criteria for success that the instructor already has in mind, and communication of the criteria is additionally facilitated by the dual role that instructors play within the program – the instructors are also raters. The initial consultation between the instructor/rater and the student provides the foundation for setting the student's performance goals and objectives over the course of the semester.

The goal of the course is straightforward: improvement across the four 20-minute presentations (followed by 10 minutes for questions and answers) that students are required to give over the course of the 16-week semester. The integration of the test with instruction is facilitated by the use of the OEPT scale to evaluate the language-specific aspects of their classroom performances. Additional criteria, addressing interactive effectiveness, are included in the presentation scales. The OEPP also has an extensive volunteer program, with undergraduates providing an audience on presentation days. These volunteers ask questions and complete evaluations, which are also based on the OEPT scale. Finally, students complete a self-evaluation for each of their performances, and again, their self-evaluations are based on the OEPT scale. (see appendix A)

> The OEPT Review, individual goal setting consultations, and the extension and expansion of the OEPT scale across assessment activities comprises a system and a set of feedback loops in which assessment is thoroughly embedded in the instructional context. You can read more about the detailed analysis of the use of objectives, goals, and formative assessment that explicates OEPP practice in these areas in Haugen (2017).

Involving stakeholders

You could effectively embed assessment activities in a program and more fully contribute to an assessment system when you design an assessment that engages all critical classroom actors: instructors, peers, and students. Brindley (1998) describes some of the ways that such engagement might occur:

> Performance assessment involves the use of a wide range of tools such as structured observations, progress profiles, various kinds of performance-based tasks and self-assessment to build up a complex and multidimensional picture of learner performance, in contrast to the single grade or score conventionally yielded by large-scale standardized tests.
>
> *(p. 46)*

You have the opportunity to involve both instructors and students in the development and evaluation of the test tasks. Instructors are most familiar with the task types that students at different proficiency levels can complete, while students can evaluate prototype tasks, provide information about relevant topics, and help to select adequate assessment methods.

Involving instructors in the test development, administration, and rating can also strengthen the link between instruction and testing. For example, instructors can contribute to the development of the rating scale by providing descriptors with which they are familiar and which they may already use during classroom assessment. Given that instructors are often raters for local tests, their participation in the scale development facilitates their interpretation, internalization, and use of the scale during the rating process.

In the following chapters, we will turn towards central aspects of the actual test development process.

Further reading

Dimova, S., & Kling, J. (forthcoming). Current considerations on ICL in multilingual universities. In S. Dimova & J. Kling (Eds.), *Integrating Content and Language in Multilingual Universities*. Dordrecht: Springer.

The book chapter provides an overview of *Current considerations on ICL in multi-lingual universities*, which includes a history of language and content integration in multilingual higher education institutions, the issues surrounding content/language integration, and the future considerations for local contexts in which content and language are integrated. The editors highlight the unique position that English holds in contexts of higher education around the world and discuss its influence on educational policy. English is introduced as an additional medium of instruction to the local or national language(s) for the purpose of internationalization of the HE, i.e., to increase international student and teacher recruitment, as well as to obtain access to research published in international journals. While context may define how we approach this undertaking, two overarching themes have become apparent: (1) student readiness for learning through an FL and (2) support for teaching content in FL. The volume provides evidence about how ICL-related concerns can be addressed using a broad range of approaches in a broad range of contexts.

Holmen, A. (2015). Linguistic diversity among students in higher education: A resource in a multilingual language strategy? In A. H. Fabricius & B. Preisler (Eds.). *Transcultural interaction and linguistic diversity in higher education* (pp. 114–161). London: Palgrave Macmillan.

The book chapter describes a project in the University of Copenhagen (UCPH) for integrating language and content. It is explained that integration of content and language (ICL) at UCPH has been developed as part of a language policy at the University, which is referred to as a policy of parallel language use. The policy states that there should be a balance between the use of English and Danish languages in both research and instruction. The chapter covers a general history of multilingualism in public universities and introduces and discusses the parallel language use policy at UCPH. The focus of the second half of the chapter is on students, first through categorizing the multilingual students in ICL settings, and then through reporting on the role of minority students in multilingual academic settings. Finally, the chapter compares student experiences in programs with different language norms and hierarchies of priority.

National Research Council. (2011). *Assessing 21st century skills: Summary of a workshop.* J.A. Koenig, Rapporteur. Committee on the Assessment of 21st Century Skills. Board on Testing and Assessment, Division of Behavioral and Social Sciences and Education. Washington, DC: The National Academies Press.

Twenty-first century skills include:

> being able to solve complex problems, to think critically about tasks, to effectively communicate with people from a variety of different cultures and using a variety of different techniques, to work in collaboration with others, to adapt to rapidly changing environments and conditions for

performing tasks, to effectively manage one's work, and to acquire new skills and information on one's own.

(p. 1)

Increasingly, these skills are incorporated into undergraduate instructional programs where their interaction with foundational language skills becomes apparent. This report synthesizes research findings related to 21st century skills and categorizes the skills into three broad categories: cognitive skills, interpersonal skills, and intrapersonal skills. Of greatest interest are those sections that address research, measurement, and policy issues associated with the assessment of 21st century skills. The report includes useful, practical suggestions, supported by research.

References

ACTFL. (2004). ACTFL proficiency guidelines (Revised). Hastings-on-Hudson, NY: American Council on the Teaching of Foreign Languages. Retrieved January 1, 2004 from the World Wide Web www.sil.org/lingualinks/LANGUAGELEARNING/ OtherResources/ACTFLProficiencyGuidelines/ACTFLProficiencyGuidelines.htm

Alderson, J. C. (Ed.). (2002). *Common European framework of reference for languages: Learning, teaching, assessment: Case studies.* Strasbourg: Council of Europe.

Angoff, W. H. (1988). Validity: An evolving concept. In H. Wainer & H. I. Braun (Eds.), *Test validity* (pp. 19–32). Hillsdale, NJ: Lawrence Erlbaum.

Black, P., Harrison, C., Lee, C., Marshall, B., & Wiliam, D. (2002). *Working inside the black box: Assessment for learning in the classroom.* London: King's College London, Department of Education and Professional Studies.

Black, P., & William, D. (1998). Assessment and classroom learning. *Assessment in Education,* 5(1), 7–72.

Brindley, G. (1991). Defining language ability: The criteria for criteria. In S. Anivan (Ed.), *Current developments in language testing* (pp. 139–164). Singapore: Regional Language Centre.

Brindley, G. (1998). Outcomes-based assessment and reporting in language learning programmes: A review of the issues. *Language Testing, 15,* 45–85.

Brown, C., Boser, U., Sargrad, S., & Marchitello, M. (2016). *Implementing the every student succeeds act: Toward a coherent, aligned assessment system.* Washington, DC: Center for American Progress.

Chapelle, C., Chung, Y., Heigleheimer, V., Pendar, N., & Xu, J. (2010). Towards a computer-delivered test of productive grammatical ability. *Language Testing, 27,* 443–469.

Cronquist, K., & Fiszbein, A. (2017). *El aprendizaje del inglés en América Latina.* Retrieved fromwww.thedialogue.org/wp-content/uploads/2017/09/El-aprendizaje-del-ingl% C3%A9s-en-Am%C3%A9rica-Latina-1.pdf

Deygers, B., Zeidler, B., Vilcu, D., & Carlsen, C. H. (2018). One framework to unite them all? Use of the CEFR in European university entrance policies. *Language Assessment Quarterly, 15*(1), 3–15.

Dimova, S., & Kling, J. (forthcoming). Current considerations on ICL in multilingual universities. In S. Dimova & J. Kling (Eds.), *Integrating content and language in multilingual universities.* Dordrecht: Springer.

Educational Testing Service. (2019). *Performance descriptors for the TOEFL iBT® test.* Princeton, NJ: Educational Testing Service.

Elder, C. (2017). Assessment in higher education. In E. Shohamy, I. G. Or, & S. May (Eds.), *Language testing and assessment* (3rd ed., pp. 271–287). Gewerbestrasse, Switzerland: Springer.

Fulcher, G. (1996). Does thick description lead to smart tests? A data-based approach to scale construction. *Language Testing, 13*, 208–238.

Fulcher, G. (1997). An English language placement test: Issues in reliability and validity. *Language Testing, 14*, 113–138.

Ginther, A. (2003). International teaching assistant testing: Policies and methods. In D. Douglas (Ed.), *English language testing in US colleges and universities* (pp. 57–84). Washington, DC: NAFSA, Association of International Educators.

Ginther, A., Dimova, S., & Yang, R. (2010). Conceptual and empirical relationships between temporal measures of fluency and oral English proficiency with implications for automated scoring. *Language Testing, 27*, 379–399.

Ginther, A., & Elder, C. (2014). *A comparative investigation into understandings and uses of the TOEFL iBT. TOEFL research report; RR-14-44*. Princeton, NJ: Educational Testing Service.

Ginther, A., & Yan, X. (2017). Interpreting the relationships between TOEFL iBT scores and GPA: Language proficiency, policy, and profiles. *Language Testing, 35*, 271–295.

Haugen, M. (2017). Objectives, goals, and formative assessment in the Oral English Proficiency Program. Unpublished dissertation.

Holmen, A. (2015). Linguistic diversity among students in higher education: A resource in a multilingual language strategy? In A. H. Fabricius & B. Preisler (Eds.), *Transcultural interaction and linguistic diversity in higher education* (pp. 114–161). London: Palgrave Macmillan.

Hymes, D. H. (1972). On communicative competence. In J. B. Pride & J. Holmes (Eds.), *Sociolinguistics: Selected readings* (pp. 269–293). Harmondsworth: Penguin.

Kane, M. (2001). Current concerns in validity theory. *Journal of Educational Measurement, 38*, 319–342.

Kane, M. (2006). Validation. In R. Brennen (Ed.), *Educational measurement* (4th ed., pp. 17–64). Westport, CT: Greenwood Publishing.

Levy, F., & Murnane, R. J. (2004). *The new division of labor: How computers are creating the next job market*. Princeton, NJ: Princeton University Press.

Messick, S. (1994). The interplay of evidence and consequences in the validation of performance assessments. *Educational Researcher, 23*(2), 13–23.

Ministry of Education. (2007). *College English curriculum requirements*. Beijing: Higher Education Press.

National Research Council. (2011). Assessing 21st century skills: Summary of a workshop. J.A. Koenig, Rapporteur. Committee on the assessment of 21st century skills. Board on testing and assessment, division of behavioral and social sciences and education. Washington, DC: The National Academies Press.

North, B. (2014). *The CEFR in practice*. Cambridge: Cambridge University Press.

OEPP. (2019). OEPT practice test and orientation website. Retrieved from http://tutorial.ace-in-testing.com/Default.aspx?p=test

Pennington, M. C., & Hoekje, B. J. (2010). *Language program leadership in a changing world: An ecological model*. Bingley, UK: Emerald Group Publishing.

Read, J. (2016). Some key issues in post-admission language assessment. In J. Read (Ed.), *Post-admission language assessment of university students* (pp. 3–20). Melbourne, AU: Springer.

Spolsky, B. (1995). *Measured words: The development of objective language testing*. Oxford: Oxford University Press.

WIDA. Alternative Access for ELLs. (2018). Interpretive guide for score reports grades 1–12. Madison, WI: Board of Regents of the University of Wisconsin System, on behalf of WIDA.

Wiliam, D. (2004). Keeping learning on track: Integrating assessment with instruction. Invited address to the 30th annual conference of the International Association for Educational Assessment (IAEA) held June 2004, Philadelphia, PA.

Wiliam, D., & Thompson, M. (2013). Integrating assessment with learning: What will it take to make it work? In C. A. Dwyer (Ed.), *The future of assessment: Shaping teaching and learning* (pp. 53–84). New York: Routledge.

Yan, X., Thirakunkovit, S., Kauper, N., & Ginther, A. (2016). What do test-takers say: Test-taker feedback as input for quality control. In J. Read. (Ed.), *Post-admission language assessments of university students* (pp. 113–136). Melbourne, AU: Springer.

3
LOCAL TEST DEVELOPMENT

You are embarking on a new test development project because you have a testing need in your local context – you need a new test or your current test fails to fulfill the testing purpose, and none of the off shelf tests seem appropriate for your context. For example, you need to screen the prospective international teaching assistants (ITAs) for oral English proficiency, but your institution lacks an oral English proficiency test or the current one has become inadequate for the intended testing purposes. You are tasked with test development, so the first question that comes to mind is: *where do I start?*

In this chapter, we will discuss the basic considerations during the development of a local language test. We will address the importance of specifying the purpose in the test specification design and the role of needs analysis in the process of item type selection and context representation.

Introduction

Test development has traditionally been viewed as a cyclical process that can be divided into three main stages: design, operationalization, and administration. Activities undertaken during the design stage include defining the test purpose, the test-takers, the task types, and the resources; activities undertaken during the operationalization stage include specifying the test structure, the tasks, and the scoring methods. The administration stage comes last, when the designed test tasks are administered and test data are collected. The data gathered in the administration stage are then evaluated to inform the further design and operationalization, which makes the process cyclical (Figure 3.1).

This model outlines the reciprocal relationships between each stage, with decisions made in one influencing activities in the next, but it also provides

FIGURE 3.1 Cyclical model of test development

information for revision of decisions made in the previous stage. However, the cyclical model cannot capture the overlap of activities in all stages of the development process of local tests. Despite best efforts to streamline the test development process into distinct stages, the design and operationalization stages tend to be blended, and test developers regularly move back and forth between decisions regarding test structure or task types, language ability descriptions, and resource allocation decisions.

Based on our experience with local tests, instead of distinct stages, we conceptualize the test development process as sets of different activities that are related to test planning, design, and implementation (see Figure 3.2). Activities related to planning include: 1) identifying the test purpose, 2) identifying the test-takers, 3) budgeting the test development and maintenance costs, 4) identifying available local resources (people, materials), and 5) building the test development team. Then, design activities relate to 1) designing tasks, 2) developing test structure, 3) establishing comparable forms, 4) establishing test administration procedures, and 5) piloting the tasks and administration. The planning and design activities, which seem concurrent in the case of local test development,

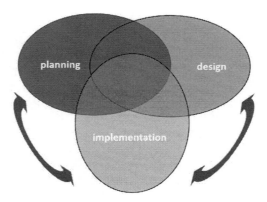

FIGURE 3.2 Local test development model

precede test implementation and continue after the test becomes operational. The blue arrows in the diagram below represent the ongoing evaluation that was represented as a cycle in other test development models.

Planning test development

In the introductory chapter, we presented the most common purposes for which tests are designed locally (proficiency, achievement, placement, and diagnosis) as well as the need to familiarize yourself with the general characteristics of the test-taker population. Therefore, in this chapter, our discussion will focus on the development and maintenance costs and resources.

Given that local tests are developed within the context in which they are used, test developers benefit from having access to available local expertise and material resources. Teachers, students, and program administrators play a central role in the planning and development process because of their knowledge of the test purposes and uses, as well as their familiarity with the policies that govern the test design, test-taker characteristics, and language uses that are specific to the local context, i.e., the target language use domain outside the test. The contextual knowledge of local expertise contributes to the design of test tasks that closely reflect local language varieties and language functions. For example, teachers of writing in university settings are familiar with the text genres that students need to produce in the writing program, and so they can contribute to the design of writing test tasks for placement in the writing program.

Development costs

The management of a test development project depends on the same constraints as any other project, namely time, cost, and scope (see Figure 3.3). In other words, you want to design a test with certain features within a given time period on a specific budget. The quality of the test will depend on how you define the scope, manage the budget, and allocate your time. Of course, to make sure your test adequately fulfills its purpose, you will need plenty of time

FIGURE 3.3 The project management triangle

and a good budget, but all resources are limited. In local test development projects, the greatest constraint is usually the budget. Schools, universities, and other institutions involved in test design have limited financial resources, and thus developing a good test can take a long time.

The project management triangle presented above is intended to highlight the trade-offs across quality, scope, time, and cost in any development project. In other words, the quality is constrained by the project's budget, deadlines, and scope (or the project size). For example, if you want to develop an inexpensive test in a short period of time, the test's scope should be reduced or a trade-off in quality should be tolerated. High-quality projects require extended time if costs are low or increased costs if time is short.

The costs are associated with test development, administration, and maintenance. When tasked with test design, test developers primarily focus on development expenses. However, it is a good idea to also plan for the test's sustainability. In other words, a local test will have to adjust to the transitions in the local context because the availability of local resources will change over time, and the test will need to accommodate technological advances and shifts in institutional policies.

While these shifts may lead to additional costs, the good news is that programs can often absorb costs by redistributing workloads and responsibilities and allowing a generous amount of time for a test to be fully embedded in the local context. As mentioned in previous chapters, the OEPT, now fully embedded in the instructional program at Purdue, is part of a larger testing system that includes a practice test, a video tutorial, a rater training program, a rating platform, and a database; however, the parts of the system were developed over a period of five years, and each part requires regular revision and updating. Unlike large-scale tests, local tests can more readily adapt to change, so test development is iterative and ongoing. In other words, it is never completely finished.

Test design activities involve the utilization of human and material resources for test development, administration, and maintenance. Human resources include both the core and external team members who participate in the different test development and administration activities, while material resources refer to equipment and space. In the following sections, we provide lists of team member roles and material resources that test developers need during different testing activities. Although you may have to outsource some of these activities and purchase new equipment, many human and material resources are probably already available in your institution. Therefore, identifying existing resources as part of your planning activities is crucial so that you can maximize their use.

If you work in a university context, for example, you may have access to a graphic design department, an IT department, or a computer science department, which can offer both human and material resources regarding test development. Your institution may have also purchased software licenses for operating systems and audio/video editing applications, as well as licenses for different learning platforms. Using rooms at your institution for test administration may be less expensive, or even free, compared to renting rooms elsewhere. In Chapter 5, we discuss in more detail how to identify and use human and material resources for development of traditional and digitally delivered language tests.

Human resources

Team members can participate in test development and administration as item writers, scale developers and raters (in case of developing in performance-based tests), graphic designers, actors/speakers and audio/video editors (if developing listening items), software developers (if designing a digitally-enhanced test), and test administrators.

The item writers are responsible for the design of the different items/tasks included in the test, which includes writing the test and task instructions, task prompts, and the actual tasks. Test instructions are the general instructions test-takers receive regarding the test structure and length (number of items and approximate time), as well as information about whether additional resources (dictionaries, conjunction tables, notes) are allowed. Test instructions may also include information about how to navigate through the test, how to play audio input, and record responses, especially when the test is digitally delivered. Item writers are also responsible for collecting existing texts, graphics, and audio and video files to include in the test.

When designing a performance-based test, some team members will be responsible for development of the rating scale, i.e., determining the scale levels and level descriptors. When responses from performance-based tests are collected, raters are trained to rate written or oral performance-based test responses and to assign scores based on established criteria. You can read more about scales, rating criteria, and rater training in Chapters 6 and 7.

Regardless of whether the test is paper or digitally delivered, it needs to be graphically designed so that the representation of textual and visual information is professionally formatted and easy to navigate. In some cases, pictures and graphics must be designed specifically for the test so that similar style is maintained across all tasks. For example, when developing an English language test for first graders in the Danish elementary schools, engaging illustrations related to different themes and pictures with recurring elements (e.g., the same character in different situations or positions) were needed so that the children would recognize characters and contexts across all tasks. For that purpose, an illustrator was hired to draw all of the pictures for the test.

When test instructions and prompts are provided in both textual and audio/video form, and if the test has listening tasks, actors may be hired to record the voiceovers or video inputs. Once the input is audio/video recorded, audio/video editors are engaged to edit the recordings. In case of digitally delivered tests, software developers are responsible for designing a platform for test delivery and response collection, as well as a system for data management.

Finally, test administrators are often clerical staff (those responsible for test registration, score report generation, and stakeholder liaison management), and test proctors (invigilators, or those who set up and monitor the actual testing session). In direct oral tests, the examiners and/or the raters may also have the role of test administrators.

Language testing team

Although the long list of roles we presented may seem overwhelming, local testing teams tend to be small, and team members usually assume more than one role related to test development and administration. For example, the same individuals can take on the roles of item writers, raters, and test administrators. Sometimes, members of the core testing team have expertise in graphic design, editing, and platform design. However, in most local contexts, these test design activities need to be outsourced by engaging local or external collaborators (Figure 3.4). For example, in the design of the first version of the OEPT, which was functional for over a decade, the software developer, the video editor, and the actors for the video input were all members of the core team. The new OEPT platform, however, was designed in 2016 by a software development company.

As mentioned earlier, an important characteristic of local testing teams is that all core team members are familiar with the local context. When the local test is embedded in a language curriculum or program, some teachers become members of the team. The inclusion of teachers in the testing team allows for the

FIGURE 3.4   Language testing team

establishment of a closer link between testing and instruction, which is one of the strengths of local language tests. Example 3.1 describes a local language testing team structure.

EXAMPLE 3.1 TOEPAS TESTING TEAM

The TOEPAS testing team

The TOEPAS is used for oral English proficiency certification of university teachers who teach in English-medium instruction (EMI) programs at the University of Copenhagen. The TOEPAS is a performance test based on a simulated lecture.

The core TOEPAS testing team consists of eight members (six testers and two administrators) who come from the local university context because some of them are also language program coordinators, teachers of English for academic or specific purposes (EAP/ESP), EMI teacher trainers, or researchers in language testing and applied linguistics. Because of their familiarity with the local context, the six testers have been involved in benchmarking, scaling, and standard setting, as well as in the development of testing protocols and procedures.

Each of the core members has a clearly defined role: test coordinator, test administrator, or rater.

- The test coordinator organizes the work of the testing team, conducts continuous test analyses, and plans test revisions and updates. The test coordinator also serves as a rater.
- The two test administrators (clerical staff) are responsible for liaising with stakeholders and external collaborators, as well as purchasing and maintaining technical equipment.
- The five raters are responsible for administering the test sessions, rating performances, recording scores, and providing written and oral feedback reports to test-takers.
- Local and external collaborators are also engaged to provide consultancy and expertise when needed.
- A local IT specialist from the IT department at the university provides consultancy regarding selection of digital, technical, and infrastructural solutions for test data recording and storage. He also liaises the communication with external software developers regarding the design and maintenance of the test database.
- External software developers were hired to design a database for storage of test data and an online interface for test data entry and retrieval.

Material resources

Material resources include the necessary equipment and space for test production. We present some of the resources in this section, but you can read about the selection of alternatives needed for the production of traditional or digitally delivered tests in Chapter 5.

The types of equipment needed for test production may include computer devices (desktops, laptops, tablets, smartphones), monitors, microphones (lapel and/or room mics), video cameras, servers (or server space), Internet routers, loudspeakers, headsets, scanners, and printers. The pieces of equipment that you need will depend on the task types and test delivery platform. For example, when developing tests of writing, video cameras, microphones, and loudspeakers may not be required if the task prompt does not include audiovisual material. Moreover, printers are rarely used if the test development is completely digitized. Purchasing high-quality equipment for test development can be expensive, and some equipment may need to be replaced in a few years when upgraded versions become available.

The equipment applied during test administration may be similar to that used during test development. The difference lies in the number of pieces and devices needed, which depends on how many people take the test simultaneously. Speakers, monitors, or projectors may be necessary if the input for listening tasks is not delivered on computer devices. For online tests and digital data storage, servers (or server space), internet routers, or hard drives may be included. Oral tests may require a microphone (lapel and transmitter if the test-taker is allowed to move) and an audio or a video recording device (e.g., camera or computer). If the oral test is digitally delivered, then a headset may be used so that the test-taker can hear the instructions and prompts and then record responses, as is the case with the OEPT. Moreover, if the recorded responses are stored remotely on a server, an internet router may be required (see Chapter 8 for data storage and management). In some cases, you can avoid purchasing equipment by having test-takers bring their own equipment (e.g., laptop, headset) to the test session, unless that compromises test security and administration consistency. In Chapter 8, we discuss the security measures test developers should implement to ensure reliable test administration.

Most of the equipment listed above functions with the use of certain software programs and applications. Computer devices, for example, need updated operating systems and different word processing applications. Software for digitizing and editing audio and video data (e.g., Adobe Premiere Pro, Corel Video Studio Ultimate, CyberLink PowerDirector), as well software programs and applications for developing digital test delivery platforms, are usually part of the test production process.

In addition to digital resources, other materials include paper and ink for printing out paper-based tests. Whiteboards, markers, and other stationery may be needed during meetings and planning activities of test production. Although test booklets and pens or pencils are common test materials in paper delivered tests, even in case of digitally delivered tests, booklets with test information and scratch paper and pencils for note taking or planning responses may be necessary. Envelopes or folders may also be needed to collect paper-based responses at the end of the testing session. Other materials could include dictionaries or conjugation tables, if such resources are allowed during testing.

When thinking about material resources, the space needed for test administration must also be considered. The building where the test is scheduled to take place should be able to accommodate the administration, and a room – or several rooms – with a specific setup may need to be booked in advance. For example, when the paper-based version of EPT was administered, a large auditorium was reserved so that the test could be administered simultaneously to many test-takers. For the administration of the OEPT, a single, relatively large (40 station) computer laboratory is reserved so that the test can be administered to many test-takers simultaneously with the use of standard university equipment. However, because only 20 test-takers are scheduled in a single session, multiple sessions must be scheduled. The TOEPAS, on the other hand, requires a different setup, i.e., a small room with long desks in the middle so that one student and one rater can sit across from each other (see Figure 3.5).

Maintenance costs

Most tests need some revision after a certain period of time due to changes in the technological infrastructure of the testing context, updates to software and applications, and the modification of institutional policies. Maintenance costs are very similar to development costs for both human and material resources. In terms of digitally enhanced tests, you will need software developers to update the digital platforms, which may involve item writers if the platform changes

FIGURE 3.5   Room setup for the TOEPAS administration

lead to item revisions. There may also be a need for software updates or purchases of additional software for test development, delivery, and response collection, as well as software needed for test data analysis (e.g., SPSS, SAS, FACETS). Therefore, you may want to plan from the beginning to establish test sustainability by acquiring financial and other resources over a certain period, so that these resources are available when the time comes for large-scale revisions. Table 3.1 provides an overview of resources related to test development, administration, and maintenance.

Test design

Once the test purpose is established and the available resources are identified, test design activities can be planned. These activities include (1) designing tasks, (2) designing the test structure, (3) developing comparable forms, (4) establishing test admin procedures, and (5) piloting the tasks and procedures. Although planning facilitates the completion of the different design activities, some re-calibration of cost and reallocation of resources can still be expected because unpredicted situations and factors may occur. For example, with the English test for elementary school children in Denmark, the technical infrastructure in the

TABLE 3.1 Resources needed for development, administration, and maintenance of tests

	development	*administration*	*maintenance*
human	item writers scale developers graphic designers actors/speakers audio/video editors software developers	administrators (clerical staff and proctors) raters/scorers	software developers (other resources as in development if items are revised)
material	equipment (computer devices, monitors, microphones, video cameras, servers, internet routers, loudspeakers, headsets, scanners, printers) software (operating systems, applications, audio/video software, software for developing digital test delivery platforms) materials for test production (paper and ink, white boards, markers, and other stationery)	equipment (computer devices, monitors, microphones, video cameras, servers, internet routers, loudspeakers, headsets) software (relevant platform for test delivery and response collection) materials (test booklets, notepads, pens/pencils, folders/envelopes)	equipment (updates of equipment purchased for test development and administration) software (updates of software used for test development and administration, plus software for data analysis)
space	team members' offices	test admin rooms	
time	continuous	scheduled test sessions	periodical

schools was analyzed when planning the test development, but the problem of intermittent internet connection was not identified before the actual pilot. This led to difficulties with test delivery and response collection, and so purchasing internet routers and wireless data was necessary. This purchase was not originally budgeted and, therefore, represented an additional cost. So, it is always a good idea to reserve part of the budget (10%) for unexpected needs.

Task design: instructions, format, input, scoring

When designing tasks, you should establish which language abilities – or aspects of the language ability – you would like to include in the test; this is known as the "construct" in the language testing field. Although different theoretical models of language ability can guide the construct definition, the ability assessed in the local context tends to be defined by the curriculum of an academic program or the language tasks test-takers are expected to perform in real life. The received approach to test development specifies the language ability that needs to be assessed before the test tasks are designed and, to a certain extent, that is the case for local tests as well. However, based on input from local teachers and other stakeholders, local test developers often define the language abilities based on test-takers' successful performances on instructional tasks or tasks observed in real-life situations.

Two approaches to task design are commonly used in language test development: specifications governed and experiential. In the specifications governed approach, a detailed description of the task purpose and characteristics guides the design of the actual item or task. The task description is usually grounded in theoretical models of the construct. The described specifications usually include the following information: (1) descriptions of the task's purpose, (2) definition of the construct, (3) characteristics of the task's setting (place, time, participants), (4) instructions for the task, (5) characteristics of input (textual, audio, visual) and response (written, spoken, multiple choice) and their relationship, and (6) method of scoring (dichotomous, partial credit, scale) (for more information about item specifications see Bachman & Palmer, 1996).

In the experiential approach, item writers design items based on their previous experiences teaching in the local language program or their familiarity with the local context, i.e., language tasks that test-takers need to perform outside of the test. Then, based on criteria related to the test purpose (i.e., ability and function), a certain number of tasks from the pool are selected for piloting and analysis. The characteristics of the well-functioning items may be described later on in the task specifications so that similar tasks can be designed for comparable forms. Figure 3.6 shows the similarities and differences between the two approaches to task design.

These two approaches, specifications governed or experiential, are not mutually exclusive and, in some cases, are informed by needs analyses conducted in the local context. Test developers observe the language uses and collect language

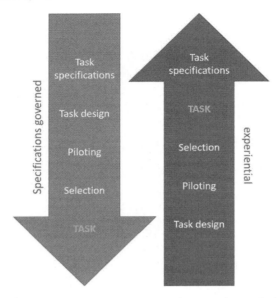

FIGURE 3.6   Specifications governed vs. experiential approach to task design

samples in order to identify the characteristics of the language in certain local situations. They then design tasks that represent the language situations and elicit similar performances. Following are three task design processes, each exemplifying a different approach (see Examples 3.2, 3.3, and 3.4).

EXAMPLE 3.2 NEEDS ANALYSIS APPROACH: TOEPAS

TOEPAS: specifications governed approach based on needs analysis

The TOEPAS is based on a 20-minute simulated lecture in which the test takers need to present new material, give instructions, and interact with students.

Based on numerous EMI classroom observations, interviews with teachers, interviews with program heads, and meetings with management across different academic disciplines, we found that certain language functions, like presentation, instructions, and interaction overlapped across different EMI classroom settings (Kling & Stæhr, 2012). Therefore, we decided to adopt a testing procedure based on a simulated lecture that elicits these common language functions. Although disciplinary teaching and content may be embedded in the testing procedure, they are not assessed (Dimova & Kling, 2018).

After we adopted the testing procedure, we defined the language abilities associated with teaching in the EMI context (construct definition) with the use of empirical data collected during piloting.

EXAMPLE 3.3 SPECIFICATIONS GOVERNED APPROACH: EPT

EPT: the specifications governed approach

The development of the English Placement Test (EPT) writing section is governed by test specifications. The test features an integrated writing task where test takers are required to read a set of six short passages (each featuring a case story, a research report, or a simple statistical graph), listen to a short lecture, and then write an essay in response to a question raised from the reading and listening input. As the EPT is administered both on-campus and online, we decided to develop a new set of essay tasks every academic year to ensure the security of the test. Each year, a team of six item writers is hired to create new writing prompts following EPT test specifications.

The test specifications include detailed information about what the prompts should be like, including selection of topic, content and linguistic complexity of reading and listening inputs, design of visual aids, and quality of audio recordings. The use of test specifications to govern the item writing process allows the item writers to develop comparable prompts. At the end of the development cycle each year, the item writers also discuss the clarity of the language in the specifications and brainstorm ways to refine the specifications.

EXAMPLE 3.4 EXPERIENTIAL APPROACH: OEPT

OEPT: experiential approach

The development of the OEPT is a good example of the experiential approach to item/test development. The test development team and the scale development team consisted of teaching assistants who were also instructors in the OEPP. They were assigned additional test development duties and provided additional compensation. Because our team consisted of graduate students, all were familiar with a broad range of instructional contexts at Purdue, either because of their own experiences or through those of students enrolled in the OEPP ITA class.

It is important to note that the OEPT is not linked to a particular context of teaching (e.g., introductory chemistry or physics), but is similar to the TOEPAS in that it focuses on common language functions across instructional contexts (e.g., stating an opinion, explicating a graph, comparing and contrasting information to make a decision, responding to a student complaint, reading aloud, and summarizing a short lecture). These tasks could be easily introduced as language activities that were essential elements in all of Purdue's instructional contexts, regardless of the particular department or program.

> All items were designed so that a test-taker can respond appropriately to the task without needing any content or disciplinary-specific knowledge, and so the OEPT is best understood as a general oral proficiency test, and not an English for specific purposes (ESP) test. In addition, we decided to not include teaching as part of the tested construct for several reasons stemming from our understanding of the broad instructional context at Purdue: (1) L1 English speaking teaching assistants are not required to demonstrate teaching proficiency before being assigned teaching duties, thus introducing a fairness issue if/when teaching is evaluated; (2) what may constitute effective teaching differs across departments (consider the importance of "chalk talk" in mathematics, linguistics, or any other domain highly dependent on problem solving); and (3) monitoring and evaluating effective teaching is a department/program responsibility.

Regardless of whether the approach taken is specifications governed, experiential, or a combination of the two, task design involves decisions related to the instructions, task format and delivery, input, and scoring method.

Instructions

Test and task instructions are important because they help test-takers familiarize themselves with the test purpose, task format, and results. When developing the instructions, you need to consider the content, specificity, language, and mode of delivery.

The kind of information included in the instructions depends on when the instructions are delivered to the test-takers, i.e., before, during, or after the testing session. Instructions are distributed before the testing session mainly to inform test-takers about the date, time, and location of the test administration, as well as information regarding what they can or should bring to the test site: identification (e.g., student ID, passport, driver's license), materials (e.g., dictionary, notes, PowerPoint), stationery (e.g., pencil, eraser), and equipment (e.g., computer, tablet, headset). These instructions are usually distributed to test-takers when they register for the test, most often in an email.

In addition to basic test instructions, information about the testing purpose, description of the test structure and tasks, explanation of the scoring system, and information about how the results are reported is useful before the test session. Sample and practice tasks, as well as sample responses and scale descriptors, help prospective test-takers not only to familiarize themselves with the tasks but also to understand the rating criteria. Finally, test-takers may need information about how the test results relate to national or international standards (e.g., linking the score bands of the test and the CEFR levels), as well as the kinds of language support that exist in the local context in case their test results are unsatisfactory.

All of these instructions can be distributed in test booklets and flyers that test-takers receive when they register. Another option is to provide these instructions on the test (or program) website so that test-takers are able to learn about the test purpose, format, and procedures before they decide to register for it. Example 3.5 discusses the distribution of instructions provided to test-takers before the test.

EXAMPLE 3.5 DISTRIBUTION OF INSTRUCTIONS BEFORE THE TEST SESSION

OEPT: instructions

When we first developed the OEPT, we were aware that, because it was a semi-direct, computer-delivered test of oral English proficiency, the format represented a radical departure from what test-takers might be expecting. While the semi-direct format has become much more familiar with the inclusion of speaking in the TOEFL iBT, we could not assume familiarity when the OEPT was introduced in 2000. The provision of adequate test preparation materials was essential.

Our first attempts included a paper booklet that described the semi-direct format, computer-based administration, tasks, and scale. This was clearly inadequate because of the mismatch across the paper-based description and the computer-based format of the test itself, but it was the best we could do at the time. In 2002, we provided prospective test-takers with a CD version of an entire practice test along with the information that was provided in the paper-based test preparation booklet. This solution was better than the booklet alone, but departments had to distribute the CDs to students and/or provide the materials in a computer lab. Test taker completion rates for the practice test were only around 50%.

Our third solution was developed in 2006. The online OEPT practice test and tutorial consists of two practice tests, the OEPT scale, two sets of sample passing responses, and a video tutorial introducing the Purdue instructional and ITA contexts. We track completion of the practice test and have achieved between 80–90% completion across departments. We believe that is about as high as it will ever be. The graduate school and departments alert incoming graduate students about the need to be certified for English proficiency, and students are also informed about OEPT test preparation materials when they register.

OEPT practice test materials are freely available and can be accessed at: http://tutorial.ace-in-testing.com/Default.aspx?p=test

The instructions provided during the test sessions are related to the overall test structure (e.g., the number and order of sections, time allotted for each section, breaks between sections, number of items per section) and the tasks (how to complete the task, and record and submit responses). Examples of tasks or warm-up questions are also included to give test-takers an opportunity to practice before they respond to rated/scored tasks. In digitally delivered tests, instructions about how to navigate the test, adjust the different settings (e.g., volume, light), record oral and written responses, and submit responses are essential (see Figure 3.7).

The instructions provided after the test usually relate to when and how test-takers will receive their results and whom they should contact if they have questions or complaints.

All instructions need to be straightforward and simple in order to avoid the possibility that the test-takers would misunderstand or overlook important information. If you include too many details, the test-takers may experience difficulties remembering them, which could result in confusion. Every attempt should be made to move the test-takers through the test as easily and comfortably as possible because you want their performance to reflect the ability being tested, not their familiarity with the format and procedure. Repeating important instructions in

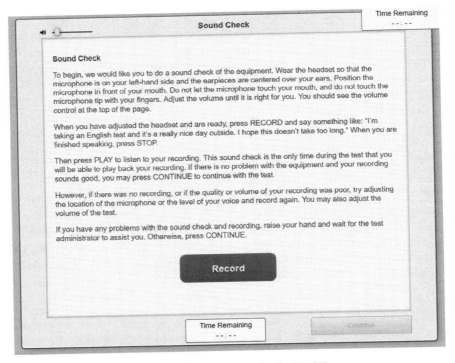

FIGURE 3.7 Example of sound check instructions in the OEPT

different places or at different points in time may also be useful. The specificity of the instructions depends on the test-takers. If they are children, then the instructions should probably be short, simple, and symbolic. Once the instructions are developed, their clarity can be confirmed through a pilot.

In local contexts where the test-takers share the same first language (L1), another consideration regarding instructions is the selection of language, i.e., L1 or target language (L2). Some would argue that providing instructions in the test-takers' L1 enhances comprehension, especially among test-takers at lower L2 proficiency levels. In many tests, general information regarding the test is provided in the test-takers' L1, while the instructions during the test are in their L2. The TOEPAS is an example where the instructions sent to the registered test-takers before the session are in both Danish and English, while the instructions during the test are in English (L2) only.

In addition to language, the selection of instruction delivery modes (textual, audio, video, visual) should also be considered. If you have a digitally enhanced test, for example, you could provide the instructions in both textual and audio modes to maximize test-takers' comprehension. Digitally enhanced tests also allow for the inclusion of video instructions, especially when the instructions are about a certain process (response recording or navigating). Video instructions may be particularly useful for younger test-takers who are accustomed to using YouTube as a source. More information about the opportunities that digitally enhanced delivery offers can be found in Chapter 5.

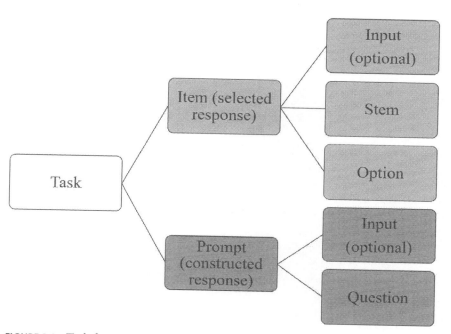

FIGURE 3.8 Task format

Task format

The task format refers to the type of output, i.e., response, it elicits, the number of language skills it involves, and the mode of delivery to test-takers. Tasks may contain items or prompts (see Figure 3.8). Items elicit selected responses (i.e., test-takers select the correct response from a multiple choice) or limited responses (i.e., test-takers insert single words, phrases, or short sentences). An example of a limited response task is the cloze test, where the test-taker is asked to enter words that have been removed from a written text in order to assess the test-taker's reading skills (see Chapter 4 for more examples of limited response). The tasks may also contain prompts that elicit constructed responses that require oral or written language production in the form of short or extended discourse; these are also known as performance-based responses (e.g., essays, presentations, dialogues) (see Chapter 4 for more examples).

In terms of number of skills, you must decide whether the tasks should focus on one skill (single-skill tasks) or whether they should involve the use of several skills (integrated-skill tasks). In single-skill tasks, the test-taker needs to activate only one language skill (e.g., speaking, listening, reading) in order to complete the task. In integrated-skill tasks, the test-taker needs to activate different language skills in order to complete the task. For instance, if test-takers are required to write an essay based on a written text, then they will not be able to complete the task successfully if they lack reading comprehension or writing skills. Understanding the text would be insufficient if the test-taker lacks the ability to write an essay, and writing an essay would be insufficient if the test-taker cannot understand the text.

The delivery mode of tasks (e.g., paper, digital, interview) can influence the facility of task administration and response collection. The design of integrated-skill tasks is facilitated in digitally enhanced tests because these tests offer solutions for multimodal representation of information. For example, the play menu and the writing field can occur on the same screen in tasks that integrate listening and writing, which simplifies the task delivery. However, despite the possible task delivery facilitation that digital devices (e.g., computers, tablets) offer, you have to consider whether digital delivery is relevant for the purpose of your test. The delivery mode is discussed in Chapter 5.

Input

The task input is the content – be it linguistic, nonlinguistic, or both – with which the test-taker is presented in order to elicit the relevant language skill for the assessment. In listening tasks, the input is the audio or video information that test-takers are required to listen to or watch and process in order to complete the task (Brunfaut & Révész, 2015; Vandergrift, 2007). The input in reading tasks is in the form of verbal (texts) and non-verbal information (e.g., pictures, graphs, tables). Factors like text length, topic, and genre familiarity may influence performance (Alderson, 2000). Test-takers are required to process the written text and non-verbal information, if present, so that they can provide responses for the reading tasks. Existing audio/video recordings or texts that are publicly available could be selected or they could be created specifically to serve as input in the reading and listening tasks. You may intuitively select existing materials or develop your own based on topics that you find suitable for your test-taker population. If you select existing materials, you need to make sure you have copyright permission to use them in the test.

In order to make sure that the input is at a specific level of difficulty, you need to analyze the lexical, syntactic, and discourse complexity, as well as the explicitness of the information. For audio/video inputs, you also need to analyze the phonological complexity, i.e., the speed, rhythm, pitch, and frequency of elisions, i.e., omissions of sounds due to uses of reduced forms (e.g., "I'm gonna" or "I'ma" instead of "I am going to"). The more linguistically or phonologically complex the input is, the more difficult it will become for the test-takers to process.

Regarding input for listening and reading tasks, the number of times that test-takers can access the input, the possibility of taking notes, and the time that the test-takers have to process the input all require consideration. For example, can the test-takers hear the audio input only once, twice, or can they replay different parts if there is a need for it? While listening to an audio input only once may increase authenticity, allowing test-takers to listen twice enhances the bias for their best performance. Allowing test-takers to take notes while listening to or watching long recordings will help them to avoid mistakes in their responses because they forgot some detail due to working memory overload.

In performance-based speaking and writing tasks, the input material that is used to elicit the extended responses may be included in the prompt. The prompt should provide sufficient contextual and linguistic cues, which will stimulate test-takers' interaction with the task in the intended manner. For example, a prompt for a writing task may include information about the context, the genre, the audience, and the length of the task response. Figure 3.9 below presents an example of a prompt for a speaking task from the OEPT. Three elements are present in the prompt: 1) introduction (establishes the context and audience), 2) input (genre and the topic), and 3) question (prompts the response). The introduction allows test developers to represent the local context in which test-takers will use the target language outside of the test. This contextualization enhances test-takers' interaction with the tasks and promotes elicitation of the relevant language functions for the assessment purpose. While the OEPT's introductions/contextualizations are minimal, test-takers appreciate having a better understanding about why they are being asked to provide a particular response. These introductions also serve to enhance test-takers' understanding of the instructional contexts in which they will be required to perform once they pass the test.

Local tests also present a unique opportunity for representation of endonormative (localized or indigenized) rather than exonormative (imported) language varieties in the task input, which has been difficult to achieve in large-scale tests because of their uses across a wide range of contexts with different linguistic norms. This opportunity is particularly useful in English as a lingua franca (ELF) contexts in which native-speaker linguistic and functional norms may not be applicable.

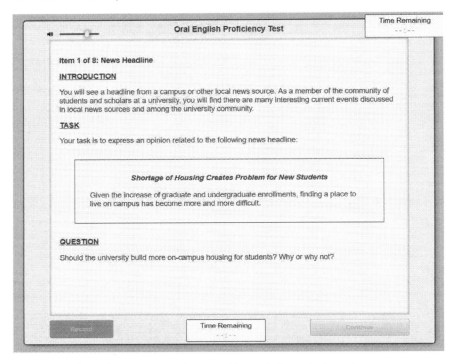

FIGURE 3.9   Example of a prompt for a speaking task from the OEPT

Scoring method

Scoring refers to assigning numerical scores based on the level of task fulfillment or response correctness. In selected or limited response types, as in multiple choice items or cloze tests, the scoring will be based on correct/incorrect or partial credit responses. If these items are digitally administered, then the scoring method may be automated so that test-takers can receive their results as soon as they finish the test. If the test has performance-based tasks, you will need to develop a rating scale and train raters to use it. Chapters 6 and 7 provide detailed information about the different types of scales, the scale development process, and rater training. You can read about result reporting in Chapter 8.

Test structure

In order to elicit test-takers' performances that include different language functions across target language domains, test developers often decide to include more than one task in the test. Most books on language test development recommend designing a detailed description, also known as "blueprint" of the test content (number and type of tasks), structure, and administration as a starting point for test development.

However, in many cases, the test writers design a pool of different tasks out of which the most relevant for the assessment purpose are selected. You will need to consider how many tasks to include and whether the order of task appearance is fixed or random. The number of tasks you include depends on whether they are sufficient to elicit all the focal language aspects that you want to assess and how long it takes to complete the test. Although a larger number of tasks can improve the test's reliability, the time and resource constraints should also be evaluated. In terms of ordering, you may apply different ordering approaches. For example, you may group tasks based on a logical thematic progression, assessed skill (or subskill), similarity, or topic. Piloting the test will help you to find out whether the number of tasks is adequate and whether the task order is appropriate.

Comparable forms

For security reasons, designing multiple forms of the language test is recommended. Two test forms may suffice in the beginning, one to administer in regular sessions and the other in case some test-takers need to be re-tested (Bae & Lee, 2011). A new form for every administration is developed when high test security is essential or when the correct task responses are made public after each test administration.

The multiple test forms have to be comparable, which means that each form must have the same instructions, structure, and task types. The comparability of test forms is analyzed by administering each of the two forms to random test-takers and then comparing each group's overall performance. The random form assignment to test-takers ensures that the two groups have equal proficiency. Any statistical differences across groups on the two test forms can be interpreted as a difference in the test forms. If the overall performance of the group who took form one equals the average performance of the group who took form two, then the forms are comparable.

You may have noticed that we are using the term *comparable test forms* instead of *parallel* or *equivalent test forms*. In order to claim that the test scores are parallel across forms, equating methods based on Item Response Theory (IRT) models are applied to resolve the statistical differences among the different forms (Boek-kooi-Timminga, 1990; Weir & Wu, 2006). In addition, equating involves the use of anchor items to compare the performance of target subpopulations over time. Large data sets are required to perform such analyses, and so they are rarely used in local testing. In addition, in local contexts, the ability to change and adapt the test to different and evolving instructional efforts is prioritized over the ability characteristics of a subgroup over time (e.g., students' performance on the Scholastic Assessment Test (SAT) in 1969 versus 2015).

Test administration procedures

When developing test administration procedures, planning the space, time, staff, and equipment, as well as the test delivery and response collection, is part of the development process. If the test is low-stakes and digitally delivered, then test-takers may complete it from home. In most cases, however, the test is administered at a specific time in a designated location.

Once you find the appropriate room(s) and decide on the time (dates and hours) for the testing sessions, you will need to determine the number of test administrators and their responsibilities before and during the test session(s). Then, decisions about check-in, seating, and test start and progression (e.g., whether everyone starts and finishes each test section at the same time or whether breaks between and within sections are allowed) can be established.

In the administration of digitally enhanced tests, the available equipment must be checked for hardware and software functionality. Having a back-up plan for response collection in case the internet is down or responses fail to register in the database is always a good idea. You can find out more about test delivery and data management (response collection and storage) in Chapters 5 and 8.

Pre-operational testing

Three types of pre-operational testing are performed to ensure the quality of the testing procedures: 1) pre-testing testing, or exploratory analysis of the tasks, scale, administration procedures, and score reporting system; 2) pilot testing, or a small scale trial used for basic item analysis; and 3) field testing, or confirmatory analysis of the test's psychometric properties (Kenyon & MacGregor, 2012). In this section, we will focus on pre-testing and pilot testing because pre-operational field testing requires the collection of large data sets, which are rarely available in local contexts. In large-scale tests, the psychometric properties of test items are further examined by embedding prospective items within a regular administration and then abandoning those items that do not work psychometrically. Local tests seldom have the opportunity to conduct extensive embedded pretesting; however, quality control can be enhanced by pilot testing.

Pre-testing of the items, test administration procedures, and score reporting system helps to examine whether all of these function according to the plan, or whether adjustments are necessary. Pre-testing of items allows test developers to identify major issues with item format and delivery, as well as response collection. The pre-test can help identify problems related to the accessibility of the test location, size of the room, seating plan, functionality of the heating/cooling system, and levels of noise or possibility for disturbance. The functionality of the equipment in the room, as well as the availability and speed of the internet should also be tested. The day and time of the administration may affect the room and equipment functionality (e.g., afternoons are noisier than mornings, the internet is slower during the weekend), and whether the day and time will affect test-takers' ability to participate in the test or their performance. Finally, the pilot allows the test administrators to try the planned procedures (check-in, seating, instructions) and figure out whether these procedures need to be adjusted. Most importantly, test administrators have an opportunity to check whether they can handle the administration alone or whether they need more staff during the administration.

Pilot testing requires the recruitment of a number of participants who are willing to try out the test in order to gather data for analysis. Whether the tasks seem adequate for the testing purpose and whether or not the tasks elicit the adequate performance can only be checked by administering them to test-takers. Identifying and keeping those tasks that give you the ability to distinguish test-takers across different proficiency levels are of particular interest. A task/item may not be useful if test-takers across all proficiency levels can complete it or if high-proficiency test-takers experience difficulties, while lower-proficiency test-takers can complete it. Piloting will also allow you to check whether the test-takers find the test and task instructions clear and easy to follow, and whether colors, fonts, visuals, and screen or page layouts are distracting. The scales for performance-based tasks also have to be piloted in order to examine whether the raters can use the scale effectively to distinguish performances across proficiency levels. You can read more about scaling in Chapter 6.

Several different data collection methods can be applied during the pilot administration: basic item analysis, observation, feedback, and questionnaires. By observing the test administration procedures, test-takers, and rater behavior, certain problems and inconsistencies can be identified and addressed before the test becomes operational. For example, you may observe some confusion during the setup of the equipment and, as a result, you develop clearer instructions. Collection of feedback from all participants in the testing process (e.g., test-takers, administrators, raters) can be performed through interviews, written comments, and focus group discussions. When a large number of test-takers participates in the pilot, feedback could be collected with the use of questionnaires. Test-takers can provide informative feedback about the functionality of the testing procedure, the difficulty or ease of tasks, equipment, and response recording, as well as test navigation and score reporting. Test administrators' feedback can include information about the functionality and order of the testing procedures, the need to include more administrative staff, and the clarity of instructions for setting up the room and equipment.

The raters, on the other hand, can discuss the ease or difficulty of using the scale descriptors to distinguish among proficiency levels, the need to include additional descriptors that underline salient features of the level, and the ease/difficulty of accessing responses and submitting scores.

Technical manuals

The purpose of the technical manual is to document the technical characteristics of the test based on the research and development work completed in the task and test development process. Therefore, technical manuals usually contain information about the purpose, content, structure, and administration of the test, as well as the scoring system and measurement properties (e.g., reliability, internal consistency, content validity). Technical manuals can also include reports on standard-setting procedures and alignment with standards (e.g., linking test scores to the CEFR). These manuals are intended for test users (stakeholders) who need information about the appropriateness of the test for their decision-making purposes and for researchers and testing specialists who want to analyze the test properties. Because tests are analyzed continually to ensure they remain reliable and valid, the technical manual needs to be updated accordingly (see OEPT Technical Manual, OEPT, 2019).

In addition to the technical manual, which is a public document, instruction manuals for internal use are quite helpful. These instruction manuals inform new testing team members about their duties and responsibilities, but they also assist the current members when performing the different tasks for which they are responsible. For example, you may need a manual for test administrators who are responsible for setting up the room and equipment for the testing session, as well as welcoming the test-takers and monitoring the testing session. The administrators will need information with technical specifications (e.g., how to set up computers, video cameras, audio players) and the different steps in a procedure (e.g., checking-in and seating test-takers). Visual representations tend to be more useful than textual explanations when providing instructions about the equipment setup (e.g., how to plug in a computer to the correct outlet) or the digital platform (e.g., how to find the application and activate the login screen). A checklist with all of the steps involved in the procedure, as well as a list of common problems and how to troubleshoot them, is also quite useful.

In the case of developing a digital test, keeping a record of the technical development of the platform and obtaining access to the source code are essential. Because test and platform revisions will be necessary after a certain period of time, the technical information and source code will be used when performing the planned changes.

Summary

In this chapter, we discussed different activities involved in the planning, design, and implementation of test development. As you may have noticed, we avoided recommending a specific order in which these activities should take place because the test development approach you take depends on the contextual factors and resources. However, we would like to provide you with a concrete example of the flow of activities undertaken in an actual test development process (see Figure 3.10) so that you can obtain an overview of the test development process in practice.

As you can see in Figure 3.10, the first stage of the development process of TOEPAS focused on the establishment of the core testing team, analysis of the local context, and description of the communicative language functions observed in teaching situations in the local university context. Based on the context

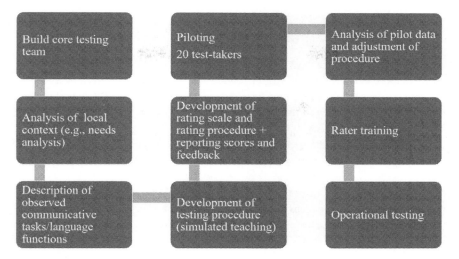

FIGURE 3.10   TOEPAS development process

analyses, a testing procedure was developed to reflect local language uses and assessment values. Then, the rating scale descriptors and the result reporting system were designed and piloted with 20 test-takers. In the last stages of the test development process, the pilot data were analyzed, and the procedure and scale were adjusted based on the results. Once the testing procedure and scale were finalized, the raters were trained before the test become fully operational.

This chapter provided a general overview of the test development process. In the following chapters, we provide more detailed discussions about task types, test delivery, scaling, and data management.

Further reading

Fulcher, G. (1997). An English language placement test: Issues in reliability and validity. *Language testing, 14*(2), 113–139.

Fulcher (1997) investigates the reliability and validity of a placement test at the University of Surrey, which is designed for decision-making regarding English language support provision for undergraduate and postgraduate students. Reliable and valid test scores are crucial in achieving the purpose of the test, minimizing the possibility of students having academic challenges or failures due to low English language ability and reliability. The author comprehensively evaluates reliability and validity by considering different quantitative estimates that complement each other, for example, obtaining correlations, inter- and intra-rater reliability, a logistic model fit, and Rasch modeling for reliability, and examining correlation, principal components analysis, cut scores, concurrent validity, content validity, and student feedback for validity. The results demonstrate how various methods are effectively used to equate test forms and investigate reliability and validity of a placement test which has a small number of examinees and logistic and administrational constraints.

Henning, G. (1987). *A guide to language testing*. New York: Newbury.

As the subtitle suggests, this book introduces the technical principles of measurement needed in the development of tests, course evaluation, and language-related research. The first chapter introduces some of the key concepts in language testing such as test purposes and test types (objective versus subjective, direct vs. indirect, discrete-point vs. integrative, aptitude, achievement and proficiency, criterion or domain referenced vs. norm-referenced, speed vs. power). The next two chapters introduce measurement scales and test data analysis. Some technical topics such as the standardization of scores, Fisher's Z – transformation, and correction for guessing formulae are described in this chapter. Some of the important topics covered in the next chapters are item analysis, correlation and regression, reliability and validity analysis, threats to reliability and validity, item response model, Rasch analysis, and teacher and course evaluations. This book can be considered an introduction to many technical and statistical principles which are important when considering test development, evaluation, and research.

Lynch, B. K., & Davidson, F. (1994). Criterion-referenced language test development: Linking curricula, teachers, and tests. *TESOL Quarterly, 28*(4), 727–743.

After presenting the difference between norm-referenced and criterion-referenced testing, Lynch and Davidson (1994) argue that criterion-referenced testing can be used to strengthen the relationship between testing and the curriculum. The authors argue that one of the most important features of criterion-referenced language test development (CRLTD) is the development of test specification and discuss the process of using CRLTD to develop and redevelop a well-written specification. They also argue that there must be clear communication between test specification writers and item writers since CRLTD's primary focus is on refining the process of specifications implementation to write test tasks. They also propose a "workshop approach" to CRLTD which can help classroom teachers develop the ability to articulate their curriculums' aims and objectives in test specifications and make connections between those objectives and the test development process. The authors mention UCLA ESLPE test and UIUC Placement Test as examples of local tests, which have used CRLTD to refine their test specifications and test items.

References

Alderson, J. C. (2000). *Assessing writing*. Cambridge: Cambridge University Press.

Bachman, L. F., & Palmer, A. S. (1996). *Language testing in practice: Designing and developing useful language tests* (Vol. 1). Oxford: Oxford University Press.

Bae, J., & Lee, Y. S. (2011). The validation of parallel test forms: 'Mountain' and 'beach' picture series for assessment of language skills. *Language Testing, 28*(2), 155–177.

Boekkooi-Timminga, E. (1990). The construction of parallel tests from IRT-based item banks. *Journal of Educational Statistics, 15*(2), 129–145.

Brunfaut, T., & Révész, A. (2015). The role of task and listener characteristics in second language listening. *TESOL Quarterly, 49*(1), 141–168.

Dimova, S., & Kling, J. (2018). Assessing english-medium instruction lecturer language proficiency across disciplines. *TESOL Quarterly, 52*(3), 634–656.

Kenyon, D., & MacGregor, D. (2012). Pre-operational testing. In G. Fulcher & F. Davidson (Eds.), *The Routledge handbook of language testing* (pp. 309–320). London: Routledge.

Kling, J., & Stæhr, L. S. (2012). The development of the Test of Oral English Proficiency for Academic Staff (TOEPAS). University of Copenhagen.

OEPT. (2019). *OEPT technical manual.* West Lafayette, IN: Purdue University.

Vandergrift, L. (2007). Recent developments in second and foreign language listening comprehension research. *Language Teaching, 40*(3), 191–210.

Weir, C. J., & Wu, J. R. (2006). Establishing test form and individual task comparability: A case study of a semi-direct speaking test. *Language Testing, 23*(2), 167–197.

4

TEST TASKS

This chapter presents a variety of task types that can be used to assess a number of language skills, including lexico-grammar, listening, reading, speaking, and writing. It briefly introduces the history of development of different task types, which is closely related to theoretical movements in linguistics and psychology. Examples of various task types designed for assessment of different languages are also presented and the advantages and disadvantages of their uses are discussed. In this chapter, we argue that, while there is no single best method to assess language ability, awareness of different assessment methods enhances one's test development options.

Introduction

There are a thousand Hamlets in a thousand people's eyes. Readers of William Shakespeare may each construct their own version of the character based on their own experiences and interpretations, even though they all read the same text. There is no single interpretation that is inherently superior to the others. While this argument speaks directly about the situatedness of interpretation, it also applies to how we judge the value and quality of test tasks. A healthy mindset for evaluating language tasks is to think that all methods can succeed and all methods can fail. Of course, it is possible to develop some criteria to evaluate the quality of a particular language proficiency measure, but that criteria should be embedded in the local context, which includes the test purpose, development and scoring resources, and the stakeholder network.

When developing a language test, you often start with tasks, especially if you already have a clear idea of what you want to assess and why you want to assess it. Sometimes, however, you might feel puzzled or even frustrated about which tasks to use. Since the beginning of language testing as a field (Lado, 1961), the tasks used in language tests have expanded from discrete-point items to open-ended, integrated tasks. In this chapter, we survey the tasks used to assess different components of language ability. Following a somewhat chronological order, we review the popular language tasks in different eras of language assessment, not to draw attention to fashions or trends, but to provide a range of options for you to contemplate as a starting point for test development. We follow the terminology in Chapter 3, *Local test development* by using *task* as an umbrella term, which is interchangeable with *item* when used to elicit selected responses, and with *prompt* when used to elicit constructed responses. Furthermore, an item includes optional *input* materials, a *stem* and *options*; a prompt includes optional input materials and a *question*.

Discrete-point lexico-grammar items

Language testing emerged as a professional field during the contrastive analysis period in second language acquisition (SLA) in the 1960s and early 1970s (Carroll, 1961; Lado, 1961), which was formed under the joint influence of behavioral psychology and structural linguistics. Contrastive analysis hypothesized that language is composed of structural elements at different levels (i.e., phonemes, morphemes, lexical categories, and sentence types) or a system of habits in communication, and that the difficulty in mastering certain structures in a second language (L2) depends on the difference between the learners' first language (L1) and the target language – the L2 that they are trying to learn. The purpose of a structuralist model of language testing is to identify and explain the features of a given target language that are difficult for learners of different L1 backgrounds to acquire. Language tasks under this approach tend to feature discrete items reflecting structural elements of pronunciation and lexico-grammar. In theory, if all learner difficulties can be predicted, then it is possible to design a sequence of language tasks that can measure the acquisition of different grammatical structures and track L2 development across stages. In actuality, however, not all learner difficulties can be explained by the differences between L1 and L2 (or *crosslinguistic influence*), although they can be to a great extent. Meanwhile, in language testing and the larger field of TESOL/Applied Linguistics, the conception of language ability has evolved to include much more than grammatical competence alone (Bachman, 1990; Canale & Swain, 1980). Researchers and practitioners are more interested in using integrated, constructed-response tasks to evaluate integrative language performance rather than the acquisition of specific grammatical structures. Because of this shift in conception and interest, the marriage between language testing and SLA has gradually dissolved.

Despite the changing conception of language ability in language testing, discrete-point items remain an effective approach to measuring lexico-grammatical knowledge. The most common types of discrete-point items include, but are not limited to, multiple-choice, true-false, fill-in-the-blank, matching, and error correction. These item-types are quite effective, especially for learners of lower-level proficiency who have not yet reached a developmental stage where they can handle more interactive, open-ended language tasks. For this reason, discrete lexico-grammar items are also popular in the assessment of foreign languages, especially the less commonly taught ones for which exposure is often restricted to the classroom (e.g., Chinese and Korean in the US). Table 4.1 summarizes the characteristics of these item-types, and an example of each type is shown in Figures 4.1–4.5. For example, in the matching item (Figure 4.2) test-takers match the pictures with the times based on the story they are listening to.

Discrete-point items are difficult to write. The challenge of writing good ("objective") items lies in the difficulty of creating good distractors that allow you to differentiate between high and low performing students. In addition, good distractors should allow test users to identify learner difficulties, thus enabling them to assess students' learning outcomes, evaluate the effectiveness of instruction, and identify areas that need instructional reinforcement or adjustment. As this chapter is only a general survey of language tasks, we will not elaborate on how to write test items. Readers can refer to Fulcher (2010), Hughes (2003), and others for guidelines on writing these kinds of items.

Integrative measures of general language ability

General proficiency measures (also referred to as *integrative tasks*) arose as a reaction to the limitations of discrete-point items and the criticism of the structuralist approach to language learning and testing. The assumption behind integrative tasks is that we often use knowledge of multiple linguistic structures and elements in combination to complete a language task. Therefore, language tests should assess language use as a whole. Some of the well-known integrative tasks include cloze, c-test, elicited imitation, and dictation. Table 4.2 summarizes the characteristics of these task types, and an example of cloze and c tests are shown in Figures 4.4 and 4.6.

While integrative tasks look rather different from one another, they are similar in that they appear to assess "everything". These measures had their heyday in language testing in the 1960s and 1970s, and remain popular options for measuring proficiency levels, especially in research contexts. Integrative tasks are quite reliable, efficient, and effective for placing students into levels and can be useful in the classroom when teachers need quick and easy-to-administer tasks to assess students' ability to use target lexico-grammatical knowledge in context. These tasks also exhibit strong correlations with other task types. However, what they are actually measuring remains a matter of debate to this very day. Regarding cloze and c-tests alike, scholars have not reached consensus as to whether these tasks measure the lexico-grammar surrounding the blanks or the ability to make meaning across clausal boundaries. While some scholars argue that the cloze test is similar to multiple-choice or fill-in-the-blank items that measure specific structural elements (Alderson, 1980), there is more recent evidence to suggest that this type of task measures test-takers' ability to

TABLE 4.1 Discrete lexico-grammar items

Item type	Prompt attribute	Response attribute	Difficulty
True–false	• The stem is often a statement that is either correct or incorrect. • The options include one *key* and one *distractor* (True vs. False).	• **Response**: Select the key from the two options. • **Scoring**: Binary (correct/incorrect)	Easy
Matching	• The task typically consists of two adjacent lists of related words, phrases, or sentences. • Since the two lists are paired, the distinction between the stem and options is less meaningful. Sometimes, the first column is called *the premises*, and the second column is called *the responses*.	• **Response**: Pair each option from one list with an option in the other list. • **Scoring**: Binary (correct/incorrect)	Easy
Multiple-choice	• The stem consists of a statement with a blank (i.e., *the stem*) and several options. • The options typically include a correct answer (i.e., *the key*) and several incorrect answers (i.e., *distractors*).	• **Response:** Select only the key from all the options. • **Scoring:** Binary (correct/incorrect)	Medium
Fill in blank	• The stem is a statement with a blank space. • The options are either not provided or provided in the form of a word/ phrase bank.	• Response: Supply the missing word or words. • Scoring: Binary (correct/incorrect) or partial credit	Difficult
Error correction	• The stem typically consists of a list of independent sentences or a paragraph. • A smaller number of words can be purposefully highlighted to limit the range of scrutiny and reduce the item difficulty for test-takers.	• Response: Identify the errors and supply a correct lexico-grammatical item for replacement. • Scoring: Binary (correct/incorrect) or partial credit	Difficult

FIGURE 4.1 True/false reading item for young learners in English and German (Tidligere sprogstart, https://tidligeresprogstart.ku.dk)

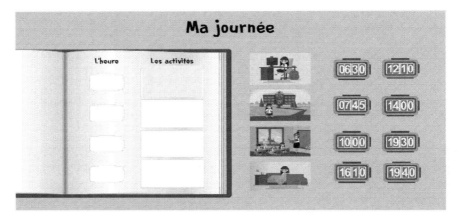

FIGURE 4.2 Matching item in listening comprehension in French (Tidligere sprogstart, https://tidligeresprogstart.ku.dk)

Me _____ Alejandro.

A. llama
B. llaman
C. llamo
D. llame

FIGURE 4.3 Sample MC item of Spanish grammar

understand language beyond the sentence level (McCray & Brunfaut, 2018; Winke, Yan, & Lee, in press). Similarly, there have been doubts about whether elicited imitation tasks measure imitation or the comprehension and reconstruction of meaning. Research findings have suggested that elicited imitation tasks are a valid measure of general language proficiency (Vinther, 2002; Yan, Maeda, Lv, & Ginther, 2016).

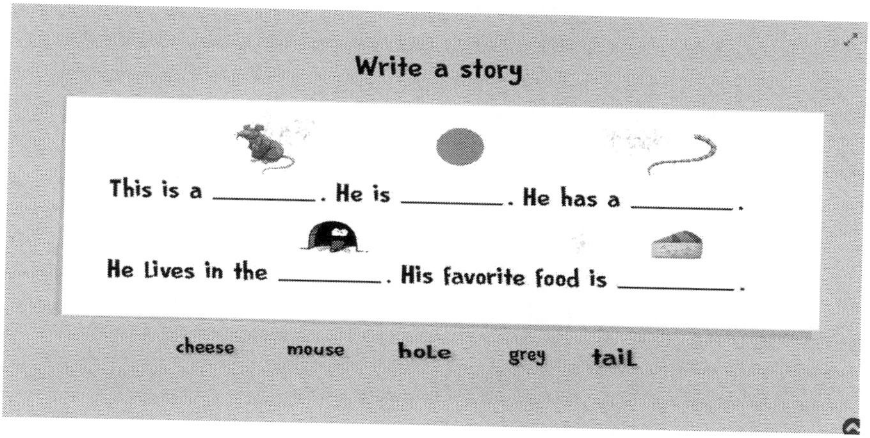

Write a story

This is a _____ . He is _____ . He has a _____ .

He lives in the _____ . His favorite food is _____ .

cheese   mouse   hole   grey   tail

FIGURE 4.4   Fill-in-the-blank/cloze test of English vocabulary for first-grade EFL learners (Tidligere sprogstart, https://tidligeresprogstart.ku.dk)

We cannot hardly expect adolescents to have respect for the
     A   B

possessions of others if they have no hope of attaining any of their
                  C   D

own.

FIGURE 4.5   Error correction in English

English 106-I is a writing course for nonnative English-speaking undergraduate students. This cou__ is desi__ particularly f__ international stud__, allowing no__ focus o__ language a__ culture. I__ is typi__ taught b__ instructors wi__ experience i__ teaching compo__ and a__ understanding o__ what i__ is li__ to wr__ in a sec__ language. F—instructional purp__. This cou__ has a__ enrollment li__ of 15 stud__ per class.

FIGURE 4.6   An example of an English c-test for university-level ESL learners

Skill-based performance assessments

Reading

In the language testing literature, it is commonplace to regard some of the general proficiency measures (cloze test, c-test) as reading tasks (e.g., Alderson, 2000). In some ways, this is reasonable, as these tasks involve the processing of a written text. However, we have classified those tasks under general language proficiency measures because of their relative simplicity in task design, as well as the skills and abilities they are claimed to measure. In this section, we introduce reading tasks that are

TABLE 4.2 Integrative language tasks

Item type	Prompt attribute	Response attribute	Difficulty
C-test	• A paragraph with the second half of every other word deleted. • The first and final sentences of the paragraph are typically kept intact to provide the context.	• **Response**: Supply the missing words. • **Scoring**: Binary (correct/incorrect)	Easy
Cloze	• A paragraph or passage with certain words or phrases removed • The words to delete can be random, systematic (every nth word), or purposeful (particular categories of word). • The options can be either fill-in-the-blank or MC items.	• **Response**: Supply the missing words. • **Scoring**: Binary (correct/incorrect)	Easy
Elicited imitation	• The task consists of a list of audio-recorded sentences. • The sentences should be long enough to prevent the test takers from repeating the sentences by simply parroting.	• **Response:** Listen to individual sentences and repeat them verbatim. • **Scoring:** Binary (correct/incorrect) or rating scale	Medium
Dictation	• The task consists of audio-recorded sentences or paragraphs.	• Response: Listen to the sentences/paragraphs and write down the sentences verbatim. • Scoring: Rating scale	Difficult

more widely understood as measures of reading fluency and comprehension. These are performance-based reading tasks that are more authentic and can be easily adapted into teaching and learning materials for reading classes.

Reading fluency is the ability to read with a certain level of automaticity. It is also a significant indicator of reading comprehension. To read a text fluently, readers need to decode written texts for meaning and create relationships between the textual meaning and the meaning gleaned from their surroundings (e.g., the readers' experiences, the reading environment). In order to focus their attention on meaning, readers need to be efficient at processing the orthography and morphosyntax of written texts. Thus, it is important to develop reading tasks that allow for the assessment of reading fluency. In general, reading fluency tasks require test-takers to read sentences, paragraphs, or passages while recording the speed of reading. The focus of the measurement is on speed while the readers read the text for comprehension. Reading fluency is often assessed through oral reading tasks. Oral reading (sometimes referred to as guided oral reading) is a popular instructional technique for teaching reading to young learners in which a teacher (or parent) reads a passage aloud to model fluent reading, and then the students reread the text (Figure 4.7). This technique has been demonstrated to be effective on adult learners as well (Allen, 2016). The key to oral reading as an instructional technique is to make sure that the text is at the appropriate reading level, so that students are able to recognize, understand, and pronounce most (95%) of the words. Using this technique, one can effectively assess the reading level of students by asking them to read aloud texts at different complexity/grade levels. By assessing the pronunciation, parsing, fluency, and disfluency patterns of the read aloud, testers are able to make judgments about the appropriate reading level of each student. When students are reading above grade level, their attention is often captured by a heavy amount of lexico-grammar decoding, which interferes with comprehension. Instructors can assess students' comprehension by asking for a summary or having them complete a comprehension task. Figure 4.7 is an example of an oral reading task in Danish as a second language.

Sneglen og rosenhækken
Et eventyr af Hans Christian Andersen (1861)

Rundt om haven var et gærde af nøddebuske, og udenfor var mark og eng med køer og får, men midt i haven stod en blomstrende rosenhæk, under den sad en snegl, den havde meget i sig, den havde sig selv.

"Vent til min tid kommer!" sagde den, "jeg skal udrette noget mere, end at sætte roser, end at bære nødder, eller give mælk, som køer og får!"

"Jeg venter grumme meget af den!" sagde rosenhækken. "Tør jeg spørge, når kommer det?"

"Jeg giver mig tid!" sagde sneglen. "De har nu så meget hastværk! det spænder ikke forventningerne!"

Næste år lå sneglen omtrent på samme sted i solskinnet under rosentræet, der satte knop og udfoldede roser, altid friske, altid nye. Og sneglen krøb halvt frem, strakte ud følehornene, og tog dem til sig igen.

"Alt ser ud, som i fjor! der er ingen fremgang sket; rosentræet bliver ved roserne, videre kommer det ikke!"

Sommeren gik, efteråret gik, rosentræet havde stadigt blomster og knopper lige til sneen faldt, vejret blev råt og vådt, rosentræet bøjede sig mod jorden, sneglen krøb i jorden.

Nu begyndte et nyt år, og roserne kom frem, og sneglen kom frem.

"Nu er De en gammel rosenstok!" sagde den. "De må snart se at gå ud. De har givet verden alt, hvad De har haft i Dem; om det betød noget, er et spørgsmål, jeg ikke havde tid at tænke over; men der er da tydeligt, De har ikke gjort det mindste for Deres indre udvikling, der var ellers kommet noget andet frem af Dem. Kan De forsvare det? De går nu snart op i bare pind! Kan De forstå, hvad jeg siger?"

FIGURE 4.7 An example of oral reading task in Danish

In contrast to oral reading (see Figure 4.7), silent reading tasks tend to be employed to measure reading comprehension. A reading comprehension task includes a reading passage followed typically by a number of selected-response or short answer items. Depending on the target proficiency level, the passage and items need to be carefully selected or modified in terms of genre (advertisement, poster, narrative, or expository writing) and complexity (language and content). The challenge in developing good reading comprehension tasks lies in both the creation of a reading passage at a particular complexity level and the creation of items following the reading passage.

There are a number of ways to manipulate the complexity level of the reading passage. You can (1) alter the length of the passage, (2) alter the use of complex syntactic structures and sophisticated lexical items, (3) manipulate the information density or content complexity of the text, or (4) select texts from different genres and registers. For example, when measuring the reading level of third-grade English language learners in the US, you might want to choose short narrative texts and avoid argumentative or expository ones. Figure 4.8 is an example of a typical

Visit Copenhagen ZOO: Best experience ever

Tickets

♦ Skip the line and buy your tickets online. We will send them to your email, SMS, or our app.
♦ Buy tickets at our many sales points downtown. Click here to find the nearest sales point.
♦ Tickets are non-refundable.
♦ Entrance is one-time only.

Opening hours

Summer (May 15-October 15)   *Winter (October 16-May 14)*

Sunday-Thursday: 10am to 8pm   Sunday-Thursday: 10am to 6pm
Friday-Saturday: 10am to 11pm   Friday-Saturday: 10am to 8pm

Closed on national holidays

Select the correct answer.

If you plan to visit Copenhagen ZOO,
   a) you can buy tickets only online
   b) you can go there any day of the year
   c) you can stay at the zoo longer in summer

FIGURE 4.8   Reading comprehension for young EFL learners in Denmark

reading comprehension task for young learners at this developmental stage. In contrast, when assessing reading skills for ESL students in higher educational contexts, it might be more appropriate to select longer argumentative texts that prompt test-takers to evaluate the quality of argumentation.

In terms of the items that follow the reading passage, a variety of task types can be used, including multiple-choice, true/false, short-answer questions, and matching or sequencing items. These tasks are typically used to measure one or more of the following subskills in reading: vocabulary, main idea (skimming), information location (scanning), and inferencing. Table 4.3 below shows the reading tasks that are commonly used to assess different subskills. While test developers have flexibility in the choice of task type, certain types of tasks are commonly used to measure particular reading subskills.

Listening comprehension

Measuring listening skills is arguably more challenging than assessing reading skills. While listening tasks tend to assess a similar set of subskills as reading comprehension tasks, they also require test-takers to attend to speech characteristics (e.g., speech rate, speaker accent) since the passage is conveyed orally. When developing listening comprehension tasks, the speech characteristics discussed below should be carefully considered.

The first speech characteristic to consider is register. In corpus linguistics and speech sciences, research has examined the differences between written and spoken discourse. In terms of complexity, written discourse tends to be structurally more complex (e.g., featuring more nominalization) than spoken discourse, whereas spoken discourse, especially dialogue, tends to feature more coordination and subordination. However, academic lectures or speeches tend to feature an "intermediate" register between written and spoken discourse (Thirakunkovit, Rodríguez-Fuentes, Park, & Staples, 2019). Therefore, depending on the

TABLE 4.3 Reading tasks

Subskills	Task	Item type
Skimming	• Identify gist or main idea(s) • Develop headings for paragraphs	• MC • Short answer
Scanning	• Locate specific details	• MC • True/False • Short answer
Coherence/ organization	• Order scrambled sentences in paragraph • Insert sentences in text	• Sequencing • Matching
Inferencing	• Guess meaning of vocabulary • Infer author's argument and purpose • Predict future event(s) in story	• MC • Short answer

target level and purposes of the test, you will need to select the register carefully and script the stimulus accordingly. To make the listening stimulus authentic, you should consider either adding disfluency features in a scripted speech or using unscripted speech. In natural speech, disfluency is ubiquitous, as it is normal for speakers to pause or repair mistakes. Thus, the listening material might sound unnatural if it is completely free of disfluencies. You might assume that adding disfluencies would confuse the listener or make the task unnecessarily challenging, but in fact, research has shown the opposite; disfluencies at expected places in speech either have little impact on listening comprehension (Wagner & Toth, 2016) or help to alleviate the processing load for the listener, thus making the task less difficult (Bosker, Quené, Sanders, & De Jong, 2014; Fox Tree, 2001).

The second characteristic to consider is the accent of the speaker. In recent discussions in the field of language testing and applied linguistics, the nature of communication and interaction in English has been problematized by views from the World Englishes (Nelson, 2012), English as an International Language (Matsuda & Friedrich, 2011), and English as a Lingua Franca (Pickering, 2006) perspectives. Researchers have gradually recognized that conversations in English happen as frequently between speakers of different varieties (e.g., British and American English) or between non-native speakers (e.g., English speakers from South Korea and Spain) as they do between native speakers of the same variety. Thus, from the perspective of authenticity, listening tasks should incorporate a variety of accents and dialects. However, inclusion of multiple varieties introduces fairness issues; while it is likely that English learners around the world are familiar with British or American accents, due largely to film and other media, it is less certain that they have heard Korean or Spanish accents before. Language testing and applied linguistics researchers have started to explore the impact of incorporating different varieties of English on test-takers' performance on listening tasks (Kang, Thomson, & Moran, 2018; Major, Fitzmaurice, Bunta, & Balasubramanian, 2005). Those studies find that listeners tend to have an advantage when processing the accent of their L1, but it remains unclear whether or not that same accent creates a disadvantage for test-takers from different L1 backgrounds. While the jury is still out on the impact of different varieties of English, test developers can justifiably incorporate them into listening tasks for a local test, especially when it is important for the students to be able to understand particular varieties represented in the local assessment and learning context. For example, when developing an occupational English test in Thailand, one might wish to include English accents from the ASEAN (Association of Southeast Asian Nations) community, as test-takers are more likely to use English to communicate with speakers from neighboring nations in Southeast Asia (e.g., Vietnam, Malaysia). In contrast, it might be problematic, or at least unnecessary, to include these same varieties in a listening test for test-takers in Latin America.

The last characteristic to consider is the inclusion of visual aids for listening tasks. With recent advances in technology, digitally-delivered language tests have become increasingly common (see Chapter 5 for more about technology). This change makes it easier to incorporate visual aids, which can provide contextual or content information. The purpose of these visuals is to either help test-takers activate their schemata (prior knowledge and experiences related to the content of the passage) or to help alleviate the cognitive pressure of processing meaning while listening.' Figure 4.9 provides an example of context visual and content visual for a listening task on the Sun, Earth and Moon for young learners. However, research has suggested that content visuals tend to have a stronger impact on test-taker performance on listening tasks (e.g., Ginther, 2002). Thus, test developers should consider the choice of visual aids according to both the complexity of the listening material and the target proficiency level of the test-takers.

Speaking

How to assess speaking is a longstanding question in the language testing literature, since it involves multiple components, including pronunciation, vocabulary, grammar, coherence, task completion and, in some cases, knowledge of a particular content domain. In linguistics, the study of language has been more concerned about how language is spoken than written. The assessment of linguistic and related psychological abilities is often mediated through the speaking mode. For example, in a particular assessment, a speaker may be prompted to pronounce minimal pairs of sound contrasts, repeat words, phrases and sentences, read aloud pre-scripted sentences and paragraphs, converse with another interlocutor, deliver a public speech, engage in a group discussion, and/or interpret from one language to another. While speaking is a productive skill, the targeted knowledge and abilities underlying this skill will vary according to the assessment context, purpose, and tasks.

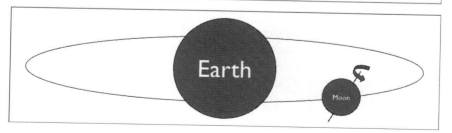

- The Moon is the Earth's only natural satellite.
- The Moon revolves around the Earth.
- The Moon also rotates on its own axis.

FIGURE 4.9 Examples of context and content visuals in listening tasks

Tasks used to elicit the production of sounds, words, phrases, or even sentences are common in linguistic and psychological experiments. These tasks are often designed to assess the knowledge of specific linguistic structures and may be viewed as quite limited or undesirable, if you consider speaking skills broadly as the ability to communicate with another interlocutor. However, these tasks can also be quite effective when your purpose is to assess subskills of oral communication such as the pronunciation of words, the automaticity of using certain grammatical structures, or sentence stress and intonation patterns. Similar to MC items, elicitation tasks are not easy to develop, as test developers need to control or take into account the impact of other linguistic structures and socio-cognitive factors in language processing. For example, it might take a group of item writers anywhere between one month to a year to develop a set of elicited imitation items for beginning-level learners in a Chinese program at an American university. Because the learners are of low proficiency and may have limited exposure to Chinese languages and cultures, item writers will need to carefully select words and grammatical structures that will both cover the key lexico-grammar in the curriculum and provide meaningful and natural sentences that are comparable to the proficiency levels of the examinees. In fact, to assess speaking, or language proficiency in general, for low-level learners, controlled speaking tasks tend to be more effective, as handling authentic and complex language tasks can be too challenging for them.

In the assessment contexts for higher-proficiency learners, speaking ability tends to be conceptualized and operationalized in a much narrower sense. That is, speaking assessment tends to involve a holistic evaluation of someone's ability to achieve a particular communicative purpose. In these contexts, controlled speaking tasks become less useful than open-ended ones; moreover, the open-ended tasks are often embedded in a specific purpose (e.g., speaking for academic study, content instruction, business transactions, and nurse-patient interaction).

Based on the interactive modes of communication, we distinguish two larger categories of speaking tasks: tasks eliciting dialogues (direct) and tasks eliciting monologues (semi-direct). Dialogues tend to be used to assess conversation skills, which can be measured in terms of both one-on-one interviews and group oral tasks. In interview tasks, the interviewer, who is often the rater/examiner as well, asks a list of questions to get the examinees to share personal information and opinions on a particular topic. In group oral tasks, the examinees are asked to share opinions on a particular topic, play a game, or work collaboratively to solve a problem. Table 4.4 illustrates the typical conversation tasks used to measure speaking ability.

Monologic speaking tasks can be classified into two subcategories: narration tasks and argument-based tasks. Narration tasks typically ask test-takers to describe a particular story or scene depicted in a picture. These tasks can be used to measure general speaking proficiency for both lower- and higher-proficiency learners and for both young and adult learners. Figures 4.10 and 4.11 show examples of picture narration tasks for adult learners and young learners respectively.

TABLE 4.4 Conversation tasks for speaking

Conversation task	Sample question
Face-to-face interview	• Tell me a little bit about your … (e.g., hometown, area of study, favorite movie) • What do you think about … ? (e.g., a current event, cultural value)

Group oral task	• Opinion exchange
	
	     ○ Current events
	     ○ Cultural values
	     ○ Educational policy
	
	 • Game
	
	     ○ Word puzzles
	     ○ Desert survival
	
	 • Problem solving
	
	     ○ Develop a lesson plan
	     ○ Develop a treatment plan for a patient

FIGURE 4.10 Picture narration task for the ESL university students

Describe the monsters

FIGURE 4.11   Picture narration task for first graders in Denmark
(Tidlingere sprogstart, https://tidligeresprogstart.ku.dk/)

Argument-based tasks tend to be used to measure language for specific purposes. The most widely assessed purpose is academic, especially in higher education. Speaking tasks in this context usually ask examinees to express their opinions on topics in a particular field of study. Among the most popular speaking topics in higher education contexts are education and information technology, public policy, psychological experiments, and economics. These topics tend to be sufficiently general and far-reaching to allow students from all majors to speak knowingly about them. While it is common to use independent speaking tasks with a very short prompt, integrated tasks, which include reading and/or listening materials, have become increasingly popular in language assessment for academic purposes. Integrated tasks are more representative of communicative contexts because, by integrating source materials (both reading and lectures), they provide test-takers with some information about the topic. This information can help ameliorate the impact of individual differences in academic interests and backgrounds, as students without relevant content knowledge are still able to speak in-depth on the topics. In addition, the source materials allow test developers to assess not only speaking skills, but also reading and/or listening skills, depending on the mode of the source materials.

In some contexts, you might be looking for tasks that assess language for a very specialized purpose (e.g., teaching, business). You might then consider developing a scenario-based speaking task that prompts test-takers to perform a particular task rather than expressing an opinion. For example, when assessing speaking ability for prospective ITAs, you can ask the examinees to do a brief teaching demonstration, explain a simple statistical graph, or respond to a student's complaint. These tasks reflect activities that all teaching assistants will likely encounter on a regular basis. Utilizing these tasks allows test developers to predict more confidently how test-takers will handle communication in real teaching contexts. In EFL contexts, or FL contexts in general, there is also a growing need to measure public speaking and oral interpretation skills. These skills differ from daily communication or general academic speaking skills, as they require more than just proficiency in the target language. For example, public speaking places a stronger emphasis on content, organization, or even the use of humor. Oral interpretation tasks often consider content or information accuracy in translation, as well as preferred register in two languages. Thus, while these tasks involve different speaking prompts and questions, they often require different rating scales.

Writing

Writing tasks vary according to the context and target proficiency level. In the beginning stages, writing tasks can include sentence completion and paragraph writing tasks. In ESL contexts, especially in higher education contexts, writing assessment typically involves composing essays, and argumentative essays in particular, to measure students' academic writing ability. However, it is also important to measure students' writing skills in other genres (e.g., email, memoir) to capture a wider spectrum of academic writing. The independent and integrated writing tasks used in English for academic purposes in higher education contexts resemble the speaking tasks discussed above, with the only differences being that (1) the task asks examinees to write an essay, and that (2) the scoring places a stronger emphasis on rhetorical features (e.g., organization and coherence) than speaking. In this section, we will focus on sentence and paragraph writing tasks and email writing tasks.

In the early stages of writing development, students learn letters, words, and then sentences. Later, they learn how to write a paragraph by composing and organizing multiple sentences around a common topic. These skills form the foundation for essay writing in different domains. Sentence and paragraph writing tasks can effectively assess foundational writing skills. Sentence writing tasks require the test-takers to know how to group individual words together in a grammatical and meaningful way. Paragraph writing tasks require knowledge about how to write an effective topic sentence, provide and elaborate on supporting details, and use discourse markers to connect sentences effectively in support of the topic sentence. Although paragraph writing is more common for lower-level proficiency learners or the earlier years of language learning, based on our experience, even students in higher education contexts can face challenges in producing an effective paragraph. These skills become more important in advanced L2 writing programs, where the ultimate goal is to prepare students to write in different genres (e.g., research paper). Thus, paragraph tasks should be under consideration when assessing writing skills for learners across multiple levels.

Another writing skill that is often overlooked is the ability to write an email. You might be tempted to think that essay writing is the most important language skill for college students, but many of them spend an average of 1 to 2

> **Email writing task**
> **Situation:** Imagine you are a graduate student in Chemical Engineering. You work in a lab under the supervision of your professor. Your parents are currently visiting you, and you would like to take them to a concert on Monday. However, the weekly lab meeting is scheduled on Monday.
> **Task:** Write an email to **your professor**, asking for a leave of absence.

FIGURE 4.12 ESL email writing task

hours per day reading and writing emails. The ability to write an appropriate email can have an impact not only on learning, but on social relations in both school and the workplace. However, in most second and foreign language education settings, email writing is not emphasized. Email writing tasks tend to be quite homogenous, with the prompt of the task creating a scenario that includes the intended audience, context, and intended speech act. The writer is supposed to make an evaluation of this information to identify the register and other pragmatic considerations, and then write the email accordingly. Thus, the scoring of email writing will likely include pragmatics, along with grammaticality. An example of an email writing task can be found in Figure 4.12.

While an email task (as in the example in Figure 4.12) appears to be easy to develop, test developers need to consider the pragmatic functions of email writing; that is, an email is often intended to achieve a specific purpose (e.g., a request) and delivered to a particular audience (e.g., professor). This differentiates email writing from other types of writing such as argumentative essays or narratives. An email task should not elicit writing performances that deviate substantially from the characteristics of an email. You might often find email writing tasks (especially for young learners) that require test-takers to write longer, narrative texts. For example, an email writing prompt might simply state, "imagine you visited Berlin last weekend. Write about what you did during the visit." This kind of prompt lacks information about the target genre or audience, making it difficult for the test-takers to write an authentic email. In addition, this type of email writing task might also elicit writing performances that are similar to a regular narrative or argumentative essay task. Thus, depending on the purpose of the local test, it might be fruitful to include a mix of essay and email writing tasks, to obtain a more comprehensive evaluation of students' writing ability.

Summary

So far, we have provided a survey of tasks that can be used to assess language performance. In this summary section, we provide a few recommendations for the selection and control of language tasks. In terms of selection, as we argued at the beginning of this chapter, all methods both succeed and fail. The selection of language tasks should be governed by the purpose of the test and the target proficiency levels of the test-takers. While certain tasks may appear to be more authentic or popular within the fields of TESOL, applied linguistics, or language testing, the selection of tasks should not be governed solely by trends. For example, research-based writing courses, which have long been the dominant approach to writing instruction in ESL writing programs in US higher education, have now spread to a number of non-Anglophone universities. While the ability to write academically in English is an important skill for undergraduate and graduate students in this increasingly globalized world, assessment tasks that require test-takers to produce a research paper can be overwhelming for those who have just graduated from high school, where writing tasks rarely go beyond the sentence or paragraph level. In this particular context, we recommend that test developers create a sequence of writing tasks of increasing difficulty and embed the assessment sequence in different placement levels within the writing program (e.g., sentence combining, paragraph writing⇒ summary⇒ literature review). Paragraph writing tasks can be used to target the lowest course/placement level to build upon students' foundational writing skills. At the higher course levels, tests can include summary writing tasks and eventually ask students to combine summaries of individual research papers into a coherent literature review. This type of assessment sequence can effectively foster longitudinal development of writing abilities among students. In contrast, when developing assessment tasks for a short, advanced-level course on academic writing, teachers and test developers can select more authentic, integrated writing tasks, since students at that level can be expected to have developed foundation skills in research-based writing. From these two examples, we hope to demonstrate that, while language tasks that are in vogue at a particular time might attract attention from a wide group of test developers and users, they are of limited value if they do not match the purpose and target proficiency level of the test.

Following the same line of reasoning, we also recommend that test developers dedicate time and effort to controlling the complexity level of the tasks. Task complexity can come from both (1) the nature of the language performance elicited by the prompt questions, and (2) the linguistic and content complexity of the input material. The careful selection of writing tasks recommended in the previous paragraph addresses the first source of complexity. To control the linguistic and content complexity of the input materials, test developers need to first identify some benchmark materials and compare the input materials they create to the benchmarks. However, the selection of benchmark materials differs across testing contexts. If the test is embedded in a local language program, we recommend using the instructional materials (e.g., textbooks, exercises) as a benchmark. If the local test is not embedded in a language program, then we recommend using materials (e.g., texts, graphs, audio) that test-takers are likely to encounter in the target language use domain as a benchmark. Of course, it is desirable that test developers simplify the content complexity of the tasks by selecting less advanced topics in the target domain. Selecting less complex content topics can ensure that content knowledge does not have a large impact on test-takers' language performance, unless the task was also developed to assess content knowledge. For example, when measuring oral proficiency for ITAs in US universities, it might be useful to ask test-takers to interpret a graph with some statistical information, as TAs are likely to encounter this type of task when teaching or tutoring students. However, it is better to control the level of statistical information embedded in the graph so that all test-takers are able to understand its content (Xi, 2010; Yan, Cheng, & Ginther, 2019). To control the linguistic complexity of the input materials, we recommend evaluating the input materials in terms of vocabulary range and sophistication, as well as syntactic complexity. If you are assessing English, there are a number of free automated tools that can be used to evaluate vocabulary use, such as *lextutor* (www.lextutor.ca/), *words and phrases* (www.wordandphrase.info/), *coh-metrix* (www.cohmetrix.com/), and *L2 lexical complexity analyzer* (https://aihaiyang.com/software/lca/). Coh-metrix is also available for the evaluation of Chinese texts. These tools are fairly reliable, as words in English are relatively easy to segment. However, we caution against dependence on automated tools to evaluate syntactic complexity, as most measures are based on length (Norris & Ortega, 2009). The assumption behind these tools is often that syntactically complex sentences tend to be longer. While this is a reasonable assumption, one cannot assume that longer sentences are necessarily complex. Therefore, a qualitative evaluation of the syntactic complexity from those who are familiar with the local testing context is more desirable. In addition, if the input material is in an audio format, the speech rate and register of the listening passage should be controlled as well.

To conclude, we have reviewed a variety of language tasks in this chapter with the hope of providing language tasks that are useful for your particular testing context or, at the very least, the range of possibilities that can occur in your local test. We hope that this survey serves as a point of departure on your quest for effective language tasks. As you continue your search, it is important to keep in mind that there is nothing inherently superior or problematic with any given language task, but its selection should fulfill the purpose of the test you envision and match the target proficiency levels of the test-takers in your own context. You should also consider the selection of test tasks in relation to factors and considerations discussed in Chapters 3 and 5.

Further reading

Alderson, J. C. (2000). *Assessing reading* (Cambridge language assessment series). Cambridge, UK: New York, NY: Cambridge University Press.

Alderson (2000) provides a clear and accessible overview of the research conducted in the field of second language reading. In *Assessing Reading*, Alderson first presents a general introduction to the assessment of reading in both first and second language learning, then discusses variables that affect the nature of reading and defines the construct of reading using the reading subskill literature. Mostly focusing on small-scale test design, in one chapter of the book, Alderson presents a critique of high-stakes summative tests. The book also contains some practical examples of reading assessment techniques for the use of teachers in their classes. Alderson's prose is very accessible to both practitioners and non-practitioners. The practicality of this work is what distinguishes it from other books related to the assessment of reading.

Buck, G. (2001). *Assessing listening* (Cambridge language assessment series). Cambridge, UK; New York, NY: Cambridge University Press.

Buck (2001) is a guide for the design and administration of listening tests, which fills a great gap in the literature by building a connection between the newly emerged need to do research in the field of listening and listening-related research that already exists in other fields. He begins the discussion by noting the different types of knowledge used in listening, i.e., the top-down and bottom-up views. The chapter goes on to introduce and discuss some of the most important, yet basic, concepts which are necessary to understand before discussing any listening-related research studies. In the subsequent chapters, Buck summarizes the research on the importance of accent, provides a historical background to the approaches used in the assessment of listening, defines the construct of listening comprehension, discusses listening comprehension task characteristics, and provides a guide to acquiring appropriate listening texts and developing a listening test. The rest of the book is devoted to a discussion about large-scale tests that involve listening comprehension: TOEFL, TOEIC, FCE, and Finnish National Foreign Language Certificate.

Luoma, S. (2004). *Assessing speaking* (Cambridge language assessment series). Cambridge, UK; New York, NY: Cambridge University Press.

Luoma (2004) relies heavily on past research and the theories driven from research. At the same time, the book is highly practical and "is aimed at those who need to develop assessments of speaking ability" (p. x). In the introductory chapter, the author presents scenarios of speaking assessment, which helps the readers have a good grasp of the variables involved in the assessment of speaking. In the subsequent chapters, various factors involved in the assessment of speaking are discussed in detail. Overall, *Assessing Speaking* is a very accessible and well-written book that is attractive for both those who want to learn more about the assessment of speaking and those who have immediate needs to assess speaking in their instructional context.

Purpura, J. (2004). *Assessing grammar*. Cambridge, England: Cambridge University Press.

It is argued by Purpura that the field of language testing needs to be better informed by research into grammar in order to improve the quality of language tests that include the assessment of grammar. Similar to the other books in Cambridge's assessment series, *Assessing Grammar* encompasses both the theoretical and the practical aspects of the assessment of grammar. The author begins the discussion by defining the concept of grammar, arguing how the elusive definition of grammar makes it hard to assess grammatical competence. Purpura explains that grammar is more than its linguistics definition, and when assessing grammar, language test developers need to consider its semantic-pragmatic meaning along with its linguistic meaning comprising only syntax and morphology. The book presents a detailed discussion of how grammar has been assessed in several language tests and is concluded by a discussion about the directions future research can take.

Weigle, S. (2002). *Assessing writing* (Cambridge language assessment series). Cambridge, UK: Cambridge University Press.

Weigle (2002) provides an excellent overview of the assessment of writing for a large audience, including test constructors, test score users, teachers, and other stakeholders. Like the other books in the Cambridge Language Assessment series, *Assessing Writing* balances between breadth and depth of treatment by covering many of the most important topics related to the assessment of writing in a good amount of detail. The book begins with an introduction to the assessment of writing by categorizing types of writing based on their purpose. In the subsequent chapters, a variety of topics are presented, including a summary of the differences between speaking and writing, the roles of topical knowledge and strategic competence in text production, writing test task design, task scoring, classroom writing assessment, portfolio assessment, and large-scale writing assessment. The author concludes the book by discussing the future of writing assessment affected by computer technology.

References

Alderson, J. C. (1980). Native and non-native speaker performance on cloze tests. *Language Learning, 30*(1), 219–223.

Alderson, J. C. (2000). *Assessing reading.* Cambridge: Cambridge University Press.

Allen, M. C. (2016). *Developing L2 reading fluency: Implementation of an assisted repeated reading program with adult ESL learners.* Doctoral dissertation: Purdue University, West Lafayette, IN, USA.

Bachman, L. F. (1990). *Fundamental considerations in language testing.* Oxford: Oxford University Press.

Bosker, H. R., Quené, H., Sanders, T., & De Jong, N. H. (2014). Native 'um's elicit prediction of low-frequency referents, but non-native 'um's do not. *Journal of Memory and Language, 75*, 104–116.

Canale, M., & Swain, M. (1980). Theoretical bases of com-municative approaches to second language teaching and testing. *Applied linguistics, 1*(1), 1–47.

Carroll, J. B. (1961). *Fundamental considerations in testing for English language proficiency of foreign students.* Washington, DC: Testing Center for Applied Linguistics.

Fox Tree, J. E. (2001). Listeners' uses of um and uh in speech comprehension. *Memory & Cognition, 29*(2), 320–326.

G. Fulcher (2010). Practical language testing. London: Hodder Education.

Ginther, A. (2002). Context and content visuals and performance on listening comprehension stimuli. *Language Testing, 19*(2), 133–167.

Hughes, A. (2003). Testing for language teachers (2nd ed.). Cambridge: Cambridge University Press.

Kang, O., Thomson, R., & Moran, M. (2018). Which features of accent affect understanding? Exploring the intelligibility threshold of diverse accent varieties. *Applied Linguistics*, online first 1–29.

Lado, R. (1961). *Language testing: The construction and use of foreign language tests*. New York, NY: McGraw-Hill.

Major, R. C., Fitzmaurice, S. M., Bunta, F., & Balasubramanian, C. (2005). Testing the effects of regional, ethnic, and international dialects of English on listening comprehension. *Language Learning*, *55*(1), 37–69.

Matsuda, A., & Friedrich, P. (2011). English as an international language: A curriculum blueprint. *World Englishes*, *30*(3), 332–344.

McCray, G., & Brunfaut, T. (2018). Investigating the construct measured by banked gap-fill items: Evidence from eye-tracking. *Language Testing*, *35*(1), 51–73.

Nelson, C. L. (2012). *Intelligibility in world Englishes: Theory and application*. New York, NY: Routledge.

Norris, J. M., & Ortega, L. (2009). Towards an organic approach to investigating CAF in instructed SLA: The case of complexity. *Applied Linguistics*, *30*(4), 555–578.

Pickering, L. (2006). Current research on intelligibility in English as a lingua franca. *Annual Review of Applied Linguistics*, *26*, 219–233.

Thirakunkovit, S., Rodríguez-Fuentes, R. A., Park, K., & Staples, S. (2019). A corpus-based analysis of grammatical complexity as a measure of international teaching assistants' oral English proficiency. *English for Specific Purposes*, *53*, 74–89.

Vinther, T. (2002). Elicited imitation: A brief overview. *International Journal of Applied Linguistics*, *12*(1), 54–73.

Wagner, E., & Toth, P. D. (2016). The role of pronunciation in the assessment of second language listening ability. In T. Isaacs & P. Trofimovich (Eds.), *Second language pronunciation assessment: Interdisciplinary perspectives* (pp. 72–92). Bristol: Multilingual Matters Ltd.

Winke, P., Yan, X., & Lee, S. (in press). What does the cloze test really test? A conceptual replication of Tremblay (2011) with eye-tracking data. In G. Yu & J. Xu (Eds.), *Language test validation in a digital age*. Cambridge: Cambridge University Press.

Xi, X. (2010). Aspects of performance on line graph description tasks: Influenced by graph familiarity and different task features. *Language Testing*, *27*(1), 73–100.

Yan, X., Cheng, L., & Ginther, A. (2019). Factor analysis for fairness: Examining the impact of task type and examinee L1 background on scores of an ITA speaking test. *Language Testing*, *36*(2), 207–234.

Yan, X., Maeda, Y., Lv, J., & Ginther, A. (2016). Elicited imitation as a measure of second language proficiency: A narrative review and meta-analysis. *Language Testing*, *33*(4), 497–528.

5

LOCAL TEST DELIVERY

This chapter addresses issues related to the selection of a test delivery platform (paper, digital, online). On one hand, it examines the advantages of technology in improving test administration efficiency. On the other, it outlines the possible difficulties test developers may encounter in the process of digital platform design, especially regarding cost-effectiveness, communication with software developers, and maintenance of the system over time. The chapter considers how the change of delivery method may elicit a different set of abilities, which may impact test-takers' success, and emphasizes the need to consider test-takers' digital literacy and the effects of the test delivery mode on authenticity, washback, and security.

Introduction

When designing the various assessment task types presented in the previous chapter, you need to think about the delivery platform, i.e., how the task instructions and the task input will be delivered to the test-takers. In this chapter, we differentiate between traditional, digitally delivered, and hybrid (or digitally enhanced) tests. Traditional test methods include paper-based written tests (e.g., multiple-choice items, performance-based writing) and oral language tests based on presentations, interviews, and conversations (see Chapter 4 for task descriptions and uses). Digitally delivered tests are those delivered via the application of electronic technology that generates, stores, and processes data using a binary system, with the digits referred to as bits (a string of bits in computer technology is known as a byte). For example, computers are digital devices because they apply this binary system to process data. We use the term "digitally delivered" instead of the more commonly used "computer-based" or "computer-assisted" because test delivery is no longer limited to computers; tablets and smartphones are increasingly being used as test delivery platforms.

Tests are often delivered in a hybrid format, utilizing both traditional and digitized elements in the task input or test delivery and data collection. Therefore, these hybrid tests may not be considered digitally delivered, but their delivery and data collection are digitally enhanced. An example of hybrid delivery is when, in a listening test, digital audio files are played on an MP3 player or similar device to deliver the task input, but test-takers have the task instructions and the items in a paper booklet where they also enter their responses. Another common example of a hybrid delivery/collection method is when writing task input is provided in a paper booklet, but the test-takers type their responses in a word processing document. You can find more information about digital test data collection and management in Chapter 8.

Selection of the test delivery platform is an important consideration because the platform needs to be compatible with the intended task format and because the task development requires various digital and programming resources. Since the decisions about the formats, the types, and the number of tasks to include in the language test depend on the test purpose, the assessed skill(s), and/or the test uses (see Introduction), the compatibility of the delivery platform with the test purpose is essential. For example, if a speaking test focuses on eliciting conversation skills and interaction, a digital delivery of tasks may not be a viable option, but digital recording of the responses might be.

In terms of resources, the delivery method influences the choice of materials needed during the test development process. It also affects decisions about response collection, rating procedures, and test data management and storage. If the local context lacks basic infrastructure for implementation of a digitally delivered test (e.g., data storage, internet access, digital devices), then the development of digitized test tasks may not be reasonable.

In the following sections, we present the digital devices used for digital test delivery, and then discuss the production, maintenance, and administration efficiency of each delivery method. We outline the challenges that you may encounter in the process of digital platform design, including cost-effectiveness, communication with software developers, and maintenance of the system over time. Then, we discuss what considerations are essential in the selection process of the appropriate platform. These include possible digital literacy, authenticity, washback effects, and test security.

Digital devices

Computers are the digital devices that are most commonly used for digital tests. When digital tests were introduced, desktop computers were the default electronic machines used for test administration because at that time, laptop processors were much less powerful and, therefore, inadequate for the delivery and collection of large data sets. In the past decade, however, laptops have almost caught up to desktop processors and, due to their portability, have become widely used. For example, if you use laptops, it will not be necessary to schedule the test in computer labs, which tend to be quite small and limit the simultaneous administration to a small number of test-takers. In fact, you may ask test-takers to bring their own laptops to the testing site and thus avoid investing in computers or laptops for digital test delivery. The advantage of desktop computers remains that they can have large monitors and full size keyboards, which may be beneficial, especially for writing tests.

In addition to desktop and laptop computers, tablets and smartphones have recently gained popularity in test administration because they contain several features that render them useful, i.e., enhanced portability, long battery life, and 4G internet connection. If you intend to administer the test in different locations, transporting a number of lightweight tablets would be much easier than transporting heavier laptops. Moreover, unlike laptops that need to be recharged after several hours of use, most tablets can go for up to 10 hours without charging. Finally, the possibility for a 4G LTE connection allows you to use a SIM card (usually inserted into the tablet) to administer online delivered tests even if there is no Wi-Fi connection. Smartphones exhibit similar characteristics as tablets, with the main difference being that they are much smaller in size.

However, tablets and smartphones have a number of limitations. First, their operating systems lack the capabilities of laptops' full-blown operating systems (e.g., Windows and MacOS), which offer extensive control over how you store and manage data and support installation of professional software. Importing documents and images from external sources is also complicated because tablets and smartphones lack USB ports, apertures for HDMI, and SD card readers. Tablets and smartphones are particularly inconvenient for writing tests because the keyboards occur on the screen and cover the writing field. Tablets can be connected with keyboards through Bluetooth, but they still remain inferior to laptops in that respect. Table 5.1 provides a comparative list of the technical features of desktop computers, laptops, and tablets and smartphones.

TABLE 5.1 Technical characteristics of different digital devices

	Desktop computers	*Laptops*	*Tablets and smartphones*
display	• large monitors • (no limitations)	• limited, dependent on laptop size	• small size
keyboard	• full size	• limited size	• on screen, small size
operating system	• all capabilities	• all capabilities	• limited capabilities
Internet	• Ethernet • Wi-Fi	• Ethernet • Wi-Fi	• Wi-Fi • 4G
portability	• static	• portable	• portable

Production of traditional and digitally delivered tests: what does it take?

Digital language tests may seem attractive due to the frequent use of technology in language teaching and learning. Numerous online resources, educational platforms, and software applications (e.g., Moodle, Blackboard) that institutions have already implemented for teaching and learning may be used for language test development and administration (Dooey, 2008; Jin & Yan, 2017; Laborda, 2007). Despite the attractiveness and popularity of digital language tests, however, many locally developed language tests are still based on traditional delivery methods because of limited local resources for digital test delivery and maintenance.

Unlike digital language tests, the production of paper delivered and traditional oral language tests requires low development and maintenance costs due to the limited use of technological resources, i.e., software, hardware, and technological expertise. For the most part, the production of paper-based test formats involves investment in graphic design, illustration, and printing. Although the printing costs may become quite high, especially if elaborate color pagination is included, the overall costs associated with production maintenance tend to be minimal.

Unless fully digitized, listening comprehension, as well as elicited imitation, tasks tend to include both traditional and digital elements because the production of task input, i.e., the information with which the test-takers are presented in order to elicit a response (Chapelle & Douglas, 2006), may entail digital resources. If the audio input is designed specifically for the test, you need to produce it in a recording studio, using professional recording and editing equipment, to ensure high quality. For the production of video input, you need human and material resources (e.g., actors to play the characters, someone to manage the audio and video recording and editing equipment). To simplify the production process, you may decide to use existing audio and video recordings that are publically available. You have to make sure, however, that you obtain copyright permission to use these recordings for testing purposes.

In traditional speaking tests, the only resources that you need are interlocutors for the oral interviews or examiners for the group discussions and simulation tasks. For some integrated oral tasks, i.e., tasks that integrate two or more language skills (e.g., reading/writing, reading/speaking), or elicited imitation tasks, i.e., tasks that require the repetition of a string of words, you can use booklets with text prompts or an audio player for the audio prompts (see Chapter 4 for task type description). Finally, to keep record of the testing sessions and assigned scores in a consistent manner, you will need to produce and print scoring sheets, as well as record-keeping and reporting forms. As mentioned earlier, traditional methods are usually digitally enhanced because, despite the traditional delivery, it is much easier to store the records in digital databases. Example 5.1 describes a traditional delivery method that is digitally enhanced.

EXAMPLE 5.1 DIGITALLY ENHANCED TRADITIONAL DELIVERY METHOD

TOEPAS: traditional delivery that is digitally enhanced

Since the TOEPAS is based on simulated lecture, it requires traditional speaking test delivery. In the first version of the test, the only resources needed for test delivery were two raters and scoring sheets. The two raters gave the instructions, asked questions during the warm-up session, and rated the performance in the simulated lecture using the scoring sheet. However, the TOEPAS could be considered a digitally enhanced method because, although the delivery was traditional, the performances were video recorded in a digital video format.

The hybridity of the test was enhanced in the second version, in which the raters use an internet interface to take notes during the performance and enter the assigned scores. The scores, reports, and digital videos are stored in the same digital database.

When digital language test methods were introduced in the last decades of the 20th century, they were deemed most appropriate for delivery and scoring of discrete-point items in grammar, vocabulary, and reading comprehension tests, rather than performance-based tests, because they did not require advanced programing and were easier to administer. The discrete-point item types can easily be contextualized with the use of visual (pictures and video) and sound files already available on the internet. According to Roever (2001), the internet can provide a highly authentic environment for language testing if the tasks involve retrieval of online information (e.g., writing emails or searching Google). With rapid advances in technology, digital delivery methods are increasingly applied in development, delivery, and scoring of performance-based speaking and writing tests.

In addition to graphic design and illustration, which are essential in traditional paper-based tests, digital test production requires careful consideration of the availability and accessibility of appropriate hardware and software for item development, as well as possible issues with browser incompatibility, test security, server failure, and data storage in the local context. In the design process, special attention must also be paid to the creation of relevant computer or tablet interface, ease of navigation, page layout, and textual and visual representation on the screen (Fulcher, 2003).

If you are developing a language test in an institution (e.g., school, university, language center) whose main activity is not language testing, then a lack of resources may be an issue; the development of digitally delivered tests requires IT expertise and software licenses that can be expensive. Institutions' limited budgets for test development tend to preclude outsourcing test digitization by hiring professional software development companies, not to mention institutions' inability to hire full-time IT specialists as part of the test development team. However, several solutions are available to overcome any possible budgetary problems, including course management systems or open source learning platforms, local IT resources, and external software developers.

One solution could be using the teaching or learning platforms or course management systems (CMS) to which your institution already subscribes (e.g., Blackboard, Canvas), as they offer some default test development tools, especially for the design of multiple-choice, fill-in-the-blank, matching, and short-answer item types. You can also explore free open-source learning platforms (e.g., Moodle, Drupal). You can use add-on extensions and plug-ins to customize and extend the features of the platform. Commercial test authoring platforms (e.g., Adobe Authorware, Articulate, Questionmark) can add more flexibility and interactiveness in the assessment task design. Although the interface used to develop a test in these platforms may not seem straightforward or intuitive, certain features are useful for determining the assessment task order (linear or random), the amount of time, and the number of attempts, as well as monitoring each test-taker's responses and progress (Douglas & Hegelheimer, 2007). To exploit the full range of feature extensions, however, you will need to have web or software design experience. With use of free, open-source platforms, you will need to investigate where and how the data collected through the test will be stored, as in some cases data are stored on unprotected public servers. Familiarization with the local requirements for personal data protection is essential in order to select the most appropriate storage and management system.

If you work in university settings, then you may have the option to collaborate with the computer science department or IT and media support department. Such collaboration would be an advantage because technical support is not only needed during test design but also for future software maintenance. Moreover, colleagues from local IT departments are aware of the technical resources that are locally available (e.g., equipment, software licenses, platforms, expertise) and can propose adequate solutions that correspond to the capabilities of the local technological infrastructure. For example, they will be familiar with the availability and the capacity of any local servers that the university possesses, the robustness of the local internet connections, possible disruptive interferences of firewalls, and the functionalities of the local hardware.

If sufficient funds for test development are available, but your test development team does not include experienced software developers, outsourcing the design of digitally delivered tests by hiring software developers is another alternative. The main advantage of this option is that you can hire software developers who specialize in, or at least have previous experience, with the development of similar testing or educational products.

Regardless of whether you decide to collaborate with colleagues from local IT departments or hire outside software developers, the design of digitally delivered platforms for test administration is a lengthy process that involves constant negotiations to adapt the envisioned task format to the technical possibilities. Such communication can be challenging because the two parties often focus on different aspects of test development; test developers focus on the effects of the task format on the elicited performance, while software developers focus on the available tools for development of the test application, often in the least elaborate way possible. Miscommunication may not be obvious in the initial discussions with software developers, and so it is essential that test developers follow every stage of the design process, which tends to be reiterative rather than linear. Example 5.2 recounts such communication between software and test developers.

EXAMPLE 5.2 COMMUNICATION BETWEEN TEST AND SOFTWARE DEVELOPERS

Development of the OEPT rater application

When we developed the first version of the OEPT rater application, we worked with three software developers from our local computer support program. After six months of weekly meetings that ended without concrete solutions, our lead software developer seemed to have an epiphany one afternoon and remarked, "Today is the first day I feel like I really understand what you do." Working with software developers, or with anyone who represents a different community of practice, can be challenging because what is obvious to one group may not be obvious to the other. Arriving at a consensus about what is needed takes time.

Another example: when we developed the latest platform, we explained that we needed item scores, not just total section scores, for item analyses. Our software developers finally understood and agreed, although the inclusion of item-level scores required extra work. To our surprise, when we were examining the first version of the new platform, we found the developers had included item-level scores but did not include a place for any total section scores. They decided that because we had item-level scores, we didn't need total scores.

Periodical software maintenance is required as operating systems, servers, and plug-ins are constantly updated. Therefore, planning the sustainability of a digitally delivered test by budgeting expenses for periodic maintenance is crucial. Finally, buying server space can also be quite costly, especially if there is a need for storage of video and audio data. In some cases, it may seem more feasible to purchase a server instead of purchasing server space. Owning a server, however, entails continuous upgrading and maintenance, which is possible only with local IT support. Example 5.3 explains the OEPT development and maintenance process.

EXAMPLE 5.3 DEVELOPMENT AND MAINTENANCE

OEPT: development and maintenance

Over the past 20 years, the Oral English Proficiency Program (OEPP) has developed a series of interconnected computer applications that support our testing program.

The OEPT.1: In 2000, the OEPP received the Multimedia Instructional Development Center (MIDC) Grant, awarded by the Information Technology center at Purdue (ITaP), to develop a computer administered oral English proficiency assessment: The Oral English Proficiency Test (OEPT). Test content was developed to introduce prospective ITAs to language tasks and activities that they would encounter in instructional contexts at Purdue. In addition to developing an instrument that would have greater validity, the development of a computer-administered platform allowed us to reduce the amount of time required to administer and rate annual examinees by approximately 30%.

The OEPT.2: In 2008, we were forced to revise the testing platform because the software used to develop the original test, Macromedia, was no longer supported and because ITaP had abandoned the mount points required for the delivery of the test on its servers. The test had to be rewritten in JAVA by a programmer provided by ITaP, who is no longer employed by Purdue. We took advantage of this opportunity to revise test items, streamline delivery, and include a post-test questionnaire. We also revised the scale from the original 4-points to the current 6-point scale.

The OEPT.3: Since the development of the OEPT, the ACE-In (see discussion below), and all related applications has occurred incrementally, the various components are related but independent. In addition, although several universities have inquired about the possibility of adopting/adapting the OEPT (e.g., Yale in 2002, Minnesota in 2004 and 2006, Michigan State in 2012, 2014, and 2015), the test is embedded in ITaP servers and cannot be liberated without a rewrite.

Changes in the operating system (OS) and hardware have made it challenging to support the OEPT and related applications. There have been several patches applied to the test program to support the system in new platforms on ITaP lab computers over the years. Changes or updates to the ITaP lab environment result in extensive quality control testing of the products in the labs to avoid surprise breakdowns in the software during actual test administration. Going forward, incompatibility of the OEPT with OS and related systems may occur and providing support would incur more cost.

The costs associated with the rebuild of the OEPT software suite and integration with the ACE-IN ($93,000.00) was covered by OEPP reserves. Thus, the OEPP is providing substantial Unit support. Ongoing support for the system will be provided through OEPP S&E.

Opportunities for innovative task design

Digitally delivered tests have an advantage over traditional tests because they facilitate innovative approaches to task design. The task input and prompts in paper delivered language tests are restricted to texts and visual elements in the form of pictures, illustrations, graphs, and figures, which poses challenges for development of integrated-skills items (Chapelle & Douglas, 2006). The task interactivity is minimal, and so tasks tend to focus on one language skill (or sub-skill) at a time and exploit multiple-choice and short response items presented in linear order (Huff & Sireci, 2001).

Digitally delivered tests also provide the possibility of overcoming the limitations of task design for paper delivered tests and allow for an improved task contextualization. For example, unlike still pictures, videos in listening tasks can stimulate the dynamic cognitive processing of multiple information sources, which reflects the listening comprehension processes occurring in real-life contexts, hence offering enhanced construct representation. Therefore, videos tend to effectively engage test-takers in the task to various degrees (Ockey, 2007).

Digital devices (computers, tablets, smartphones) facilitate the delivery of integrated skill tasks, i.e., tasks that involve two language skills (e.g., listening/reading with speaking/writing). The availability of multimedia and access to digital information support rich input design with different types of textual, graphical, video, and audio material that test-takers need to understand, select, evaluate, and synthesize in their oral or written responses as part of the task completion. Integrated skill items are considered to enhance the representation of real-life contexts since separate language skills rarely occur in isolation (Sawaki, Stricker, & Oranje, 2009).

When it comes to the nature of input and the type of expected response, digital devices offer a wide range of advantages. Zenisky and Sireci (2002) provided a non-exhaustive list with 21 item types (pp. 340–341). Some items require the use of a mouse to manipulate information on the screen as part of the task completion. Examples of mouse use in test items include: 1) drag and drop items, where an element (text or other stimuli) is moved from one place to another in order to specify relationships, order or re-organize information, sort information, insert words/phrases/sentences in larger texts, or develop a concept map; 2) highlight texts; 3) click on the correct element (hot spot) on the screen; and 4) delete text. The mouse can also be used to click on recording buttons for oral tests, where test-takers' spoken responses are digitally recorded. Due to the growing use of touchscreen technology for tablets and smartphones, many test-takers, especially those from younger generations, may lack experience using a mouse. Instead, as Example 5.4 below suggests, they may be more comfortable using their fingers to drag and drop elements, as well as highlighting and pressing the correct elements on the screen.

EXAMPLE 5.4 SELECTION OF DIGITAL DEVICE FOR TEST DELIVERY

English test for first graders in Denmark

The English test for first graders in ten public schools in Denmark contains several items that require responses by clicking on pictures, dragging and dropping elements, and clicking on the correct answer. For example, in the item "My family", the students had a picture of a family on the screen and were required to click on the correct character (hot spot) in the picture as they listened to a recording that named family members.

The first version of the test was designed for computer-delivery, and so the students needed to use a mouse to click on the picture. During the pilot, the testing team realized that, although the students were familiar with the item type, they had never used a mouse because they had played similar games on a tablet or a smartphone. Therefore, the second version of the test was designed for tablet-delivery so that the students could use their fingers to respond on the touchscreen.

Control over task delivery and task completion processes can easily be supported with technology (Ockey, 2009). For example, the mouse-over functionality can be applied to provide instructions in both the target language and test–takers' L1, which minimizes the possibility that test–takers' misunderstanding of instructions will affect their task performance. Technology can also provide access to different digital resources and tools, such as dictionaries, conjugation tables, glossaries, thesaurus, or tutorials.

Test administration

The functionality of test administration is another aspect to consider when selecting traditional or digital platforms for test delivery. Digital platforms may be preferred because they tend to facilitate test administration. However, traditional test delivery platforms may be maintained or enhanced with digital data collection. Following is a typical process of paper test delivery.

Once the test booklets are printed, they need to be distributed to the testing site, i.e., the place where the test-takers will take the test. In high-stakes test situations, the transport of the test booklets must be secured to protect unauthorized access to the tasks before the scheduled administration. After the tests are distributed and responses are collected, they need to be delivered to the raters. Sometimes rating sessions are organized with raters gathered to rate the responses, or else the tests are sent to raters who perform the ratings individually and then send the results back to the testing coordinators. When the rating is completed, the results are recorded manually, and the test booklets are stored according to the planned storage procedures (see Chapter 8 for data management and storage). Given the need for large storage spaces, sometimes decisions are made to destroy actual test responses after a certain period of storage. The manual transportation, processing, and storage of secured physical data may compromise the data security and complicate the analysis of response data over longer periods of time. To minimize possible complications with test security and handling of data, numerous working hours of continuous involvement of dedicated administrative staff is unavoidable.

The administration of traditional oral language tests could be extremely time-consuming for the interlocutor and the examiners. For example, it will take at least 5 hours to administer a 15-minute test to just 20 test-takers, not to mention the additional time to record the results. Oral language test administrations are time-consuming and therefore expensive. In many local contexts, the test administrators are language teachers who do not receive a course release, and the oral test administration may be considered an additional professional activity. To ensure test quality through teachers' full engagement with the testing activities, institution or program leaders must account for the expenses related to teachers' test administration and rating time.

When planning the test administration, it is also important to consider interlocutor and examiner fatigue as a factor that negatively affects the consistency of test administration, also known as reliability. Fatigue can lower examiners' attention and affect their rating behavior, which can lead to inconsistent test administration and rating. In other words, test-takers' performances and results may not depend solely on their language proficiency but also the part of the day when they took the test (Ling, Mollaun, & Xi, 2014). To avoid compromising the consistency, you may need to engage several interlocutors and examiners or, if a limited number of test administrators are available, you need to arrange for frequent pauses. Unlike traditional test methods, digital platforms allow for simultaneous administration of performance-based tests to many test-takers in multiple testing sites. An added advantage of oral test administration is that digital delivery minimizes the interlocutor effect that can occur in traditional oral test settings. Example 5.5 exemplifies the use of digital platforms for test administration efficiency.

EXAMPLE 5.5 ORAL TEST ADMINISTRATION EFFICIENCY WITH DIGITAL DELIVERY

OEPT: a digital oral English proficiency test

The OEPT is a semi-direct, computer-delivered test for screening international teaching assistants. It was designed to replace the Speaking Proficiency English Assessment Kit (SPEAK), an institutional version of the Test of Spoken English (TSE) designed by the Educational Testing Service (ETS) because of its inadequacy for use in the local context. The SPEAK was administered one-on-one, i.e., one test administrator administered the test to one test taker. It took around 40 minutes to administer the test to each individual test taker.

The OEPT is administered in a computer lab, where around 20 students take the test simultaneously. The latest version of the OEPT is timed and test takers complete the entire exam in about 30 minutes. In approximately 1 hour, responses from 20 test takers are collected. In a traditional oral test setting, at least 7 hours would be needed to test 20 people.

In terms of writing tests, internet technologies provide the possibility for test administration in multiple sites, as the only requirements are a digital device and internet access (Example 5.6). This means that some screening for course or program admission or for the identification of language support needs at universities could be performed even before students arrive on campus, which would greatly facilitate early course and program planning.

EXAMPLE 5.6 WRITING TEST DELIVERY EFFICIENCY

Summer Online EPT for Early Advising

Over the years, The EPT at the University of Illinois at Urbana-Champaign (UIUC) has evolved from a traditionally delivered, paper and pencil writing test to a semi-enhanced online writing test. The change occurred as a solution to the early advising need for undergraduate students at the university. In recent years, most US universities have started offering early advising sessions at the college and even department level so that students can receive information and guidance regarding coursework in their majors before they arrive on campus. As undergraduate students have to fulfill the first-year composition course requirement, an important topic during early advising sessions is the ESL courses that they may need to take during their freshman year. To facilitate this effort, in 2014, we decided to offer bi-monthly online test administrations to undergraduate students so they can take the test on their own laptops or computers in their home countries and then receive course placement prior to the advising sessions. This change has allowed us to test over 200 students within a 24-hour window, without requiring them to arrive on campus early or having to wait until August to take the test. As a result of this change, the vast majority of the undergraduate test takers (80–95%) now choose to take the test during the summer before their freshmen year.

Collecting written responses through a computer improves the data management system and the response evaluation process. Digital devices' role in speaking tasks is particularly useful because these devices assist in the digital recording of responses, provide secure storage, and are easily accessed for rating purposes. The digital format of oral and written responses and the digital rating platforms facilitate the rating process for human raters, which minimizes scoring errors resulting from data mishandling and score recording (see Chapter 8 for a detailed discussion on data management and storage).

Digitally delivered testing has evolved to the point of developing automated scoring systems for performance-based tests of writing and speaking. By using computational linguistics and speech recognition technology, machines are "trained" to recognize certain written or speech characteristics that can characterize language performances at different proficiency levels and assign scores accordingly. The purpose of automated scoring systems is to improve rating efficiency and consistency, hence score reliability, and to reduce the expenses related to engaging human raters (Ockey, 2009). At this time, automated scoring systems are rarely used in locally developed language tests because the development of such systems is very expensive and time-consuming. In fact, the necessity to have large amounts of data to "train" the machine prevents local test developers from working on such systems, as data generation tends to be more limited in local test administration than in large standardized tests such as the TOEFL. These limitations may be overcome if you have local resources, like language technology labs, computational linguistics programs, or natural language processing programs.

Table 5.2 provides a comparison of traditional and digital test delivery platforms in terms of development costs and resources, administration, elicited response types, data storage, and maintenance. Traditional platforms are cost effective and do not require many resources for development and maintenance, but they offer limited task innovation and response types. Digital delivery platforms, on the other hand, provide the possibility for task innovation and various response types, but their development and maintenance may require costly resources.

TABLE 5.2 Summary of the characteristics of traditional and digitally delivered tests

	Traditional	*Digital*
development	• cost effective • low resource • limited task innovation • limited interactivity	• costly • high resource (hardware, software, expertise) • varied task formats • high interactivity
administration	• high resource • time-consuming	• low resource • efficient
response types	• limited	• varied
data storage	• manual storage and manipulation	• easy to store, retrieve, and analyze
maintenance	• low maintenance	• high maintenance

Selection of test delivery format: what to consider

In addition to development, response types, administration, and management, you will also need to consider test-takers' digital literacy and the effects of the test delivery mode on authenticity, washback, and security.

Digital literacy

If you are planning to develop a digitally delivered test, it is important to take into account the effects of digital literacy on test-takers' task completion and over-all test performance. Depending on the purpose of your test and the language skill(s) you want to assess, you may consider including digital literacy as an integral part of the assessed skill or else minimizing its effects. Lack of digital literacy could result in differential test performance, which means that test-taker performance may be influenced by their digital literacy proficiency rather than their language proficiency (Chapelle & Douglas, 2006; Jin & Yan, 2017; Roever, 2001).

Digital literacy is defined as "a person's ability to perform tasks effectively in a digital environment" (Jones & Flannigan, 2006, p. 9). This means that digital literacy is not confined to familiarity with and the ability to use computers, the internet, or software; it includes the ability to find, understand, evaluate, and use information available in multiple formats via computers, tablets, smartphones, and the internet (Buckingham, 2007; Jones & Flannigan, 2006). Van Deursen and Van Dijk (2009) operationalized digital literacy as a set of different skills: operational (using computer hardware and software), formal (accessing computer network and web environments), and informational (finding, selection, evalu-ation, and process information). As part of information, Ananiadou and Claro (2009) added the ability to restructure and transform information to develop knowledge, i.e., information as a product (p. 20).

Given the recent expansion of computer and internet use among different test-taker groups, including the claim that the younger generations are "digital natives", the term digital literacy has evolved from skills-oriented concepts (computer literacy, media literacy) to more process-oriented concepts that involve understanding and organizing digital information. For instance, the Danish writing tests that students take at the end of their obligatory education in Denmark require searching for, evaluating, and using relevant information from the internet rather than just typing responses into a word processor.

Despite the widespread use of digital devices, you still need to examine the operational literacy of test-takers in relation to the particular digital device and software applications that you want to use. For example, when piloting a digitally delivered English language test for first graders in the Danish elemen-tary schools (see Example 5.4), we realized that, although the students were exposed to computers and videogames daily, they experienced difficulties using a mouse for tasks that involved drag-and-drop elements because they had been used to completing such tasks on touchscreen smartphones or tablets. In other words, the test-takers lacked operational digital literacy for computers.

In order to ensure operational digital literacy, you need to provide opportunities for test-takers to familiarize themselves with the technology used, especially when it is not necessarily embedded in the communicative situation represented in the task (Csapó, Ainley, Bennett, Latour, & Law, 2012). For example, test-takers need to use a play button to hear the oral input and record buttons to record their responses in a speaking test. To prevent unfamiliarity with the recording process from interfering with task performance, test-takers should have an opportunity to practice using the audio play/record menu on the screen. Opportunities for familiarization can be offered through instructions (see Example 3.5 in Chapter 3) and practice items that are not rated.

Assessment of writing is a testing domain in which technology may or may not be used by all test-takers. Some writers use word processors exclusively at every stage of the writing process, while others may use word processors scarcely or only for final drafts. For example, university students may use word processors exclusively, while elementary school children may still handwrite texts before typing them up. Regardless of whether the writers belong to the first or the second group, they need to familiarize themselves with the writing tools on the digital device, especially if the test system uses writing tools that are different from the commercial word processors, like Microsoft Word (Csapó et al., 2012).

When technology is embedded in the task (e.g., the task requires computer mediated communication, or CMC), traditional test methods may be irrelevant because they will not elicit the expected performance. Digitally delivered tasks need to reflect these online environments, and so task contextualization cues in the prompt are essential. For example, you may decide to include tasks that reflect online environments that have become commonplace with the emergence of social media (e.g., Facebook, Twitter, Instagram) and telecommunication apps (e.g., Skype, Viber, Whatsapp), as well as the accessibility of digital information in different forms: textual, visual, and audio. For such tasks, familiarization may not be essential, but should still be considered.

Changing the modality of test delivery

If you want to change the test delivery mode from traditional to digital, you first need to think about whether and how the change of delivery method may elicit a different set of abilities, which may impact test-takers' success. In a manner similar to investigations in writing studies of the shift from composing by hand to composing on a word processor, language testing researchers in the 1980s and 1990s investigated how the transition from paper and pencil to computer-delivered tests might affect test-takers' performance because of preference for one delivery system over the other or lack of digital literacy (Bangert-Drowns, 1993).

While comparisons of direct (interviews) and semi-direct (digitally administered) assessments of speaking have found the methods highly correlated, additional qualitative analyses have revealed that the different methods produce different response characteristics (see Ginther, 2003, for a review). In addition, discussions regarding digital speaking tests have also focused on restrictions imposed by the delivery method in relation to limitations on interactivity (Galaczi, 2010; O'Loughlin, 2001). Regarding the assessment of writing, Leijten, Van Waes, Schriver, and Hayes (2014) held that writing ability models need an update to include the effect that technologies have on the cognitive processes involved in writing. They called for the inclusion of subprocesses that account for online searches, motivation management, and the construction of verbal and visual content, or design schemas (pp. 324–326). The comparability of offline reading to reading in a digital environment has also been challenged. Research findings have suggested that readers need a new set of skills and strategies to successfully comprehend digital texts (Afflerbach & Cho, 2009a, 2009b; Coiro & Dobler, 2007). Although readers may be quite proficient offline readers, they may experience difficulties not only when searching for textual information online (Eagleton & Guinee, 2002), but also when they are required to critically evaluate and understand search results (Coiro, 2011; Fabos, 2008; Henry, 2006). Spiro (2004) argued that, unlike the processing of offline reading, the cognitive processing of online texts presents a more demanding task for readers because they need to respond and adapt to various contextual cues that arise from the multi-layered and more complex representations of information that occurs in digital environments. In preparation for the introduction of the TOEFL iBT, Taylor, Jamieson, Eignor, and Kirsch (1998) and Powers (1999) found debilitating effects for computer familiarity on TOEFL iBT performance but maintained that, because the effects were negligible, no additional preparation materials would be required in support of the TOEFL iBT.

It is likely the case that differences between traditional paper and pencil and digital delivery formats attract the most attention in times of transition. Certainly, while the role of computer familiarity in the composition process received a great deal of attention as word processing programs were being introduced and adopted, discussions now focus on the cognitive processes underlying language production in the digital domain. Indeed, the differences between direct and semi-direct speaking assessment formats no longer receive the same attention they once did, despite the fact that the inclusion of interactivity remains an issue with respect to construct representation. Technological advancements and the widespread use of CMC (e.g., blogs, YouTube videos, Skype) have resulted in a situation where the impact of digital delivery has been ameliorated. Nevertheless, the absence of delivery format effects cannot be assumed and should be taken into consideration, especially when switching from one test delivery format to another.

Authenticity

Test-takers engage with the intended language domains if test tasks include sufficient contextual cues that elicit their background knowledge of the communicative situation (Douglas, 2000). These interactions with the tasks help to elicit relevant language performances that will be used to make assumptions about test-takers' ability to communicate in real-life situations. Therefore, the degree to which the test format (traditional or digital) represents that situational characteristics (setting, participants, content, tone, and genre) and enhances test-takers' interaction with the task is vitally important (Bachman & Palmer, 1996; Chapelle & Douglas, 2006; Douglas, 2000).

Digitally delivered tests, more so than paper delivered tests, offer possibilities for a wide range of innovative tasks that facilitate the inclusion of relevant contextual cues and promote interactivity through exploitation of multimedia. Local test developers can take full advantage of multimedia to design input with graphic and audio enhancements, which enables them to maximize task authenticity. However, although digital devices can assist in accomplishing realistic representations of the real-world situations in which the communication takes place, they may not be preferable for every testing situation. For instance, simulated role-plays may be included in language for specific purposes (LSP) tests or tests for employment certification because certain communicative tasks need interlocutors to represent interactions across modalities in the communicative contexts (Norris, 2016, p. 232). Paper delivered tests may also be relevant when testing young learners because they allow for the inclusion of tasks that require drawing and coloring.

The development of digital and web-based tasks is essential when measuring test-takers' abilities to participate in computer-mediated communication (CMC). The characteristics of CMC language discourse differs from discourse in other domains, and so tasks need sufficient clues to allow test-takers to differentiate these domains in digitally delivered tasks. For example, the search, selection, and evaluation of online texts as information sources requires a different set of abilities than those needed for using paper-based textual sources. For that reason, using a paper delivered test may lack authenticity because it fails to engage test-takers with the task in the intended manner.

Security

Regardless of the local test delivery methods (traditional or digital), an important consideration is ensuring the security of test items, item responses, and test-takers' personal information. Lack of test security can compromise the results and affect the test consequences for individuals. For example, if test-takers have access to test tasks, then opportunities for cheating are created, which means that scores will not accurately reflect their abilities. Unauthorized access to personal data, including both personal identifiers and test result information, breaches data confidentiality and results in unethical testing practices and negative consequences for test-takers.

With paper delivered tests, item security can be maintained if new items are selected from a large item pool or new items are created for each test administration. Although these strategies may enhance security, the drawback is insufficient data for item analysis. In local test development, the opportunities to run trial items before their actual uses are limited, as you do not have access to large numbers of test-takers Therefore, although items can be trialed before use, the data collected may be insufficient for closer analyses of consistency, item difficulty, and discrimination. Further security precautions include test booklet distribution to and from testing sites in sealed envelopes or boxes and test storage in locked cabinets and rooms.

One issue with the security of online delivered tests is that the use of applications and machine translation programs, such as Google Translate, equals cheating, although they have been found to assist communication for L2 beginners (Garcia & Pena, 2011). Similarly, questions of authorship are real threats that can compromise test security (Chapelle & Douglas, 2006), and it is believed that the internet access leads to increased instances of plagiarism (Evering & Moorman, 2012; Pecorari & Petrić, 2014). Having an internet connection makes it possible for students to copy large amounts of text. Cheating by sharing can also be enhanced, as it is difficult to monitor test-takers' accesses to social platforms.

Issues with test security have received much attention in regards to large-scale standardized English proficiency tests. Given that these tests are administered at different testing sites, concerns about the identity of test-takers, fraudulent exam invigilators/proctors, and collective memorization of test items have been raised (Watson, 2014; Xinying, 2015). Rigorous measures against identified fraudulent activities may have negative consequences for all test-takers, including those who did not cheat, as testing agencies lose credibility and stakeholders begin to mistrust the test results (Wilkins, Pratt, & Sturge, 2018). Although security measures in local tests may not receive public attention, it does not mean that security precautions are less important in such contexts.

Test security may be an issue, especially in locally developed computer-delivered tests, as a lack of awareness is present regarding how and where test data are stored and how easy unauthorized access of data is. It is essential that you familiarize yourself with the institutional, national, and international laws and regulations for the handling and manipulation of personal and sensitive data to ensure appropriate collection and storage. For example, specific regulations may exist regarding the location and ownership of the servers on which test data are stored. This means that some of the freely or commercially available test development platforms and applications may not satisfy legal security requirements.

Notwithstanding the legal requirements, development of computer/tablet-, web-based and, most recently, cloud-based tests needs to follow the general security procedures in a digital or online environment. According to the *Code of practice for information security management* (ISO/IEC 27000, 2009; ISO/IEC 27001, 2005; ISO/IEC 27002, 2005) the basic information security components for the online environment include: 1) confidentiality, 2) integrity, 3) availability, 4) authenticity, and 5) non-repudiation.

Confidentiality, integrity, and availability refer to the assurance that test data are not released to unauthorized individuals, processes, or devices, that they have not been modified or destroyed, and that they are reliably and timely accessible (ISO/ IEC 27001, 2005; ISO/IEC 27002, 2005). In other words, only assigned examiners can access the test data in their original form on approved machines (e.g., personal computers, tablets), and that computer-, web-, or cloud-based test delivery to test-takers is unobstructed and reliable. In web-based and cloud-based testing, digital identities need to be created for each test-taker.

While authenticity is required to check the identity of users, be they test-takers, examiners, or administrators, non-repudiation is the ability to obtain proof of delivery and reception (ISO/IEC 27000, 2009). Establishment of a digital identity to secure authenticity and non-repudiation is crucial (Raitman, Ngo, Augar, & Zhou, 2005). Digital identities are certain data attributes or distinctive characteristics (e.g., usernames and passwords, test IDs, rater IDs, date of birth) that allow for the assessment, validation, and authentication of test-takers when they interact with the testing system on the internet (Bertino, Paci, Ferrini, & Shang, 2009).

Usernames and passwords are the most basic way to authenticate users for test-taker authentication and authorization to access the assessment tasks, as well as to authorize registered examiners and test administrators to enter and access test data. Clear definition of the different user roles in the data management system is an imperative so that users are granted access only to authorized information. For instance, test-takers' logins allow them to access the tasks assigned to them, while raters' logins authorize them to access the responses they are assigned to rate (see Chapter 8 for examples of secure data management systems). Example 5.7 illustrates how test security could be breached if the password protection system does not function properly.

EXAMPLE 5.7 SECURITY ISSUES WITH AUTHENTICATION

OEPT security issues

Just the other day we found that our computer system had been used in ways we did not anticipate. At first, it looked like we were hacked when three students signed on to our rater training program rather than the practice test. The URLs are similar, and our software developer actually left the backdoor open by not restricting access to the rater training system. All three of the students logged out when they realized they were in the wrong program; however, one later returned.

The student who returned opened the test prep program and the rater training program at the same time and was able to listen to different responses at different levels of the scale. The student listened to many failing sample responses before closing both programs and logging out. She then took the test the next day.

Finally, you may face the dilemma of whether to develop test tasks that require finding and using internet sources for task completion. While these tasks authentically reflect CMC or writing with digital sources, internet access compromises test security. You will have to decide whether to consider online dictionaries, conjugation websites, and translation websites as test security threats, or whether these resources strengthen the authenticity of the test as L2 writers constantly use them in real-life situations. The major security threat with internet access is the possibility of using Google Drive, Dropbox, or similar cloud-based storage domains and devices to exchange task responses with other individuals. This could be prevented by blocking the access to these websites or by using window or keystroke tracking programs. These programs keep logs of the websites that test-takers access or the words they type up during the test session, which can reveal any cheating practices.

Washback

Local language tests are often used to inform educational programs or to support larger language programs by providing formative feedback, language courses, or individual instruction. In such cases, you may reasonably expect that the task type and delivery platform would have an impact on teaching and learning, i.e., the test washback effect (Bailey, 1996; Cheng, 2013). Since learning with informational technology (IT) has become one of the main curricular goals across educational levels (elementary to university), implementing digital language tests may help you to integrate the IT goals with the language learning goals in the curricula and, in that way, create opportunities for positive washback effects on teaching and learning (Chapelle & Douglas, 2006).

One positive washback effect of digitally delivered language tests is the access to digital resources (e.g., dictionaries, conjugation tables, language corpora, translation applications) as well as digital information sources. Inclusion of such digital resources in language tests may raise awareness about their legitimacy in language teaching and learning. Teachers may include more activities that develop learners' abilities to apply the digital resources effectively (e.g., how to use language corpora for learning collocations or how to find relevant synonyms in dictionaries), but also activities that improve learners' understanding of privacy, copyright, and plagiarism issues related to digital source use.

Digitally delivered language tests also enable language programs to develop platforms for systematic data collection, which can help track learners' progress and provide continuous diagnostic feedback, as well as develop adequate instructional goals and objectives. Such a platform can facilitate the model of *Cognitively-based assessment* of, for, and as learning, the purpose of which is to document what students have achieved (of learning), how to plan instruction (for learning); and what is a worthwhile educational experience in and of itself (as learning) (Bennett, 2010).

Despite the above-mentioned possibilities for positive washback effects, digital language tests may also negatively affect language teaching and learning. Since some digital test tasks deliver restricted representations of complex language abilities, it is possible that they may limit the instructional attention only to those language aspects that the tasks represent. For example, if digitally delivered speaking tasks elicit monologues, then language instruction may focus primarily on longer monologues instead of interaction. This could be problematic if one of the intended instructional goals is effective communication with one or more interlocutors.

Summary

This chapter has discussed the advantages and disadvantages of traditional and digital delivery of language tests, as well as fundamental considerations regarding digital literacy, authenticity, security, and washback. Deciding on the delivery method is a crucial step that determines the task design, test administration, and maintenance. Therefore, you should examine the availability of human and technological resources and the adequacy of the technological infrastructure at your institution before making any decisions about the test delivery platform. If you are considering changing the delivery method of an existing language test from traditional to digital, you should first investigate the degree to which this change will affect test-takers' performance and whether it aligns with the testing purpose.

Further reading

Chapelle, C. A., & Douglas, D. (2006). *Assessing language through computer technology.* Cambridge, UK: Cambridge University Press.

Chapelle and Douglas (2006) present and discuss the most recent developments in computer technology and how technology has affected language test development and delivery. The first chapter introduces the topic of technology in relation to language assessment and explains which groups of people might benefit from reading this book. The next chapters touch upon a variety of topics related to technology in language testing, including how the interaction between input and response can be different when a test is technology-based, and what the threats to test validity are when technologies such as automated scoring or adaptive item selection are used. There is a chapter that is closely related to the needs of classroom teachers to computerized testing which works as a step-by-step guide to creating computer-based tests on a commercial platform. The administration of computerized tests is also discussed. The final chapter concludes the discussion by explaining how promising the future of computerized language testing looks with the fast-increasing transformative power of technology.

Chapelle, C. A., & Voss, E. (2016). 20 years of technology and language assessment in Language Learning & Technology. *Language Learning & Technology*, *20*(2), 116–128.

Chapelle and Voss (2016) examine the use of technology in language testing by synthesizing language assessment research published in *Language Learning & Technology* (LLT) from 1997 to 2015. The authors selected 25 articles and reviews for the synthesis and categorized them into two main themes: technology for efficiency and for innovation. The scholarship that emphasizes technology to improve test efficiency covers research on adaptive testing, automated writing evaluation (AWE), and comparability of different test versions. Going beyond the efficiency, research on technology for innovation opens opportunities to connect language testing, learning, and teaching. Examples include individualized assessment and feedback within AWE systems and the new learning and assessment environment in distance-learning contexts. The technology-mediated assessment leads to redefining language constructs and introducing novel task designs (e.g., an asynchronous online discussion) as well as attending to consequences of innovative technology-based assessment and evaluating authoring software. The authors call for more field-wide efforts to develop expertise of appropriately coping with issues in technology-mediated testing.

Douglas, D., & Hegelheimer, V. (2007). Assessing language using computer technology. *Annual Review of Applied Linguistics*, *27*, 115–132.

After a brief review of Jamieson's famous (2005) article on computer-based language assessment, the authors discuss both the promises and threats associated with computer-based tests. Their discussion includes the definition of the construct measured in computer-delivered tests, and how the nature of language construct is different in these tests from paper and pencil tests. The authors also make a technical discussion about the authoring tools that are being used in computer-based or web-based tests. When it comes to computer-based tests, a discussion of how scoring and reporting procedures are different from traditional paper and pencil tests is inevitable. Automated scoring of speaking and writing is briefly touched upon in this section of the paper. The last section of the article is about the validation issues that surface in computer-based testing. In this section, the authors argue that research to validate the specific interpretation of a computer-delivered test is of utmost importance. This discussion is supported by examples of validation research conducted by various researchers to validate TOEFL iBT.

Fulcher, G. (2003). Interface design in computer-based language testing. *Language Testing*, *20*(4), 384–408.

Fulcher (2003) describes the three phases of developing a computer-delivered language test interface. The author states that the article is unique due to the fact that interfaces used for computer-based language tests are not publicly available for use by other test developers. Phase I in interface design is introduced as "planning and initial design" when a preliminary version of the test interface is drawn with the consideration of the computer software and hardware specifications necessary for running the test. The second phase is called "usability testing" and consists of looking for problems in interface design and solutions to those problems. The author highlights the importance of usability research in this phase of interface design. Phase III is called "field testing and fine tuning" which is "required for scaling the test and ensuring that the logistics of data collection, submission, scoring, distribution and retrieval, and feedback work as planned" (p. 403). The author states that the three-phase model introduced in this article can be used for any interface development in future computer-based tests.

Jamieson, J. (2005). Trends in computer-based second language assessment. *Annual Review of Applied Linguistics*, 25, 228–242.

Jamieson (2005) discusses the "value-added" benefits of computer-delivered tests over the traditional paper and pencil tests with a focus on adaptive testing technologies which can make the tests shorter and more efficient. She also mentions that technology enhances language test developers' chances of testing abilities more accurately relevant to the target language use domain when compared to paper and pencil tests. Score reporting can also be more accurate in computerized testing since test-takers can be given more specific feedback about their performance on a computer-delivered test. Finally, the author discusses a number of possible future applications of technology in test computerization, including the use of corpora to develop more authentic language tests, the use of virtual reality in realistic simulations of discourse, and the use of natural language processing technologies in automated scoring of tests. The author also briefly discusses the possibility for the adaptation of multimedia computer-assisted language learning in developing multimedia language tests.

Ockey, G. J. (2009). Developments and challenges in the use of computer-based testing for assessing second language ability. *The Modern Language Journal*, *93*, 836–847.

Ockey (2009) discusses the contributions and limitations of computer-based testing (CBT) to medium- and large-scale second language (L2) ability assessments, focusing on delivery, computer-adaptive testing (CAT), and language skill assessments. The changes of delivery from CD-ROM-based to web-based testing in CBT systems improved test security and cost-effectiveness while decreased construct validity concerns over computer familiarity. CAT, a main CBT system, has expected advantages (e.g., higher test security, individualized level of challenging test-takers, implementation of different question types). However, CAT, in fact, is technically challenging because statistical assumptions on which CAT is based, unidimensionality and local independence, are possibly violated. Huge item banking requirement and computerized storing and retrieving of tests and scores add security concerns while developing numerous items and guaranteeing test-taker identity pose practical issues. CBT also brought innovations to language skill assessments mainly in terms of new independent tasks types, skill integration, and automatic rating. While addressing concerns related to the innovative tasks and rating, the author predicts continued growth in CBT as technology advances.

References

Afflerbach, P., & Cho, B. (2009a). Determining and describing reading strategies. In H. S. Waters & W. Schneider (Eds.), *Metacognition, strategy use, and instruction*, (pp. 201–225). New York: Guildford Press.

Afflerbach, P., & Cho, B. Y. (2009b). Identifying and describing constructively responsive comprehension strategies in new and traditional forms of reading. In S. E. Israel & G. G. Duffy (Eds.), *Handbook of research on reading comprehension*, (pp. 69–90). New York: Routledge.

Ananiadou, K., & Claro, M. (2009). *21st century skills and competences for new millennium learners in OECD countries.* OECD Education Working Papers, No. 41, OECD Publishing. Doi:10.1787/218525261154

Bachman, L. F., & Palmer, A. S. (1996). *Language testing in practice: Designing and developing useful language tests.* Oxford, UK: Oxford University Press.

Bailey, K. M. (1996). Working for washback: A review of the washback concept in language testing. *Language Testing, 13*(3), 257–279.

Bangert-Drowns, R. L. (1993). The word processor as an instructional tool: A meta-analysis of word processing in writing instruction. *Review of Educational research, 63* (1), 69–93.

Bennett, R. E. (2010). Cognitively Based Assessment of, for, and as Learning (CBAL): A preliminary theory of action for summative and formative assessment. *Measurement, 8* (2–3), 70–91.

Bertino, E., Paci, F., Ferrini, R., & Shang, N. (2009). Privacy-preserving digital identity management for cloud computing. *IEEE Computer Society Data Engineering, 32*(1), 21–27.

Buckingham, D. (2007). Digital media literacies: Rethinking media education in the age of the internet. *Research in Comparative and International Education, 2*(1), 43–55.

Chapelle, C. A., & Douglas, D. (2006). *Assessing language through computer technology.* Cambridge, UK: Cambridge University Press.

Cheng, L. (2013). Consequences, impact, and washback. In A. J. Kunnan (Ed.), *The companion to language assessment* (Vol. 3, pp. 1130–1145). Chichester and UK: John Wiley and Sons.

Coiro, J. (2011). Predicting reading comprehension on the internet: Contributions of offline reading skills, online reading skills, and prior knowledge. *Journal of Literacy Research, 43*(4), 352–392.

Coiro, J., & Dobler, E. (2007). Exploring the online reading comprehension strategies used by sixth-grade skilled readers to search for and locate information on the internet. *Reading Research Quarterly, 42*(2), 214–257.

Csapó, B., Ainley, J., Bennett, R. E., Latour, T., & Law, N. (2012). Technological issues for computer-based assessment. In E. Care, P. Griffin, Patrick, & M. Wilson (Eds.), *Assessment and teaching of 21st century skills* (pp. 143–230). Dordrecht, NL: Springer.

Dooey, P. (2008). Language testing and technology: Problems of transition to a new era. *ReCALL, 20*(1), 21–34.

Douglas, D. (2000). *Assessing languages for specific purposes*. Cambridge, UK: Cambridge University Press.

Douglas, D., & Hegelheimer, V. (2007). Assessing language using computer technology. *Annual Review of Applied Linguistics*, 27 (2007), 115–132. Doi:10.1017/S0267190508070062

Eagleton, M. B., & Guinee, K. (2002). Strategies for supporting student internet inquiry. *New England Reading Association Journal*, 38(2), 39–47.

Evering, L. C., & Moorman, G. (2012). Rethinking plagiarism in the digital age. *Journal of Adolescent & Adult Literacy*, 56(1), 35–44.

Fabos, B. (2008). The price of information: Critical literacy, education, and today's internet. In J. Coiro, M. Knobel, D. Leu, & C. Lankshear (Eds.), *Handbook of research on new literacies* (pp. 839–870). Mahwah, NJ: Lawrence Erlbaum.

Galaczi, E. D. (2010). Face-to-face and computer-based assessment of speaking: Challenges and opportunities. In L. Araújo (Ed.), *Proceedings of the Computer-Based Assessment (CBA) of foreign language speaking skills* (pp. 29–51). Brussels and Belgium: European Council.

Garcia, I., & Pena, M. I. (2011). Machine translation-assisted language learning: Writing for beginners. *Computer Assisted Language Learning*, 24(5), 471–487.

Ginther, A. (2003). International teaching assistant testing: Policies and methods. In D. Douglas, (Ed.), *English language testing in US colleges and universities* (pp. 57–84) Washington, DC: NAFSA.

Henry, L. A. (2006). SEARCHing for an answer: The critical role of new literacies while reading on the internet. *The Reading Teacher*, 59(7), 614–627.

Huff, K. L., & Sireci, S. G. (2001). Validity issues in computer-based testing. *Educational Measurement: Issues and Practice*, 20(3), 16–25. Doi:10.1111/j.1745-3992.2001.tb00066.x

ISO/IEC 27000 (2009). *Information technology – Security techniques – Information security management systems – Overview and vocabulary*. *2009*. ISO/IEC 27000:2009(E).

ISO/IEC 27001 (2005). *Information technology – Security techniques – Information security management systems – Requirements*. *2005*. ISO/IEC FDIS 27001:2005(E).

ISO/IEC 27002 (2005). *Information technology – Security techniques – Code of practice for information security management*. *2005*. ISO/IEC 27002:2005(E).

Jin, Y., & Yan, M. (2017). Computer literacy and the construct validity of a high-stakes computer-based writing assessment. *Language Assessment Quarterly*, 14(2), 101–119.

Jones, B., & Flannigan, S. L. (2006). Connecting the digital dots: Literacy of the 21st century. *Educause Quarterly*, 29(2), 8–10.

Laborda, J. G. (2007). From Fulcher to PLEVALEX : Issues in interface design, validity and reliability in internet based language testing. *CALL-EJ Online*, 9(1), 1–9.

Leijten, M., Van Waes, L., Schriver, K., & Hayes, J. R. (2014). Writing in the workplace: Constructing documents using multiple digital sources. *Journal of Writing Research*, 5(3), 285–337.

Ling, G., Mollaun, P., & Xi, X. (2014). A study on the impact of fatigue on human raters when scoring speaking responses. *Language Testing*, 31(4), 479–499.

Norris, J. M. (2016). Current uses for task-based language assessment. *Annual Review of Applied Linguistics*, 36(2016), 230–244.

O'Loughlin, K. J. (2001). *The equivalence of direct and semi-direct speaking tests*. Cambridge, UK: Cambridge University Press.

Ockey, G. J. (2007). Construct implications of including still image or video in computer-based listening tests. *Language Testing*, 24(4), 517–537.

Ockey, G. J. (2009). Developments and challenges in the use of computer-based testing for assessing second language ability. *Modern Language Journal*, 93(SUPPL. 1), 836–847.

Pecorari, D., & Petrić, B. (2014). Plagiarism in second-language writing. *Language Teaching*, 47(3), 269–302.

Powers, D. E. (1999). Test anxiety and test performance: Comparing paper-based and computer-adaptive versions of the GRE general test. *ETS Research Report Series, 1999* (2), i–32.

Raitman, R., Ngo, L., Augar, N., & Zhou, W. (2005). Security in the online e-learning environment. In *5th IEEE International Conference on Advanced Learning Technologies : ICALT 2005: proceedings: 5–8 July, 2005*, Kaohsiung, Taiwan (pp. 702–706).

Roever, C. (2001). Web-based language testing. *Language Learning & Technology, 5*(2), 84–94.

Sawaki, Y., Stricker, L. J., & Oranje, A. H. (2009). Factor structure of the TOEFL internet-based test. *Language Testing, 26*(1), 5–30.

Spiro, R. (2004). Principled pluralism for adaptive flexibility in teaching and learning to read. In R. B. Ruddell & N. Unrau (Eds.), *Theoretical models and processes of reading* (5th ed., pp. 654–659). Newark, DE: International Reading Association.

Taylor, C., Jamieson, J., Eignor, D., & Kirsch, I. (1998). The relationship between computer familiarity and performance on computer-based TOEFL test tasks. *ETS Research Report Series, 1998*(1), i–30.

Van Deursen, A. J., & Van Dijk, J. A. (2009). Using the internet: Skill related problems in users' online behavior. *Interacting with Computers, 21*(5-6), 393–402.

Watson, R. (2014, February 10). Student visa system fraud exposed in BBC investigation. *BBC News.* Retrieved from www.bbc.com/news/uk-26024375

Wilkins, H., Pratt, A., & Sturge, G. (2018, August 29). TOEIC visa cancellations. Retrieved from https://researchbriefings.parliament.uk/ResearchBriefing/Summary/ CDP-2018-0195.

Xinying, Z. (2015, October 12). Examiners get tough on students who cheat. *China Daily.* Retrieved from www.chinadaily.com.cn/china/2015-10/12/content_22159695.htm

Zenisky, A. L., & Sireci, S. G. (2002). Technological innovations in large-scale assessment. *Applied Measurement in Education, 15*(4), 337–362.

6
SCALING

This chapter focuses on the different types of language test scoring systems, with particular attention to scale design for performance-based tests in speaking and writing. Alongside the presentation of the different types of scales (analytic, holistic, primary-trait), this chapter discusses different scale design methods (data-driven, theory-driven) and benchmarking, i.e., finding representative performances of each scalar level. It argues that although the choice of approach depends on the resources available in the local context, it is important to consider three main components throughout the scale development process: (1) alignment between the scale and theories of language and language development, (2) ability of the scale to distinguish levels of test-taker performance, and (3) scale usability for test raters. The chapter ends with a discussion on the issues that must be considered during scale validation, and the unique challenges and opportunities for scaling in local testing contexts.

Introduction

To many language teachers and program administrators, scoring language performances might seem like an easy task. Some may wonder why much effort needs to be dedicated to scoring, as "the data (performance) will speak for itself." This may be true if you are measuring weight, height, or even diabetes, as there are widely accepted objective measurements for these biological or physiological traits. However, the evaluation of psychological constructs, such as language ability, is a "complex, error-prone cognitive process" (Cronbach, 1990, p. 584). Oftentimes, the test performance is too complex to convey a clear picture of the examinee's language proficiency without interpretation from experienced and well-trained experts, or else our current understanding of language proficiency as a construct is not sufficiently developed to allow us a consensus in our evaluation of the test performance.

Making a fair and appropriate judgment about language ability is not easy. The difficulty stems from at least three reasons. The first reason is the continued expansion of our profession. As the fields of Teaching English to Speakers of Other Languages (TESOL) and Applied Linguistics continue to explore new territories and embrace new philosophies, models, frameworks, and approaches to inquiry into languages and language learning, our understanding of language ability is becoming increasingly fluid and expansive. Thus, trying to reach a consensus on an operational definition of language ability has become an almost Herculean task. However, without an operationalizable definition, it is impossible to score language performance and compare the meaning of the scores across contexts.

The second reason that making principled judgments is difficult pertains to those who conduct the scoring. In local assessment contexts, be it placement, screening, certification, or proficiency tests, language instructors are the major group of raters or examiners. While instructors bring valuable experience and insights about the target test-takers to the table, they are not necessarily equally familiar with best practices in scoring test-taker performances. They need to be trained as raters to score test performances according to the operational definition of language proficiency for the test, which can be somewhat different from the teachers' own definition in the classroom. In other words, the test might ask raters to prioritize different subskills on a test than in the classroom. For example, in a speaking class, teachers might consider extra-linguistic factors (e.g., eye-contact, posture, body language) when helping students prepare for presentations, but in a testing context, where language performance is central, such factors tend to be de-emphasized. While teachers do not necessarily change the way they teach, they have to adopt a different approach for rating a test. Sometimes, more experienced teachers can be the most resistant to change. This is similar to martial arts training, where it is easier to teach one style of Kung Fu to children without any foundations than to experienced martial artists who are experts in a different style.

The third reason lies in the rating process. Language ability is multi-dimensional (involving a range of subskills), and so scoring language performances within time constraints is expected to be difficult by nature. For example, when describing the challenges in writing assessment, Hamp-Lyons (1995) wrote:

> When we assess writing, we engage in another complex and multifaceted activity:
> judging another person's text. Into that text has gone not only that person's grammatical ability, their reach of word knowledge and control, their sense of what a unified subject is, their factual knowledge about the subject, but also their understanding of the world and their place in it, their exploration of ideas, and their feelings.
>
> *(p. 760)*

Imagine that you have to evaluate a 500-word essay in 10 minutes while considering all of the above criteria; you might think "it is impossible to summarize everything with a single score," but you could probably bite the bullet and finish the task, even though it required great concentration. If you are asked to evaluate ten essays per day for a week, however, you might start to ignore the criteria and instead rely solely on your general impression to assign the scores. Of course, as you are using this coping strategy, you might question the value of language testing and want to run away from assessment for good. Indeed, scoring language performance should not be merely about quantity, but the above situations, emotions, and strategies are common among language teachers and program administrators, especially when appropriate design and quality control are missing during the scoring process.

One way to address these problems is to design an effective rating scale to guide the scoring process. In this chapter, we will delineate what scaling entails by introducing the advantages and disadvantages of rating scales, the types of rating scale used in assessment practice, and different approaches to scale development and validation. At the end of the chapter, we will discuss the unique challenges and exciting opportunities in scale development for local language tests.

Why do we need a rating scale?

There is no definitive answer as to when the first numerical scale was used to measure a variable, although some have speculated that it dates back to the Greco-Roman physician Galen in the 2nd century A.D. (McReynolds & Ludwig, 1987). The first formal application of a numeric rating scale to evaluate a psychological construct was done by the German Enlightenment philosopher, Christian Thomasius (1655–1728), who devised a set of rating scales to measure personality in the late 17th century (see McReynolds & Ludwig, 1987, for a brief historical review of rating scales). Yet, after centuries of use, exploration, and reflection, scaling still remains one of the fundamental and essential problems in psychological measurement, suggesting the levels of complexity that can go into the scoring process of psychological tests.

In language teaching and assessment, rating scales are most commonly used in the assessment of speaking and writing abilities. However, it was not very long ago when the assessment of language performance, including speaking and writing skills, still relied heavily on tasks that only elicited responses indirectly related to actual writing and speaking performances/abilities (e.g., multiple-choice items or short-answer questions). Scoring for such language tasks was reliable and easily automatable through the invention of stencils on paper and pencil tests or later on the use of simple matching algorithms when computer-delivered tests became available. As modern language testing moved towards the communicative era (starting in the 1970s), more authentic, complex, and performance-based speaking and writing tasks became commonplace in language teaching and assessment. These tasks tend to be more open-ended in nature, eliciting an extended spoken or written response from the test-takers.

Alongside the communicative approach, systematic inquiries into the development, validation, and use of rating scales also emerged. While the response process on these tasks appears closer to what language communication looks like in real life, it adds a great challenge to the reliability, or consistency, of the scoring process. As Upshur and Turner (1999) outlined (see Figure 6.1), the scoring process for performance-based language assessment is not only affected by examinee ability and task difficulty; the rating scale and raters also play a role. If you recall the three reasons we listed at the beginning of this chapter for why evaluating language performances is challenging, the provision of a rating scale is the first solution to the scoring problems in language testing. As the evaluation of language performance is based on systematic, principled judgment, raters need some criterion or guidance to help them avoid excessive randomness or subjectivity when evaluating test performances. Also, a rating scale lifts part of the burden from the raters by limiting the elements they need to focus on during the scoring process. Furthermore, the rating scale is also a means of communication between the test developers, raters, and test users, who are all interested in the inferences and decisions made from the scores. The descriptors can provide some meaning or justification for the users' decisions, provided that the scale is used effectively.

Different types of rating scales

With decades of improvement in development and use, rating scales have evolved. You might have seen a wide variety of rating scales and wonder which one to use for your local testing context. You might also wonder whether there is any type of scale that is superior to other types. The answer is a qualified no.

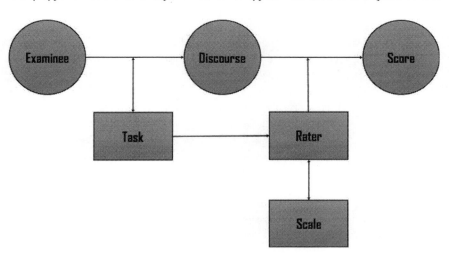

FIGURE 6.1 Factors affecting the scoring process
(adapted from Upshur & Turner, 1999)

There is no scale type that is inherently better than others; however, depending on the purpose and resources available for your local test, there is usually a better option that can meet your assessment needs. This section will introduce different types of rating scales commonly used in language testing, along with the kinds of information they can provide. From the perspective of measurement, all abilities can be assessed on four levels of measurement: namely, nominal, ordinal, interval, and ratio scales (Stevens, 1946). In language testing, there are a wide variety of rating scales used in scoring language performance. However, they all belong to two general categories of rating scale: holistic and analytic. A *holistic scale* features a single construct, and raters only need to assign one score to each performance; in contrast, an *analytic scale*, also referred to as *multiple-trait scoring rubric*, has more than one (sub-)construct, and raters need to assign a score to each aspect of the assessed ability or skill, and then derive a total score by either summing the subscores or weighing among different subscores to obtain some kind of an average score.

As research gradually uncovers different factors within the design of language tasks that may affect language performance and the evaluation of it by human raters, *primary trait scales* have been developed. This type of rating scale is a variety of holistic scale but is developed specifically for each prompt or task. Primary trait scales can provide rich, prompt-specific information about the performance at each level, although it is important to note that this kind of scale can be time-consuming to develop. Thus, it is not widely used in large-scale language tests. However, it can be useful in local contexts, given the narrower scope of the test. For example, a post-admission writing placement test can include two writing tasks: (1) email writing, which assesses students' pragmatic knowledge of daily written communication, and (2) integrated argumentative essay, which assesses students' command of lexico-grammar and knowledge of the rhetorical structures of academic writing. As the two tasks assess fairly different writing skills, it might be desirable to develop a separate scale for each task.

As language is complex and involves many subcomponents, the development and use of hybrid scales has become a common practice. Testing researchers and practitioners have explored the development and application of a *hybrid holistic scale*. This type of scale features lengthy or rich descriptors for each level, covering a range of analytic components. An example of the hybrid holistic rating scale can be found in the Oral English Proficiency Test (OEPT) at Purdue University, which was developed to measure the English speaking skills of prospective international teaching assistants (see, Bailey, 1983, for a review of the history behind oral proficiency testing for international teaching assistants in the US) (see Example 6.1). The scale levels and descriptors are presented in Figure 6.2 (taken from Kauper, Yan, Thirakunkovit, & Ginther, 2013).

EXAMPLE 6.1 A HYBRID HOLISTIC SCALE

OEPT: A hybrid holistic scale

The scale used for rating performances on the OEPT is hybrid holistic because it is a holistic rating scale that has specific descriptors for several analytic components, namely, pronunciation and intelligibility, fluency, lexical sophistication and accuracy, grammatical complexity and accuracy, coherence. In other words, the raters assign a holistic score for each item performance and an overall holistic score, but they take into consideration the analytic components in their score decision process.

This hybrid scale is used for scoring speaking performances in both the OEPT and the classroom-based assessments in the related ITA speaking courses, as it covers the core speaking (sub)constructs targeted in the Oral English Proficiency Program. The holistic nature of the scale allows the raters to assign a holistic score in a timely manner to accommodate efficient placement and certification during busy testing season; meanwhile, the comments raters make based on the analytic components provide detailed diagnostic information about each student when used in the classroom setting.

The field has also witnessed the use of a *binary analytic scale*. Like regular analytic scales, this type of scale still requires a score on each criterion, but reduces the scale to a set of binary questions or options to lower the difficulty in rating. Two types of binary analytic scales are common in language testing. The first type is called an *empirically-derived, binary-choice, boundary-definition (EBB) scale*, developed by Upshur and Turner (1995). An EBB scale is a task-specific scale that decomposes a holistic construct or scale into "a hierarchical (ordered) set of explicit binary questions relating to the performance being rated" (p. 6). The answer to each question breaks the performances into two levels. The first question often constitutes the most important cut on a holistic element (e.g., is the speech comprehensible?). As the level progresses, the questions become more fine-grained (analytic). By answering these questions in the specified order, the raters are guided to assign a holistic level to a particular language performance at the end. For demonstration purposes, Figure 6.3 presents an example of a simplified 4-point EBB scale for speaking ability. The speaking ability was decomposed into two levels of binary choices, with a total of three binary questions. The questions start from a holistic element (i.e., comprehensibility) and gradually move down to more specific elements (i.e., coherence and lexico-grammar at the second level).

The other type of binary analytic scale is called a *performance decision tree*. Similar to the EBB scale, performance decision trees also features a number of binary questions. However, in a decision tree, the raters have more flexibility in choosing the order by which they answer the binary questions, and raters need to sum the points from different questions at the end of the scoring process to derive holistic

OEPT2 HOLISTIC SCALE
revised 11-8-2012

Level	General Proficiency Level / Requirements of Listener / Performance of Speaker
60	*Excellent and Consistent across items. Majority of items 60.* *Minimal listener effort required to adjust to accent.* Frequent displays of lexico-syntactic sophistication and fluency. Speaker is at ease and confident fulfilling task, elaborating a personalized message, using accurate English. Errors are minor and few.
55	*More than Adequate. Mix of 55, 60, with a few 50 if any. Little listener effort required to adjust to accent/prosody/ intonation.* Consistently intelligible, comprehensible, coherent. Strong skills across items. Wide range of vocab and syntactic structures, generally sophisticated responses. Speaker may exert some noticeable effort or show minor fluency issues in elaborating clear message to fulfill task. Errors are minor.
50	*Adequate and ready for the classroom without support. Majority of items 50, possibly some 55 or very few 45. Acceptably small amount of listener effort required to adjust to accent/prosody/intonation.* Consistently intelligible and comprehensible. Speaker may exert a little noticeable effort, but despite minor errors of grammar/vocab/stress/fluency, message is adequately coherent, with correct information, some lexico-syntactic sophistication, and displays of automaticity and fluency.
45	*Borderline - Inconsistent – Minimally adequate for classroom with support. Mix of 45 and 50, very few, if any, 40. Tolerable listener effort required to adjust.* Consistently intelligible. Strengths & weaknesses across characteristics or items. Message is generally coherent, but may require more than a little noticeable effort for speaker to compose, or delivery may be slow. Or message may be clear and expressed fluently, but language use is somewhat simplistic.
40	*Limited - Not ready for the classroom. Mix of 40 and 45, or a few 35, if any.* Able to address prompts and complete responses. *Consistent listener effort may be necessary.* Message may be simplistic/unfocussed/incomplete/ incorrect. May struggle somewhat to build sentences/argument or to articulate sounds. May be occasionally unintelligible, incomprehensible, or incoherent.
35	*Restricted - May need more than 1 semester of support. Mix of 35 and 40. Listening may require considerable effort.* May be unintelligible or incoherent more than occasionally OR have marked deficiencies in at least 3 other areas: fluency, vocabulary, grammar/syntax, listening comprehension, articulation/pronunciation, prosody. May have difficulty completing responses.

FIGURE 6.2   The hybrid speaking scale for the Oral English Proficiency Program

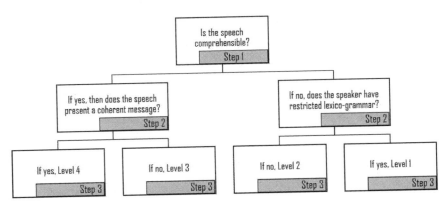

FIGURE 6.3   An EBB scale for speaking ability

scores. The principles behind performance decision trees are similar to those for EBB scales. That is, the scale helps simplify or decompose the holistic construct into analytic questions. However, as compared to EBB scales, performance decision trees are composed of more analytic questions and elements, and these questions do not necessarily form a hierarchy. Because of this flexibility, performance decision trees can be used to tackle more complex diagnosis of language performance (e.g., the processing of specific lexico-grammatical items, and the sequencing of turns in conversation). Moreover, raters do not have as much pressure to keep a holistic view of the performance during the scoring process; instead, they can focus on more fine-grained performance characteristics that are relevant to the target language ability and work on the holistic score as the last step. An example of a decision tree can be found in Figure 6.4, which is a performance decision tree for the English Placement Test at University of Illinois at Urbana-Champaign that was developed to help raters derive subscores on argumentation and lexico-grammar and decide on the relative strengths and weaknesses of the two criteria.

So far, we have browsed through a variety of rating scales commonly used in language assessment. You might be overwhelmed or confused about which type to use in your own local context. Sometimes, it is difficult to choose a clear winner from these scales or to make connections among them, as they look quite different. In theory, however, all of these scales can be placed along a continuum of specificity, with holistic scales being the least specific and analytic scales being the most specific (see Figure 6.5). Nevertheless, in practice, it

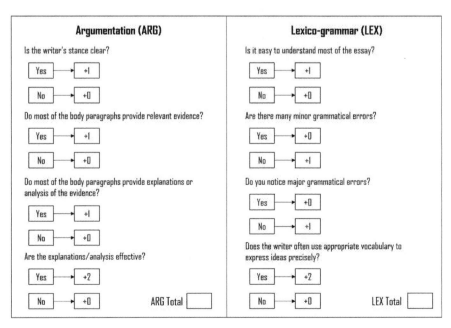

FIGURE 6.4   The performance decision tree for the English Placement Test at UIUC

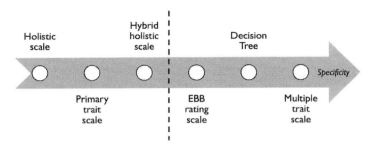

FIGURE 6.5 Different types of rating scale on the same continuum

is still convenient and perhaps more meaningful to classify rating scales according to the holistic vs. analytic dichotomy. If you need fine-grained information or diagnosis from assessment results, you will fare better with an analytic type of rating scale. Conversely, if you need a rather efficient and effective measure to place students into different levels, a holistic scale is the better option. We will introduce different approaches that you can employ to develop a rating scale from scratch in the following section.

Approaches to scale development and validation

Similar to the choice of rating scale, there are different approaches to the development of rating scale as well, and the choice of approach depends on the resources available in the local context. However, regardless of the approach you select, it is important to consider three main components throughout the scale development process: (1) alignment between the scale and theories of language and language development, (2) ability of the scale to distinguish levels of test-taker performance, and (3) scale usability for test raters. One disclaimer on the importance of theory in scale development and validation before we introduce the specific approaches: As rating scales and the rating process only deal with real performance data, it is reasonable to expect any rating scale to be guided or have some level of appeal to theories in language learning and development. However, as we mentioned at the beginning of the chapter, our field does not have a unified set of theories regarding language learning and development, making completely theory-driven scales difficult to achieve in language testing. If they are possible, then they tend to stay at a very general level. However, theory should inform or have a place in all approaches to scale development. Fulcher, Davidson, and Kemp (2011) classified scale development methods in language testing into two general approaches: the measurement-based approach and the performance-based, data-driven approach.

The measurement-based approach

The measurement-based approach is probably the oldest and most commonly used method to construct a scale. This approach relies on the intuitions of "experts", often experienced language teachers. To develop a measurement-based rating scale, you first need to form an expert committee to identify the target linguistic knowledge and skills for the assessment, which will become the criteria in the scale. Then, based on their knowledge and experience with language teaching and learning, the experts decide on the levels of performance needed in the scale. Once identified, descriptors are developed for each level of performance. No real linguistic or technical analysis is required for this method of scale development, but the committee refines the scale based on repeated use over time.

Due to the subjective nature in developing rating criteria and descriptors, such "a priori" developed scales have been criticized for being less specific and more imprecise, thus resulting in inconsistent ratings across raters (Knoch, 2009). A number of language testing scholars have pointed out that the language used in these scales are developed based on neither theory nor empirical data. The scale descriptors are often relativistic, abstract, and impressionistic, which does not foster a strong link between the scale (meaning) and performance (score) of intuitively developed scales (Fulcher et al., 2011; Pollitt & Murray, 1996), thereby losing explanatory power regarding the language performance of the test-takers (Knoch, 2009). Some have also expressed concerns over the reliability of the scale, questioning whether raters would be able to reliably distinguish performances across levels or criteria across performance levels (Brindley, 1998; Upshur & Turner, 1995).

Whether scales developed in the measurement-driven approach are atheoretical resembles a chicken or egg problem. Theory comes from the accumulation of and reflection on real-life experience. A theory is never sound unless it can be empirically validated. Thus, when experts' intuitions and experiences are used with caution, we cannot argue that the scales developed from the measurement-driven approach is utterly atheoretical. However, because of the skepticisms reviewed above, scale developers have become more attentive to the psychometric quality of rating scales, i.e., how well a rating scale can distinguish the levels of performances specified in the scale. More and more rating scales developed in a measurement-driven approach undergo an additional measurement analysis stage, often times through Rasch analysis, to ensure that the scale can differentiate real test performances across the predetermined levels in a reliable manner.

Performance-based, data-driven approach

Unlike the measurement-based approach that relies on intuitively derived, predetermined scale criteria and levels, a performance-based, data-driven approach is a bottom-up method. In this approach, you start from collecting and analyzing actual performance samples. Through the analysis of real language performances, you should try to find out if any linguistic performance features can help distinguish performances across levels. These features will become the basis for the scale descriptors. Your goal is to describe these features for performances at each level and to ensure that the scale descriptors can be easily interpreted by other raters, so that they can identify these key features easily when scoring the test performances. Once the scale descriptors are established, the scale levels should also be empirically established using statistical analysis (e.g., discriminant function analysis). This procedure helps to reveal the number of performance levels that the scores, based on the scale, can statistically distinguish.

In practice, how the features are identified can vary depending on the extent to which the developers appeal to theory during the development stages. For example, when developing a scale for more domain-specific language tests, the developers often refer to theoretical discussions about language performance in those specific domains to identify key knowledge and skills. They may also evaluate performances of high-proficiency speakers to identify representative performance features of the key knowledge and skills. In contrast, when dealing with the assessment of general language skills or proficiency, scale developers are often left with only one option; they have to evaluate and rank order the sample performances based on impressionistic ratings. Once consensus is reached regarding the rank order, they then go about describing the differences across those performances in an effort to uncover features that can differentiate performances between adjacent levels.

In either approach, the key features are further classified and interpreted to form the scoring criteria. Oftentimes, the performances will undergo a stage of fine-grained analysis based on those key features. Then, these features will be quantified and subjected to statistical analysis to reveal the number of performance levels that are statistically distinguishable. This step helps to identify the scale levels. Once the levels of performance are decided, the key performance features identified in the first step are used to describe each level in the scale. Even though this method allows for a close analysis of actual performance samples and strengthens the link between scale and actual performance, it is not without criticisms; researchers have noted that the data-driven approach to scale development can be time-consuming, and it produces analytic descriptors – often linguistic constructs – that human raters might find difficult to use in real-time rating (e.g., Banerjee, Yan, Chapman, & Elliott, 2015; Fulcher et al., 2011; Upshur & Turner, 1999). In this regard, the measurement-driven approach has more advantages, as scale descriptors developed by experienced instructors tend to be based on their teaching experience and thus more teacher-friendly. Since teachers form the main group of raters in local language programs, scales developed from the measurement-driven approach are more usable for the raters.

Combining the best of both worlds: a hybrid approach

The most important difference between the measurement-driven and performance data-driven approaches is that, while the former is more attentive to raters' perception and use, the latter is more diligent in ensuring the link between the scale and the language performance data. Here, we would like to introduce a third option: a hybrid development approach that combines the best of both worlds by involving experienced teachers and testers to evaluate sample test performances during the scale development process. In doing so, the scale development process should triangulate input from three information sources to reach an optimal outcome: theory, rater, and performance. An example of the application of this approach can be found in Banerjee et al. (2015, p. 8), where they consider input from the three sources in revising the rating scale for the writing section of the Examination for the Certificate of Proficiency in English (ECPE).

As Banerjee et al's (2015) study dealt with scale revision rather than scale development (although the two processes share more commonality than dissimilarities), we will sketch out a more general scale development process using the hybrid approach based on their model. More importantly, they dealt with a large-scale testing context. In local contexts, an additional source that we need to consider is the alignment between assessment and instruction. This brings up a vital point about scale development in local language programs; that is, teachers and testers should collaborate in the process as they complement each other in terms of their expertise. While testers can ensure the process is guided by sound assessment principles, teachers know the curriculum and the students better. The following is an example of a hybrid scale development (Yan, Kim, & Kotnarowski, in press). The stages of the scale development process are represented in Figure 6.6.

EXAMPLE 6.2 HYBRID SCALE DEVELOPMENT

EPT: a hybrid approach to scale development

We used a hybrid approach to scale when developing a profile-based rating scale for EPT, the ESL writing placement test at the University of Illinois at Urbana-Champaign.

In the first stage, our task was to identify the key constructs, which included triangulating information gathered from three steps: (1) reviewing theoretical models of language ability or domain-specific skills, (2) analyzing the curriculum and course syllabi in the local language program, and (3) asking experienced teachers (and administrators when appropriate) to reflect upon the range of language performance they typically observe in the classroom and the kinds of information about the students teachers would like to receive from the test.

In the second stage, a committee of experienced teachers (and testers, if available) was formed to evaluate sample performances. The performance samples were representative of the writing performance in the language classes and were rated in several rounds to allow for discussion and changes. While rating, the committee members simply ranked the essays based on their impressionistic judgment of the overall quality and noted the reasons behind the ranking (e.g., Essay A is ranked higher than Essay B because it has a clear paragraph-level argument structure). After each round of rating was done, the committee met and tried to reach consensus regarding their rankings. During this discussion, the committee members noted the reasons for both the consensus and disagreement among their rankings. The agreed-upon reasons were maintained to develop scale descriptors, while disagreement was discussed and revisited in the subsequent round to see if consensus could be reached. The goal was to reach alignment but, at the same time, allow all members to freely explain their own rationales in case disagreement occurred. Until all members could reach consensus on most of their evaluations, they needed to revisit the performances and consider how many levels they could differentiate among the performances and whether performances at each level shared similar characteristics. If such features did exist at each level, the committee members tried to describe those features in concise and precise language, and those descriptions formed the initial draft of the rating scale.

The third stage was the piloting phase. Once the scale was drafted, the developers pilot-rated more performances using the new scale to see if it could be applicable to a larger pool of test performances. More teachers who are novice to the new scale were invited to see if the new scale allowed them to capture the differences among those performances as did the committee members. In this process, feedback was gathered and, based on that feedback, adjustments to the scale were made.

After a couple of iterations of piloting and refining, the scale was launched for operational use (the fourth stage). At this point, the developers should start creating rater training materials and activities to help new raters learn to use the scale. The specific procedures during the rater training were similar to those in the second stage. However, the difference was that, at this stage, new raters were assigned to benchmark performances, i.e., essays that show the typical performance characteristics of each level and received the same scores from the majority of the experienced raters. The use of benchmark performances during rater training was crucial, as new raters could be easily overwhelmed by the number of performance features to which they needed to attend. Thus, using benchmarks could help raters ease into the rating scale by simplifying the variability among examinee performances while still maintaining the full range of performances represented on the test.

Issues to consider during scale validation

After more operational test data become available, the developers normally perform a set of measurement, linguistic, and statistical analyses to examine the reliability and validity of the scale. Scale validation can be an ongoing and rather long process because it involves the examination of a wide range of inferences and decisions to be made about the test performance. Since the focus on this chapter is on scale development, we will not discuss these analyses further in this

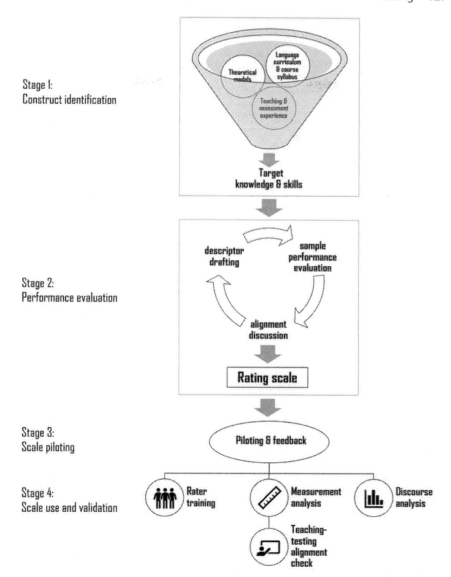

Stage 1:
Construct identification

Stage 2:
Performance evaluation

Stage 3:
Scale piloting

Stage 4:
Scale use and validation

FIGURE 6.6 A hybrid approach to scale development and validation

chapter. Some general frameworks for validating rating scales and language tests can be found in Chapelle, Chung, Hegelheimer, Pendar, and Xu (2010), Knoch and Chapelle (2018), and Yan and Staples (forthcoming). However, we will briefly discuss a few important issues or guiding questions to consider during scale development. For each issue, we will first explain the necessity of addressing it, and then offer a technical solution (one that involves expertise that goes beyond language pedagogy), as well as a less technical one.

Rater behavior on a rating scale

As we mentioned at the beginning of the chapter, performance-based language assessments normally rely on principled judgments by human raters. Nevertheless, they are susceptible to a variety of rater effects. A more detailed account of these rater effects will be provided in the next chapter, but as a preview, rater effects typically manifest in their *severity* (whether they are unfairly penalizing certain groups of performances), as a function of *intra-rater reliability* (whether raters assign the same score to performances at the same level), or as a function of *inter-rater reliability* (how raters agree with each other), as well as *scale use patterns, rating bias and strategies* (e.g., *central tendency, halo effect,* and *rater interaction;* see the next chapter for more detailed explanations). The effect on rater performance can vary according to rating workload, rating experience, rater and examinee background, as well as the quality of the rating scale. Some rater effects are easy to observe during or after the scoring process; other effects are difficult to detect unless the raters are asked to score language performances in an experimental setting targeting those effects, or unless the test administrators or rater trainers conduct a measurement analysis of rater behavior. For languages tests, Rasch modeling is a widely used measurement model to analyze a range of rater effects on the use of a rating scale. This kind of analysis requires at least 100 exams or scores assigned by raters, and so it is commonly practiced after each large test administration or each round of rating exercises during training where each performance is rated by all raters. In low-stakes settings, however, less technical solutions are also feasible. After each test administration, rater trainers can examine rater agreement statistics and check whether they use all levels of the scale. Normally, a rater's score assignment should resemble a normal distribution across the scale levels. During rater training sessions, rater trainers should also learn to be sensitive to rater behaviors, checking if the raters show different severity levels to different groups of examinees or on different tasks. They should also meet with individual raters regularly to understand their concerns about the scale and the scoring process.

The psychometric quality of a scale

In addition to rater reliability, a scale needs to be able to reliably distinguish examinees at different proficiency levels on all criteria, regardless of examinee backgrounds and other construct-irrelevant factors. To ensure these psychometric qualities of a rating scale, test developers often perform a series of post-hoc analysis of test scores to make sure the scale functions as intended. Normally, Rasch analysis covers this type of analysis, including whether and the extent to which (1) the scale can statistically distinguish examinees of different levels, (2) different rating criteria function differently if an analytic sale is used, and (3) a rating scale has unintended biases given factors such as testing conditions or rater and examinee backgrounds. This is a technical solution. However, when sufficient examinee population and the needed resources are lacking, as is often the case for local testing programs, we need to look for viable alternatives. One way to examine the psychometric quality of a rating scale is to look at the raw scores that examinees receive. First, the distribution of the final score can be calculated to check whether examinees' scores on the test follow a normal distribution. A highly skewed distribution tends to suggest low discrimination power for the scale. To examine how a scale functions across criteria, test conditions, or examinee backgrounds, we can divide examinee scores by those factors and then examine the average and distributions for each condition or group to determine whether examinees tend to receive the same, similar, or consistently higher or lower scores across conditions. Put simply, the score distribution and descriptive statistics are very useful information to examine the psychometric quality of rating scales, and thus should be employed in all contexts.

Link between scale descriptors and linguistic performance

So far, we have focused mainly on the psychometric quality of the rating scale, which is a very important aspect of scale validation. However, a rating scale needs to be valid with respect to the target language performance characteristics. In formal scale validation procedures, this is often done by a corpus-based analysis of examinee performances. First, the scale descriptors need to be deconstructed to identify an array of relevant linguistic or extralinguistic features. Then, corpus linguistics techniques will be employed to extract those features in a sample of examinee performances. Usually, these features will be quantified and subjected to some form of statistical analysis to help interpret whether the performance features correspond to the scale descriptor patterns at each level. As with measurement-based analyses, this procedure requires expertise in corpus linguistics. A non-technical alternative to a corpus-based analysis is to decompose the rating scale into a smaller number of rating criteria (e.g., decomposing a holistic writing scale into three rating criteria: source use, argument development, and lexico-grammar) and then rate the sample essays analytically. Although the analytic scores do not provide information about fine-grained performance features, as compared to holistic scores, they do provide more detailed information regarding examinee performances.

Alignment with national/international standards

As we discussed in previous chapters, local tests are developed in many parts of the world with close attention to national or international standards for language teaching, learning, and assessment. By linking a local test to national/international standards, we can extend the use of its scores beyond the local contexts (e.g., the use of local test scores for employment at trans-national companies in Europe). The spread of the Common European Framework of Reference (CEFR) is a good example of the need for such international standards. In

Europe, it is normal for local tests to be aligned to the CEFR. However, to create an alignment between local tests and the CEFR, a *linking study* needs to be carried out, often by a group of content and testing experts who are familiar with both the local test and the CEFR, in order to examine the benchmark language performances at each scale level and to identify the corresponding level on the CEFR (Council of Europe, 2011). It is important to note, however, that the CEFR is not a rating scale. When assessment expertise and resources are lacking in local contexts, it is possible, for simplicity's sake, that language teachers and program administrators choose to use the CEFR directly to rate language performance. However, this option is highly undesirable, as the CEFR is not developed with a particular test in mind, and its level descriptors tend to be purposefully generic to account for different types and levels of tests. These descriptors will not be closely linked to language performances in the local testing context. Example 6.3 describes the purpose and the process for TOEPAS scale alignment with the CEFR.

EXAMPLE 6.3 SCALE ALIGNMENT WITH CEFR

Linking the TOEPAS with CEFR

The main purpose of aligning the TOEPAS scale to the CEFR levels was to achieve transferability and transparency of the test results. Based on interviews regarding the uses and consequences of the TOEPAS with lecturers certified through the TOEPAS for teaching EMI, we found that these lecturers have the need for international recognition of their proficiency level (Dimova, 2017). They express concern that stakeholders may be unable to recognize their proficiency levels based solely on the TOEPAS scale, so they need the reported results to be trans-institutionally and trans-nationally recognizable.

As proposed by the manual *Relating Language Examinations to the Common European Framework of Reference for Languages: Learning, Teaching, Assessment* (CEFR) (Council of Europe, 2009), the linking procedure, which consisted of four stages (familiarization, specification, benchmarking, and validation) was performed by a panel that consisted of 12 members (six already familiar with the TOEPAS scale and six unfamiliar with the TOEPAS scale but experienced with the use of CEFR). The alignment took place over a three-day standardization event. While Day 1 focused on familiarization with the CEFR scales, Day 2 was dedicated to training, and Day 3 to benchmarking. The specification stage was completed before the three-day event in collaboration with the test designers and coordinators because they were most familiar with the different aspects of the test content and tasks. The TOEPAS specifications were presented to the panel judges on Day 2 before benchmarking local samples. Procedural validation data were collected during the event, but the analysis was performed after the event ended.

Based on the results of the alignment procedure, we found that the TOEPAS scale ranges from B2 to C2 level on the CEFR, with the cut-score set right between B2 and C1 (B2+/C1).

Unique challenges and opportunities for scaling in local testing contexts

As we mentioned repeatedly in previous chapters, there are many challenges when it comes to scale development for local testing contexts: lack of experience, resources, and motivation, to name but a few. In some ways, these challenges also create opportunities for interesting explorations and inventions of rating scales and/or language assessment practice in general. Here, we will discuss three potential challenges and the opportunities they yield.

Restricted range of proficiency and different profiles in the same classroom

In educational and employment contexts, students and employees are often selected from a larger pool of applicants that tend to represent a full range of proficiency or ability for the particular academic or professional purposes (e.g., graduate study in Biology or air traffic control). The selection procedures, while allowing school administrators and employers to select the qualified candidates, create a narrower range of proficiency or ability (we call this *restricted range of proficiency* resulting from direct selection). Many large universities in English-speaking countries have set minimum cut-off test scores to screen the applicants by their English proficiency (e.g., TOEFL or IELTS scores). At the same time, these schools often require students who score lower than a certain required test score on a local placement test/exam to receive additional language support by taking courses in their ESL program. For instance, UIUC requires international undergraduate students who score below 103 in total, and below 25 on either speaking or writing sections of the TOEFL iBT (below 7.5 in total and below 7 on either speaking or writing sections of the IELTS) to take the EPT (https://linguistics.illinois.edu/languages/english-placement-test). Purdue University also requires undergraduate students who score 100 or less on TOEFL iBT, or less than 7.5 on the IELTS, to take the institutional English for Academic Purposes placement test (www.purdue.edu/place/courses/index.html). Therefore, students who end up taking the ESL courses are within a restricted range of proficiency with little variance in their performance (roughly with an overall score of 80–100 on TOEFL), which provides unique challenges for local ESL programs.

When examining speaking or writing performances, many local programs rely on or adopt existing rating scales from large-scale tests like TOEFL, which target a fuller range of proficiency. This may be largely due to budgetary reasons, lack of experience, and/or the amount of time and effort involved in creating new rating scales. Even though the use of existing rating scales can have many advantages and has also been well researched, these scales are not necessarily sensitive enough to capture the nuance of language performances among students within a restricted range (Bridgeman, Cho, & DiPietro, 2016; Cho & Bridgeman, 2012; Ginther & Yan, 2018). As most university-level ESL students fall within the high intermediate to low-advanced proficiency group, such scales tend to have limited use. Despite this restricted range of proficiency, however, there are often different profiles that exist within the same level of classes, which may benefit from different instructional approaches and focuses. These profiles might become more prominent because of the restricted range of proficiency, thus offering unique and interesting scaling possibilities that large-scale tests do not.

Participation of teachers: language assessment literacy in the classroom

In language programs, it is commonplace to involve teachers in different stages of test development. In scale development, it would be ideal and beneficial if teachers could collaborate with testers, who are more familiar with the best practice in rating and scaling, whereas teachers are more familiar with the test performances and target test-takers in the classroom. Admittedly, teachers' assessment literacy has been questioned, which raises concerns about their value/qualification for test development (Popham, 2001). Teachers themselves, or non-testing specialists in general, might also feel less confident or comfortable about their assessment knowledge or skills. However, there are benefits of involving teachers more in the test development process. One of the biggest strengths that teachers bring is their knowledge of both the students (language learners) and the local context. As such, they are able to identify the students' profiles (strengths and weakness) and apply this knowledge to assessment practices (Purpura, 2004). The experience of being involved in various stages of test development enables them to better connect teaching and assessment (Yan, Zhang, & Fan, 2018), and also provides an opportunity to better understand their students within the restricted range.

Next, involving teachers in actual assessment practices can enhance their assessment literacy. Teachers need to acquire skills including developing, administering, and scoring writing tasks, as well as the ability to recognize components of a good paper or good writing (Weigle, 2007). They can also develop good intuitions about assessment concepts and principles by participating in various assessment practices. These iterative, accumulated assessment experiences would enable them to feel more "empowered" as teacher-assessors (Crusan, Plakans, & Gebril, 2016; Lee, 2010).

Teacher-tester collaborations can also be beneficial to testers, as teachers can contribute knowledge about their students and develop descriptors aligned with the assessment language used in the classroom. The collaboration in assessment practices thus helps bridge the gap between the two groups and increases the usability and interpretability of the rating scale. As such, communication between teachers and testers should be promoted in order for successful collaboration in assessment practices (Jin, 2010).

The combination of placement, diagnosis, and more in the rating scale

Another challenge for local language tests is the need to serve multiple purposes. For example, a post-admission language test often needs to provide not only placement decisions but also diagnostic information for language instructors about students' actual language performance and skills. Oftentimes, post-admission language tests focus on a holistic score to provide placement decisions, but they are not specifically designed to provide specific diagnoses of students' language profiles. Here, we define a profile as a description of the strengths and weaknesses in students' language performance. As a result, finer-grained diagnosis of students' language ability often takes place in classrooms, and teachers need to elicit and assess students' language performances for diagnostic purposes. As local tests are often embedded in language programs, these tests tend to be learning-oriented and would benefit greatly from combining placement and diagnostic purposes (Purpura, 2004).

The diagnostic function of language tests is important in local testing contexts. The nature of language proficiency changes across speakers of different proficiency levels, and different learner profiles exist even within the same proficiency group due to varying strengths and weaknesses in subskills. For instance, within the intermediate-advanced proficiency range, some students have strong receptive skills (reading and listening), while showing contrasting weakness in productive skills (speaking and listening) (Bridgeman et al., 2016; Ginther & Yan, 2018). Different profiles also exist on individual skills when we look at the relevant subskills (e.g., lexico-grammar and argumentation in writing; see Jarvis, Grant, Bikowski, & Ferris, 2003). These profiles can have different implications for instruction. Therefore, in order to fully capture the subtle profile differences in test-takers' performances, rating scales for local language tests need to explore the possibility of identifying learner profiles, which can offer both placement and diagnosis for the examinees.

Summary

This chapter introduced the fundamental concepts, procedures, and issues related to scaling for local language tests. If you are reading this chapter for a general learning purpose, we hope that you have obtained a general sense of what scaling entails in practice and why the procedures involved in scale development and validation are necessary. If you are reading this chapter to find a solution to a practical scaling problem, we hope that we have offered possible solutions to your problem.

In any case, following a systematic approach to scale development and use is essential. The development, implementation, use, and validation of a rating scale should be an iterative process. During this process, the scale developers should keep in mind that theory cannot be ignored, and teaching and assessment experience is just as informative as the analysis of performance data.

Lastly, through the iterative discussions during scale development, implementation, and use, teachers and testers can help standardize the conceptualization and operationalization of language ability in both assessment and instructional contexts. The involvement of different stakeholders in scale development and validation can promote collaborative dialogue and practice in language assessment among stakeholder groups. Ultimately, this collaboration will strengthen the alignment between assessment and pedagogy in local language programs.

Further reading

Alderson, J. C. (1991). Bands and scores. In J. C. Alderson & B. North (Eds.), *Language testing in the 1990s: The communicative legacy* (pp. 71–86). London and England: Macmillan.

Alderson (1991) discusses the purposes, uses, and issues centered around band scores of language tests, particularly focusing on the ELTS Revision Project. After providing background on language test proficiency scales (e.g., the InterAgency Language Roundtable scales, the Australian Second Language Proficiency Ratings, and ELTS bands), the author introduces three main purposes of scales (i.e., user-oriented, assessor-oriented, and constructor-oriented), each of which has the functions of reporting test results, guiding assessing process, and controlling test construction, respectively. The author also addresses issues that impede successfully achieving the functions and purposes, for example, inconsistency between performance descriptions in scales and actual performance elicited by test tasks, and mismatch between components in rating scales and reporting. The author further discusses the process and issues of arriving at finalized performance-based test band score descriptors as well as converting of comprehension-based test raw scores into band scores. The author points out the commonality in the issues of band and test scores and emphasizes the benefits of using scales for various stakeholders.

Fulcher, G., Davidson, F., & Kemp, J. (2011). Effective rating scale development for speaking tests: Performance decision trees. *Language Testing, 28*(1), 5–29.

Fulcher et al. (2011) present the development of a Performance Decision Tree (PDT), a speaking test rating scale from a performance data-based approach. The authors begin with comparing performance data-based and measurement-driven approaches in designing and developing scales. The authors argue for performance data-based approaches because performance data-based scales provide sufficient descriptions directly linked to examinee performance, which enables rigorous inferences from scores to domain-specific performance, whereas measurement model-based scales misrepresent language abilities as simplified linear levels and offer decontextualized description of abilities. Hence, the authors developed PDT, which features as binary choice-based decision-making and rich description based on a thorough review of literature on interactional competences in service encounters domain (e.g., discourse competence, discourse management competence, and pragmatic competence) and analysis of performance data. The authors claim superior validity and efficiency of PDT to assess communication competence in service encounters in management contexts and call for continued research on performance data-based scales.

Upshur, J. A., & Turner, C. E. (1995). Constructing rating scales for second language tests. *ELT Journal*, *49*(1), 3–12.

Upshur and Turner (1995) introduce "empirically-derived, binary-choice, boundary-definition (EBB) scales," (p. 6) to remedy reliability and validity issues of using standard rating scales in instructional settings. The authors argue that theory-based approach of standard ratings does not reflect actual learner performance due to characteristics inherent to instructional settings, for example, narrow proficiency ranges and frequent interactions between teaching conditions and progress. The authors propose EBB scales as an alternative, which consists of binary questions in a hierarchically ordered decision-making structure. The authors developed two EBB scales to respectively assess grammatical accuracy and communicative effectiveness of a story-retell task that 99 French ESL fifth graders took. They provide detailed descriptions of the test development and administration procedures, and report high reliabilities for both communicative effectiveness ($r=0.81$) and grammatical accuracy ($r=0.87$). The authors highlight that focusing differences and boundaries between scale categories rather than the midpoint of a category and using precise and simple descriptors improved rater reliability. They also stress the positive influence of locally developed scales on enhancing validity of ratings.

References

Bailey, K. (1983). Foreign teaching assistants at US universities: Problems in interaction and communication. *TESOL Quarterly*, *17*(2), 308–310.

Banerjee, J., Yan, X., Chapman, M., & Elliott, H. (2015). Keeping up with the times: Revising and refreshing a rating scale. *Assessing Writing*, *26*, 5–19.

Bridgeman, B., Cho, Y., & DiPietro, S. (2016). Predicting grades from an English language assessment: The importance of peeling the onion. *Language Testing*, *33*(3), 307–318.

Brindley, G. (1998). Outcomes-based assessment and reporting in language learning programmes: A review of the issues. *Language Testing*, *15*(1), 45–85.

Chapelle, C. A., Chung, Y. R., Hegelheimer, V., Pendar, N., & Xu, J. (2010). Towards a computer-delivered test of productive grammatical ability. *Language Testing*, *27*(4), 443–469.

Cho, Y., & Bridgeman, B. (2012). Relationship of TOEFL iBT® scores to academic performance: Some evidence from American universities. *Language Testing*, *29*(3), 421–442.

Council of Europe. (2009). *Relating language examinations to the common European framework of reference for languages: Learning, teaching, assessment. A manual.* Strasbourg: Language Policy Division.

Council of Europe (2011). Common European Framework of Reference for Languages: Learning, Teaching, Assessment. Council of Europe.

Cronbach, L. J. (1990). *Essentials of psychological testing.* (5. Baskı) New York, NY: Harper Collins Publishers.

Crusan, D., Plakans, L., & Gebril, A. (2016). Writing assessment literacy: Surveying second language teachers' knowledge, beliefs, and practices. *Assessing Writing*, *28*, 43–56.

Dimova, S. (2017). Life after oral English certification: The consequences of the test of oral English proficiency for academic staff for EMI lecturers. *English for Specific Purposes*, *46*, 45–58.

Fulcher, G., Davidson, F., & Kemp, J. (2011). Effective rating scale development for speaking tests: Performance decision trees. *Language Testing*, *28*(1), 5–29.

Ginther, A., & Yan, X. (2018). Interpreting the relationships between TOEFL iBT scores and GPA: Language proficiency, policy, and profiles. *Language Testing*, *35*(2), 271–295.

Hamp-Lyons, L. (1995). Rating nonnative writing: The trouble with holistic scoring. *Tesol Quarterly*, *29*(4), 759–762.

Jarvis, S., Grant, L., Bikowski, D., & Ferris, D. (2003). Exploring multiple profiles of highly rated learner compositions. *Journal of Second Language Writing*, *12*(4), 377–403.

Jin, Y. (2010). The place of language testing and assessment in the professional preparation of foreign language teachers in China. *Language Testing*, *27*(4), 555–584.

Kauper, N., Yan, X., Thirakunkovit, S., & Ginther, A. (2013). *The Oral English Proficiency Test (OEPT) technical manual.* (pp. 21–32). West Lafayette, IN: Purdue University Oral English Proficiency Program.

Knoch, U. (2009). *Diagnostic writing assessment: The development and validation of a rating scale* (Vol. 17). New York: Peter Lang.

Knoch, U., & Chapelle, C. A. (2018). Validation of rating processes within an argument-based framework. *Language Testing*, *35*(4), 477–499.

Lee, I. (2010). Writing teacher education and teacher learning: Testimonies of four EFL teachers. *Journal of Second Language Writing*, *19*(3), 143–157.

McReynolds, P., & Ludwig, K. (1987). On the history of rating scales. *Personality and Individual Differences*, *8*(2), 281–283.

Pollitt, A., & Murray, N. L. (1996). What raters really pay attention to. *Studies in Language Testing*, *3*, 74–91.

Popham, W. J. (2001). *The truth about testing: An educator's call to action.* Alexandria, Virginia, USA: ASCD.

Purpura, J. E. (2004). *Assessing grammar.* New York: Cambridge University Press.

Stevens, S. S. (1946). On the theory of scales of measurement. *Science*, *103*(2684), 677–680.

Upshur, J. A., & Turner, C. E. (1995). Constructing rating scales for second language tests. *ELT Journal*, *49*(1), 3–12.

Upshur, J. A., & Turner, C. E. (1999). Systematic effects in the rating of second-language speaking ability: Test method and learner discourse. *Language Testing*, *16*(1), 82–111.

Weigle, S. C. (2007). Teaching writing teachers about assessment. *Journal of Second Language Writing, 16*(3), 194–209.

Yan, X., Kim, H., & Kotnarowski, J. (in press). The development of a profile-based writing scale: How collaboration with teachers enhanced assessment practice in a post-admission ESL writing program in the USA. In B. Lanteigne, C. Coombe, & J. Brown (Eds.), *Issues in language testing around the world: Insights for language test users*. New York: Springer.

Yan, X., & Staples, S. (2019). Fitting MD analysis in an argument-based validity framework for writing assessment: Explanation and generalization inferences for the ECPE. *Language Testing*, 0265532219876226.

Yan, X., Zhang, C., & Fan, J. J. (2018). "Assessment knowledge is important, but ... ": How contextual and experiential factors mediate assessment practice and training needs of language teachers. *System, 74*, 158–168.

7

RATERS AND RATER TRAINING

This chapter discusses the process of rater selection, initial training, and continuous norming. It addresses the different methods of rater training and the importance of rater agreement for the reliability of test results and the different instruments and methods that can be employed for the analysis of rater behavior and inter- and intra-rater reliability. More specifically, the chapter presents how to perform consensus, consistency, and measurement estimates, as well as rater effects from the local testing context. The chapter ends with an overview of best practices for rater training, including rater cognition, benchmarking, as well as establishing a rater group as a community of practice.

Introduction

In local testing, be it for placement, screening, or certification purposes, the raters are usually language teachers. While teachers are familiar with test-takers and test-taker performance in the local context, they need training to rate test performance in a consistent manner. When rater training is not in place, we might observe two kinds of raters or rater behavior. The first kind of raters appear quite confident about how the scale works, but their ratings show that they do not apply the scale and interpret scale descriptors in the intended way. The other kind of raters are opposite to the confident raters; they are less confident or comfortable with the rating scale (or new scales in general). When structured rater training is not in place, they may avoid using the scale and instead resort to their regular assessment practices in class or their own conceptualizations of language proficiency to evaluate language performances. In either case, because of the lack of standardized rater training, we might observe a great degree of individual variation in their scores and scoring behavior. This does not necessarily mean that teachers do not know what language ability is. In fact, if teachers are asked to rank a batch of language performances, they are usually able to distinguish between high and low proficiency performances. However, agreement on the evaluation of mid-level performance can be difficult to achieve. Unfortunately, this level or range of proficiency is what you might be dealing with in a local testing context. However, given teachers' background in language pedagogy and sensitivity to different profiles of language performances, with a structured rater training program, they can be easily trained to reach consensus on the meaning and value associated with language proficiency in the particular local context and on aspects of language performances to focus on during evaluation.

If you are a teacher working predominantly in language classrooms, you might also wonder why rater agreement is important for local tests. It is a common attitude or stance regarding assessment among teachers and teacher educators that teachers should have the freedom to hold assessment close to their own values and beliefs; they should not be standardized in terms of how they evaluate students' performance, as long as learning takes place. In fact, standardization and freedom do not necessarily form a relationship of opposition. A teacher should be granted freedom in terms of instructional approach and materials selection. However, when multiple sections of the same class are taught by different instructors, when students need to be placed or advanced into different levels of courses, or when the instructional program is required to achieve certain teaching or learning goals, standardization in assessment procedures becomes important for program evaluation purposes (see Chapter 8 for program evaluation). Similarly, in the classroom, teachers interact extensively with the students and can repeatedly observe (that's what assessment entails, in a broad sense!) student performance across contexts. Their evaluation of the students is less likely to be *biased* and more likely to reflect the students' true knowledge or skills. Thus, in classroom-based assessment contexts, educational expertise and experience should be valued, and teachers should be encouraged to use their daily observations to complement the formal assessments that they use to evaluate students' learning outcomes. In measurement terms, if repeated testing or assessment provides similar test scores, the test or assessment possesses high *test-retest reliability*. However, the assessment context for a local language test is different. Teachers often do not know the examinees or have more than one shot to accurately assess their language abilities. Instead, they have to use a standardized rating scale to evaluate examinees' performance. During the scoring process, teachers' instructional experience and familiarity with student performance profiles in the courses can still be valuable for helping them distinguish examinees across levels. However, rater training is needed to ensure that they use the rating scale in similar ways.

Rater training for large-scale and local language tests can be very different. First, large-scale tests tend to have large rater pools and thus can afford to select the most reliable raters for each test administration. Local tests tend to have small pools of raters and, for practical purposes, must employ all raters for operational scoring. Thus, rater training tends to be more intensive as the goal is to align all raters to the scale. However, compared to local tests, large-scale tests lack the ability to make finer distinctions among a subpopulation of examinees because they lose the rich information that the test scores can provide about the examinees and the opportunities the examinees can be given, as well as the resources and support they can access. Because of their experience and familiarity with the local context, language teachers or other local members (e.g., other stakeholders in the local context) often possess sensitivity during the scoring process to the strength and weaknesses of the examinees' linguistic knowledge, as well as their impact on language performance. Such sensitivity can contribute to the design of tasks, scoring methods, and even research projects for local language testing. However, all of these benefits are conditioned upon raters' ability to reliably rate test performances in the local context. In this chapter, we will discuss rater behavior and rater training models that are suitable for local language testing.

The promise and perils of rater-mediated language assessment

Because of human raters' sensitivity to a wide range of performance characteristics and individual difference in cognitive capacity, scoring styles, and preferences, rater-mediated language assessments offer both advantages and disadvantages. In the previous chapter, we talked about the importance of rating scales, citing Upshur and Turner's (1999) model of scoring to illustrate the factors that influence the quality of scoring. As can be seen from their model (Figure 6.1), the impact of most factors is mediated through raters. When discussing the development of rating scales, we also pointed out that, no matter how adequate a rating scale is, it has to be useable for raters. In fact, any test that utilizes constructed-response items (e.g., short-answer questions, essay tasks) will require scoring by raters. These tests are therefore called *rater-mediated assessments*. Performance-based language assessments such as an essay writing test or an oral interview test are examples of this type of assessment.

An important advantage of rater-mediated assessments is that raters can use their prior knowledge, expertise, and experience to assist with scoring. Performance-based tests rely on the use of rating scales to define the assessed knowledge and skills and to guide raters to focus on the target performance characteristics. However, for practicality, the scale descriptors are often kept simple and brief, and may not indicate a clear one-to-one correspondence to those who lack the relevant content knowledge. Raters' prior experience and expertise can help to bridge the gap between the descriptors and the target behavior or performance characteristics for the test.

However, because raters have different values, philosophies, and preferences based on their prior experiences, they might also emphasize different aspects of the rating scale and test performances, thus arriving at different scores on the same test performance. It is hard for test developers to strike a balance between the scale, rater, and rater training. We want to make sure that the raters assign the same score to the performance to ensure that they are using the scale consistently. In other words, we want to make sure that, regardless of which rater rates the performance, the test-taker receives the same score. This expected agreement between raters is referred to as *rater reliability* in language testing or psychological measurement literature. If two raters regularly assign different scores to the same examinees, then the test scores will become less reliable and meaningful, and the quality of the test will be compromised. In practice, if the examinee takes a test twice with two different and unreliable raters, s/he will likely receive two different scores. In that case, which score would be a better reflection of his or her knowledge or skills? You might be tempted to average the scores between the two raters, but oftentimes, this is not the best option and should be the last resort before exhausting other possible ways to improve rater reliability. This assessment principle applies to both large-scale and local language tests.

The involvement of teachers as content experts or raters who are familiar with the local contexts can bring both benefits and challenges to the scoring process. Unlike large-scale tests, local tests typically cannot afford to lose raters, even though some raters do not exhibit satisfactory rater reliability. They all have to rate most of the time. Thus, rater reliability becomes essential to the accuracy of test scores. However, the reliability of local tests often depends on the group dynamic among the raters, as well as their individual differences. It is within this constraint that rating and rater training for local language tests often reside, but this constraint also gives the rater group a strong sense of community and makes rater training a much more communal practice. When raters are familiar with the local context, they are more aware of the purposes and uses of the test. This awareness can keep them on track when scoring language performances, rather than focusing on criteria not included in the rating scale. Moreover, involving members in the local context can help to reinforce positive test impact. If the test purports to place students into different ESL courses, and the raters are instructors of those courses, then it is possible that they can enhance the alignment between teaching and testing.

In summary, the involvement of members in the local context is often a characteristic of the scoring process for local language tests. While local members are fallible as raters, their involvement makes raters and rater training a much more integrated system than the scoring process for large-scale language tests.

Rater behavior: a catalog of rater effects

Just as every language class needs some form of assessment, there also needs to be some measures to assess rater reliability. When we think about rater agreement, it is not difficult to envision two dimensions. First, raters need to agree with each other on most of the exams they score. Second, individual raters need to assign the same score to exams at the same level. In the measurement literature, we call agreement between raters *inter-rater reliability* and agreement within individual raters *intra-rater reliability* or *internal consistency* of raters. The most commonly used indicator of rating quality in rater-mediated assessments is rater agreement. There are different ways of estimating rater agreement. Stemler (2004) classified these estimates into three large categories: namely, *consensus estimates*, *consistency estimates*, and *measurement estimates*. We will not provide much statistical detail about these estimates, but will instead explain what these estimates represent, how they should be interpreted, and why they are needed in the assessment of rater performance.

Consensus estimates

Consensus estimates reflect the percentage of agreement between the scores assigned by two or more raters. Some commonly used consensus estimates include exact agreement (percentage), adjacent agreement (percentage), and kappa statistics. While exact agreement is defined as the percentage of exams on which two or more raters assign exactly the same scores, adjacent agreement refers to the percentage of exams on which the scores assigned by two raters are only one point apart. For example, if two raters assign a 3 on a 5-point rating scale for a particular examinee, then we consider that the two raters have reached exact agreement on that examinee. If, however, one rater assigns a 2, whereas the other assigns a 3, then we would consider the two raters to have reached adjacent agreement. For some tests, the sum of exact and adjacent agreement percentage is used as the estimate of rater reliability to allow for humanistic errors/individual variations because it is rather difficult to reach exact agreement on all occasions, even if the two raters might have similar qualitative evaluations of the same performance. In contrast, Kappa statistics take an extra step to account for agreement by chance in the calculation of agreement percentage. Kappa statistics assume that raters play a guessing game while scoring examinee performances. Thus, among the three consensus estimates, Kappa statistics is the most conservative because it tends to be lower than the exact agreement statistic. Nevertheless, the interpretation of these estimates is the same; that is, the closer to 1, the higher the level of rater agreement. To showcase an example of consensus estimates of rater reliability, we present in Table 7.1 the rater agreement statistics used to examine rater performance for regular test administrations of the English Placement Test at UIUC.

TABLE 7.1 Consensus estimates of rater reliability on the EPT

Agreement	Explanation	Frequency (n)	Percentage (%)	Cumulative percentage (%)
Exact	exactly the same	35	53.03	53.03
Adjacent	1 point apart	23	34.85	87.88
Discrepant	2 points apart	7	10.61	98.49
Conflicting	>2 points apart	1	1.52	100

Consistency estimates

The assumption underlying consistency estimates is that raters need to demonstrate a similar or consistent way of ranking examinees according to the scale. That is, more proficient examinees should receive higher scores than less proficient examinees, even though two raters might not assign the exact same scores to the examinees. Thus, consistency estimates differ from consensus estimates, as they represent the extent to which raters rank order examinee performances in a consistent manner. The most commonly used consistency estimates are variations of the correlation coefficient, including Pearson's r, Spearman's rho, and Cronbach's alpha. Both Pearson's r and Spearman's rho are correlation coefficients that are commonly used to estimate inter-rater reliability. The difference is that, whereas the computation of Pearson's r is based on the raw scores of the examinees, Spearman's rho is calculated based on the ranking of the examinees. To understand the real difference between Pearson's r and Spearman's rho requires some foundational knowledge in statistics. However, a rule of thumb for the choice of reliability coefficient is that, if the raw scores are not normally distributed, then Spearman's rho is recommended. While the first two coefficients apply to a pair of raters, Cronbach's alpha is applicable to a group of raters, indicating the extent to which the raters are functioning interchangeably or aligned to the rating scale. All three of these consensus estimates range from 0 to 1 and are interpreted in the same way. That is, the closer to 1, the more aligned the raters are to one another or to the rating scale. Keep in mind, however, that it is very unlikely to achieve 100% exact agreement, regardless of how hard you train the raters. You should consider your training a success if you can achieve 50% exact agreement. If two raters do not give the same scores, you can always assign the exam to a third rater and then assign the final score more conservatively. This procedure is common for local language tests.

You might think that consistency estimates are a less strict version of consensus estimates. However, this is not the case. One drawback of consensus estimates is that, if they are used as the only criteria to evaluate rater performance, then raters may choose to use strategies to "game" the evaluation system. For example, suppose we are training raters to use a 6-point rating scale to evaluate essay performances, and we set as the goal for the rater training program that, by the end of the training, raters should achieve 40% exact agreement. This is not an easy task for a local test, especially when you have 6 levels on the scale. To game the evaluation system, a rater can play it safe by assigning only 3s and 4s to the exams s/he is assigned to rate (i.e., the middle categories or the center of the scale). If the scores on a test follow a normal distribution (i.e., most scores are distributed around the center of the scale, and very few scores are distributed on both ends of the scale), then there is a good chance that this rater will hit the target of 40% exact agreement. This kind of playing-it-safe is a well-known rating strategy or pattern called the *central tendency* effect. If we only use exact agreement consensus estimates, we would perhaps not detect this strategy and conclude that the rater's performance is satisfactory. However, consensus estimates would be able to detect this effect as the rater's score assignment might not show a similar rank order as other raters, even though the exact agreement is high.

Another advantage of consistency estimates is that they allow you to check whether certain raters assign consistently higher or lower scores than other raters. This is called the rater *severity* effect. That is, a rater is more severe or harsh if s/he consistently assigns lower scores than other raters or more lenient if the other way around. By identifying such an effect, rater trainers can work with the rater individually to help him/her align more closely to the rest of the group.

However, consistency estimates are not without weaknesses. An important disadvantage of this estimate for local language testing is the impact of a restricted range of proficiency. In the previous chapter, we have explained what a restricted range of proficiency entails and the kind of impact it has on scaling. The same thing happens with consistency estimates in that, if a test has restricted range of proficiency among the examinees (a common characteristic of local tests), then the consistency estimates tend to underestimate rater reliability. Thus, it is recommended that consensus and consistency estimates should be used in tandem to evaluate rater performance on a local language test.

Measurement estimates

In contrast to consensus and consistency estimates, measurement estimates are a third category of complex procedures that analyze rater performance at a much more fine-grained level and often provide rich information about rater behavior. We won't elaborate on these estimates in this book, but some of these procedures include the *many-facet Rasch measurement model, generalizability theory*, and *factor or principal component analysis*. However, we will introduce two additional rater effects that these measurement estimates often analyze and discuss how they can be detected using less complicated methods.

First, imagine that raters are assigned to rate a speaking test using a 6-point rating scale. This scale has four different criteria: pronunciation, fluency, vocabulary, coherence. Each criterion requires raters to assign an independent score. Suppose you have to finish rating 100 speaking performances; that would mean 500 scores (4 criterion scores plus 1 total score multiplied by 100). Would you be tempted to assign the same scores across the 4 criteria just to speed up the process? In fact, it could happen that raters do assign similar scores across criteria. In the measurement literature, the phenomenon that score assignment on one criterion affects score assignment on other criteria is called the *halo* effect. Because the halo effect tends to involve multiple criteria, it occurs mostly in analytic scoring (recall this term from Chapter 6). The occurrence of a halo effect often defeats the purpose of analytic scoring. Because the rationale behind analytic scoring is to provide more fine-grained information regarding different aspects of examinees' language performance, allowing test users to make judgments about the performance profiles (i.e., strengths and weaknesses) of each examinee. If raters consistently assign similar scores across criteria, we would lose the ability to identify variability in examinee profiles from the test scores. Admittedly, it is possible that some examinees will have an even profile; however, it is generally the case that some variation exists among their performance profiles. The interesting phenomenon is that, sometimes, a halo effect can happen without raters' awareness. In fact, depending on the presentation sequence of rating criteria, raters can even demonstrate a slight halo effect in different directions (Ballard, 2017). The many-facets Rasch measurement model can detect the halo effect to some extent. However, you can also examine halo effect by computing correlation coefficients among the criterion scores for each rater. We would typically expect scores on different criteria to be somewhat different, and so the correlation coefficients should not be very strong.

Next, imagine that you are a rater for an English speaking test who also speaks Mandarin Chinese as either an L1 or L2. Would it be easier for you to understand English speech produced by low-proficiency, Chinese-L1 speakers? The answer is oftentimes "yes". Now, would you give a higher speaking score to a low-proficiency Chinese speaker than you would to a comparably low-proficiency Korean speaker (supposing that you do not speak Korean as well)? The answer is often "yes" in this case, too. The differential score assignment or severity effect by examinee L1 background is called *bias*. Bias can occur as raters interact with different characteristics of the task (e.g., whether a task involves graphs), the scale (e.g., whether different types of raters may focus on different criteria), and the examinee (e.g., whether the raters share a similar language background with the examinees). Both the Rasch model and generalizability theory can provide in-depth analysis regarding rater bias.

Rater biases can also be checked by looking at the raw scores and score distribution by different raters, examinees, or testing conditions. For example, if you would like to see whether a graph-interpretation speaking task is biased against examinees who do not have much familiarity with statistical graphs, you can ask examinees to indicate their familiarity with graphs and group them based on their response or simply separate them by academic background (e.g., science/engineering vs. humanities/liberal arts). Then, you can examine the score distribution of different examinee groups on this item. If the humanities/liberal arts students indeed show a notably lower average score, then you might want to scrutinize the content of this item for potential bias (e.g., the graph is too complex; the interpretation or discussion of the graph requires statistical knowledge). As there can be many factors that influence test performance and rater scoring, you should take the interpretation of these statistics with a grain of salt. However, that does not mean that this approach always leads to meaningless speculations about rater biases.

Rater effects from the local testing context

In addition to these universal rater effects, there are also rater effects that might be associated with the unique local testing context. It is not uncommon for teachers or non-testing experts to consider testing as a peripheral component of their professional life. When they are involved in the scoring process, some of them may have low motivation to learn about and use a new rating scale, especially when the rating scale differs from their regular assessment activities or approaches. Below, we list a few quotes from language teachers to indicate their motivation, attitudes, and beliefs toward (scoring) speaking or writing assessment. These are important factors to consider when examining rater performance and reliability in local testing contexts.

- We are language teachers, not testers. We should not be asked to rate writing or speaking tests *(both speaking and writing, low motivation)*.
- We teach writing, not language. We should only rate argument development, not lexico-grammatical correctness *(writing, attitudes toward different criteria in the rating scale)*.
- This essay is very strong. It has five paragraphs, a clear stance at the end of the introductory paragraph, and a topic sentence in each body paragraph *(writing, a very structural approach to argument development, without looking into the content of the essay)*.
- I cannot understand anything he says. His accent is too strong *(speaking, focusing on accent instead of intelligibility)*.
- I don't find the grammatical errors problematic. Everything she says is intelligible to me *(speaking, focusing only on intelligibility)*.
- I just disagree with this argument *(speaking and writing, evaluating test performances on ideas rather than language)*.

The above statements are not meant to provide an exhaustive list of rater issues that you are likely to encounter in local testing contexts. However, they are listed here to demonstrate the need for ongoing rater training for local language tests. More importantly, the purpose of these example statements is to encourage you to consider the background, work context, and prior experiences of the raters in their local context and anticipate potential issues raters and rater trainers might encounter during the rating and rater training process. As a rater trainer, you should keep in mind that rating for a local test can be time-consuming and that teachers should be compensated for scoring the test; alternatively, the hours they need to spend on test scoring should be included in their normal workload. When giving feedback on the teachers' rating performance, you might also want to strike a balance between positive and negative comments to prevent them from developing negative feelings towards the task. Low motivation among teachers might make rater training difficult initially, but this issue usually improves over time if you continue to communicate with the teachers about their concerns and needs.

Why do we need rater training? Does it really work?

Rater training is a journey of reflection and discovery. It is not only a way to examine whether raters are on the same page about the operationalization of the assessed knowledge and skills (i.e., language ability) on the local test, but also a communal expedition that leads to a better understanding of language learners and users, which thus demands collaborative effort from all members of the local (rater) community. Through conversations on the analysis of examinee performance, new knowledge can be co-constructed in a bottom-up fashion about the practice of rating to the scale, the placement of different examinee profiles, the instructional activities for certain language issues, and more. This is why we strongly advocate for rater training as an ongoing, regular quality control procedure for local tests. We will elaborate on the best practice of rater training at the end of this section, but before we make our recommendations, a general introduction of what rater training entails and whether it is effective in practice is in order.

As the name suggests, rater training is a quality control procedure where raters are trained to rate performances. In performance-based assessments, a common goal of rater training is to develop a satisfactory level of consistency and alignment among the raters in terms of their interpretation and application of the scale. In order to do so, raters have to minimize any rater effects they display in their rating behavior. That is, rater training should help raters recognize effects such as rater severity, rater bias, central tendency, and halo effect, and then negotiate a set of effective training activities to help them reduce these rater effects and achieve higher rater agreement. In theory, rater training should focus on the analysis of test performances and reflection upon rating behaviors. However, in practice, rater training for local language tests often goes beyond the immediate assessment situation, tapping into other related settings within the local context where the test has an impact. This practice is a distinct feature of rater training for local tests, where raters participate in assessment-related conversations as both raters and their regular roles in the local context. This kind of practice can ultimately create a community of practice by helping both raters to integrate language assessment into their professional life and test developers to improve the quality of the test in a sustainable way.

Interestingly, the field of language testing does not seem to have a broad consensus regarding the effectiveness of rater training. While the majority of the research in language testing has indicated that rater training helps to improve rater reliability (Weigle, 1994), some researchers have failed to find a meaningful effect of rater training on rater performance (Elder, Barkhuizen, Knoch, & Von Randow, 2007; Vaughan, 1991). Woehr and Huffcutt (1994) conducted a meta-analysis on the effectiveness of rater training for performance appraisal. Their study revealed that, on average, rater training appears to have a moderate effect on rating accuracy, rater severity, and halo effect. However, there is considerable variability in the design and implementation of rater training (e.g., content, intensity, and duration of training). These characteristics can have an impact on the effectiveness of rater training (Ivancevich, 1979). Interestingly, if we look at rater training across fields, we may be surprised to find out that the length and frequency of rater training can range from a one-time, 5-minute briefing to a repeated training module that lasts for an entire semester or year.

In language testing, rater training is rarely done in the course of a few minutes. However, in the published studies, rater training is often a one-time event. Based on our experiences in different contexts, it is difficult to see an immediate effect of rater training for language tests, and that effect rarely lasts long if it is provided only once. Research in the assessment of other psychological traits has reported similar findings (e.g., Ivancevich, 1979).

The challenge of making rater training effective with a single meeting makes sense from a rater cognition perspective. Cronbach (1990) argues that rating is "a complex, error-prone cognitive process" (p. 684; later echoed by Myford & Wolfe, 2003). The rating process for language tests is arguably more challenging than other psychological constructs (for reasons highlighted in the beginning of Chapter 6). A quote on writing assessment from Hamp-Lyons (1995) explicates the difficulties in rating essay performances:

> Writing is a complex and multifaceted activity. When we assess writing, we engage in another complex and multifaceted activity: judging another person's text. Into that text has gone not only that person's grammatical ability, their reach of word knowledge and control, their sense of what a unified subject is, their factual knowledge about the subject, but also their understanding of the world and their place in it, their exploration of ideas, and their feelings.
>
> *(p. 760)*

Because writing tends to be more carefully planned than speaking in terms of rhetorical structure and lexico-grammar, the interaction among the writer, the text, and the reader makes the assessment of writing more challenging than the assessment of speaking. Rater effects can occur when they make a judgment on any of the aspects of writing ability, as listed above. In fact, your rating might change easily if you take a second look at an essay due to the level of complexity involved in written language. Therefore, it would be impossible to address rater effects in one sitting; it takes time to detect and resolve rater effects that arise in practice. It is a long process of negotiation and collaboration between raters and rater trainers. This is why we recommend implementing a rater training program as an integral part of the quality control procedures for a local language test.

Best practice for rater training

Rater training focuses on how raters approach the task of scoring and evaluating performances. Its utmost purpose is to help raters make sense of the scale and the relationship among scale levels, descriptors, and benchmarks. In light of this overarching goal, rater training should start by asking raters to rank benchmark performances from different levels, so that they can develop a clear understanding of the level differences in the scale. As raters become more aware of the full range of the scale, the training can move on to finer details, namely, distinguishing perform-ances between adjacent levels and characterizing performances at each level.

Example 7.1 presents rater training in a local testing context, i.e., the written section on the English Placement Test (EPT) at the University of Illinois at Urbana–Champaign.

EXAMPLE 7.1 THE EPT RATER TRAINING PROGRAM

EPT rater training

The EPT is a post-admission English Placement Test for ESL undergraduate and graduate students at UIUC, which is designed to place students into appropriate levels of ESL writing and speaking classes. The EPT has a semester-long rater certification program for its written section where novice raters meet on a monthly basis for training. The raters for the EPT are all instructors (full-time lecturers and graduate teaching assistants) for the ESL writing program in the Department of Linguistics.

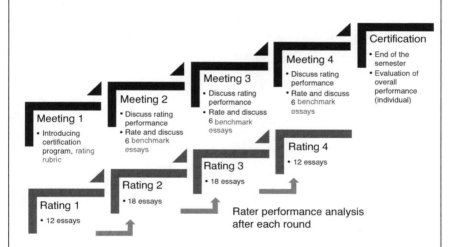

During each month of the training program, the raters are asked to rate a sample of benchmark essays individually and receive feedback from the rater training regarding their performances. Then, they meet at the end of each month to evaluate and discuss a smaller set of benchmark essays as a group during the meeting. They are asked to provide justifications for the score each essay receives, as a way to achieve a mutual interpretation and application of the rating scale. During the meeting, the discussion often starts with raters identifying performance characteristics that are aligned to the scale descriptors. However, as soon as they have developed a good intuition about the scale, the raters would draw on their relevant teaching experience in the classroom to identify student writing profiles that correspond to different levels of the scale and reflect upon the students' learning needs and instructional activities that can help them improve the target writing subskills.

The EPT rater training helps foster mutual assessment knowledge and practices among language teachers and testers (or *language assessment literacy* as a technical term in the language testing literature, Davies, 2008; Fulcher, 2012; Inbar-Lourie, 2008; Yan, Zhang, & Fan, 2018), ultimately leading to alignment between teaching and testing within the ESL writing program.

There is not really a single model of best practice for rater training. However, we would like to recommend a few important considerations when developing a rater training program for your own language test.

Rater cognition

One cannot overstress the fact that rating is a complex cognitive process. This is, first and foremost, the factor that should guide the consideration of all other factors listed below, as well as the overall design and implementation of your rater training program. As much as you might like to address all rater effects during rater training, it is highly unlikely that you will be able to achieve this goal. Take baby steps and give yourself time to develop rater reliability and confidence. Based on research findings on longitudinal development of rater performance (Lim, 2011), raters tend not to develop a firm grasp of the rating scale until the third or even fourth time practicing with it. Therefore, if you have an analytic scale or a hybrid holistic scale with analytic components (refresh your memory about the different types of scales from the previous chapter if need be), you will need to have patience with the raters and allow them enough time to explore and internalize the rating scale.

Rater background

Before you design or deliver rater training, you should consider the background of the raters. Human raters are not machines. When they read an essay or listen to a speech sample, they will develop assumptions, hypotheses, and attitudes toward the examinee based on their personal, linguistic, cultural, educational, professional backgrounds. This is human nature. However, while some of these perceptions are relevant to the language ability of the examinee, others are biases that need to be recognized and minimized. Thus, an understanding of rater backgrounds is likely to help develop training materials and activities to prevent certain biases from surfacing.

Benchmarking

Another important suggestion for rater training is benchmarking. In a language test, benchmarks usually refer to the most typical test performances at each level of the rating scale. Because they are typical to a particular level, these perform- ances tend to render higher rater agreement (they can also be envisioned as the center of each level, if we think of scale levels as bands). When training raters to the scale, especially during the initial stage of training, it is very important to use benchmark test performances and provide the "correct" scores to the raters.

In contrast to benchmarks are *borderlines*, which are test performances that are not typical of a particular level and display characteristics of performances at both of the two adjacent scores or levels. These performances tend to be less frequent and representative of the examinee population than benchmarks. Thus, borderline performances should not be used during rater training. In addition, we recommend using only benchmark performances because rater training is not a guessing game or a test for raters, although certain stakes are inevitable for rater training in some contexts. Rater trainers should not use borderlines to trick the raters or force them to agree on these essays. In fact, because of the cogni- tive load of scoring language performances, it is not an easy task to align raters to the rating scale, even when using benchmarks.

Training intensity, length, and frequency

Effective rater training should not have a high level of intensity, and a certain amount of time should be dedicated to guiding raters through the analysis of test performances using the rating scale. In this regard, the analysis of benchmarks at each scale level as a group is essential to rater training. You should not, how- ever, overwhelm the raters with too many test performances at a time. Rating a large number of exams in one sitting usually leads to low agreement and morale, and raters may get tired easily (*rater fatigue* is the technical term in meas- urement). Even if a certain training effect is achieved in this kind of intense training, the effect rarely lasts long. A more sustainable model for rater training prefers quality to quantity. If possible, you should focus on different levels of the scale during different training sessions. That will allow time for raters to discuss and reflect upon their scoring processes and identify areas for further improvement.

When evaluating benchmark performances, you should allow some flexibility and freedom for raters to engage in meaningful conversations about language ability and the various test performance characteristics that mark different levels of language ability. Ongoing, repeated practice of rating and justifying those rat- ings is key to reinforcing the training effect over time. In doing so, you are more likely to encourage raters to consider scoring or assessment as a regular part of their job. Example 7.2 outlines the OEPT rater training intensity, length, and frequency.

EXAMPLE 7.2 THE OEPT RATER TRAINING PROGRAM

OEPT rater training

OEPT rater training begins with a 20-hour online program that prospective raters complete individually. The program introduces prospective raters to the scale with a sample of benchmark performances at each level of the scale for each item. Trainees begin with justifications; that is, they are asked to explain why performances were given a particular score. They are not asked to rate until they are familiar with all benchmarks and levels. Raters are also required to transcribe a set of item responses during the familiarization stage of the program, which we have found to be an effective method to get trainees to listen more carefully. Once familiarization is complete, trainees are asked to set selected sets of exam responses. The first sets represent each score level, and raters need only rank exams in the correct order; the second sets highlight differences between levels; and the third sets include responses at each level but are presented in ways that mimic actual administrations with more exams at the pass/no pass boundary (45/50). Once trainees reach 80% agreement, which is almost always achieved, they are cleared to rate as apprentice raters during the August administration of the test. At that time, we rate about 300 exams in the week before classes begin. Raters are certified only after completing the rater training program and rating as an apprentice during our largest administration of the test.

Even after achieving agreement with the scale, rater training continues. Raters complete a set of exams each month, and these are discussed in monthly rater training meetings. Over time, we have amassed many rater training sets. Some focus on the entire scale, while others focus on particular levels or examinees of different language backgrounds.

Community of practice

If you consider all of the factors above, you are likely to have a positive, or at least less negative reaction, from your raters regarding scoring and rater training. There is, however, more that you can do to make scoring, rater training, and even language assessment a more communal experience. To do so, you should seek frequent feedback from raters about the scale and make adjustments accordingly. This can help the raters to develop a sense of ownership of the scale or test. Raters should be encouraged to express their intuitions, hypothesis, and opinions regarding the scale. They should be encouraged to develop their own internalized versions of the rating scale (e.g., tweaking scale descriptors or developing their own "decision trees" for score assignment), as long as these internalized versions are largely aligned to the original scale. Raters are not machines, so don't try to make them interchangeable, because you are bound to fail. In fact, if you allow some freedom during rating and rater training, you might be surprised to find out that there are many occasions when the raters' voices can lead to an improved version of the rating scale. Therefore, developing some level of autonomy and ownership among the raters can create a community of assessment practice. As we discussed in previous chapters, the raters for local language tests tend not to be very confident about their language assessment literacy. This kind of rater training practice can help develop language assessment literacy in the local context.

That said, while granting teachers a certain level of autonomy, raters must be trained to be willing to accept majority rule during rater training. When a rater assigns a different score from the rest of the community, you should try to prevent that rater from going into *defense* mode. Ideally, when discussing raters' scores and comments on certain test performances, you should keep the ratings anonymous. After all, rating is a shared practice, and it should not be about getting the "right" answer. Example 7.3 describes the development of a rater community of practice in the case of the TOEPAS.

EXAMPLE 7.3 THE TOEPAS RATER TRAINING PROCEDURES

TOEPAS rater community of practice

The TOEPAS rater team has spontaneously developed as a community of practice in which the members have opportunities to collaborate, share knowledge, and build a shared rater identity. Several features of the test development and rating procedure have provided opportunities for development of a rater community of practice: group training sessions, post-score discussions, and collaborative writing of feedback reports.

The rater training program consists of an intensive four-day group program, followed by individual rating practice. The training program includes:

1. **Introduction to the basic principles of language testing**. Raters tend to lack sufficient assessment literacy, and so they are introduced to fundamental concepts in language testing such as rater reliability, test validity, and test consequences.
2. **Overview of the purpose and history of the TOEPAS**. Raters are briefly introduced to the development of the TOEPAS, the local policies that led to its establishment, and score uses.
3. **Familiarization with the TOEPAS scale**. Raters familiarize themselves with scale descriptors through group discussions and activities.
4. **Familiarization with benchmark performances**. Raters watch benchmark performances and try to use the scale descriptors to describe the performances in a group.
5. **Rating and discussion of performances**. Raters watch performances, use the scale to rate them, and then discuss the performances in a group. Then,

raters try to write feedback reports in which they describe the performance they watched.

6. **Observation and rating of a live TOEPAS session.** New raters observe a live TOEPAS session administered and rated by two experienced raters. They also practice rating the observed session.

7. **Individual rating.** After the intensive four-day sessions, new raters are assigned performances that they rate individually. New raters are certified when they achieve 80% agreement.

In addition to the initial group training and regular group norming sessions, raters further develop collaboration through post-score discussions and feedback report writing. More specifically, after independent score submission, the two raters discuss the performance to decide on the final score that will be reported to the test-taker. These post-score discussions allow raters to adjust their uses of the scale and their shared understanding of the scale descriptors. These discussions also help the raters to relate scale descriptors to concrete examples (quotes) from the performance in order to produce the written feedback report that test-takers receive as part of the test results.

Summary

This chapter discusses issues related to raters and rater training. We have introduced a catalog of rater effects that can occur during test scoring, their impacts on test scores, and ways to address them during rater training. It is important to keep in mind that rating is a complex cognitive process and that training takes time to affect rater performance and reliability. Equally important is the fact that, although we cannot treat human raters as machines, it is important to develop a mutual understanding among them of what constitutes language ability for the particular assessment purposes and how to assess strengths and weaknesses in language performances. It is important to embed these questions in their daily professional lives so that the language test becomes a living organism that grows and integrates itself into the local context.

Further reading

Carey, M. D., Mannell, R. H., & Dunn, P. K. (2011). Does a rater's familiarity with a candidate's pronunciation affect the rating in oral proficiency interviews? *Language Testing, 28*(2), 201–219.

Carey, Mannell, and Dunn investigate how examiners' familiarity with examinees' interlanguage affects pronunciation assessment ratings in International English Language Testing Systems (IELTS) and oral proficiency interviews (OPI). Ninety-nine IELTS examiners across five test centers (Australia, Hong Kong, India, Korea, and New Zealand) participated in the study by rating three candidates' OPI performance, whose first language is Chinese, Korean, and Indian, respectively. Most examiners are native speakers of English, except for the Indian center, but their levels of familiarity to the non-native English accents varied. The results showed that examiners' interlanguage familiarity had significant positive associations with pronunciation ratings across languages. Examiners with higher familiarity to the candidate's interlanguage tended to give higher pronunciation ratings. In addition, the location of test centers was significant to the inter-rater variability, independent of the interlanguage familiarity. Examiners' ratings were significantly higher when they rated the candidate's pronunciation in their home country, for example, when the Chinese candidate's performance was rated in the Hong Kong center. The authors suggested language test development, rater training, and research consider interlanguage phonology familiarity and the test center effect as an important source of bias in the OPI test.

Davis, L. (2016). The influence of training and experience on rater performance in scoring spoken language. *Language Testing, 33*(1), 117–135.

Davis (2016) investigates the effects of rater training, rating experience, and scoring aids (e.g., rubrics, exemplars) on rater performance in the TOEFL iBT speaking test. Twenty native speaking English teachers participated, who have varied teaching and rating experience but no previous TOEFL speaking rating experience. Each rater scored 400 responses over four scoring sessions and took one rater training. The training effects were investigated via rater severity, internal consistency, and accuracy of scores. Multi-faceted Rasch measurement analysis results showed little effect of training and experience on overall rater severity and internal consistency. However, increases were detected in pairwise inter-rater correlations and inter-rater agreements over time. In addition, scoring accuracy measured by correlations and agreement with previously established reference scores was significantly improved immediately after the rater training. The frequency of using exemplars was associated with extreme raters: most accurate raters referred to exemplars more frequently and longer than the least accurate raters did. Using scoring rubrics also increased the score accuracy. The study reassures positive rater training effects on rater performance found in previous literature while providing new insights into the relationships between using scoring aids and rating performance.

Deane, P. (2013). On the relation between automated essay scoring and modern views of the writing construct. *Assessing Writing, 18*(1), 7–24.

Deane (2013) examines the writing construct measurement in automated essay scoring (AES) systems. After reviewing definitions of writing as a construct, the author discusses the construct that AES system measures, focusing on the e-rater scoring engine. AES systems primarily measure test production skills or text quality (e.g., the text structure, linguistic features) but do not directly measure other writing skills such as deploying meaningful content, sophisticated argumentation, or rhetorical effectiveness. While acknowledging the limitations of AES systems, the author highlights fluency and language control as important components. The author provides literature that supports a strong correlation between efficient text production skills and other cognitive skills necessary for successful writing, which connects AES and human ratings. The strong correlations exist because mastery of core text production skills enables writers to use more cognitive resources for socio-cognitive writing strategies, which otherwise needs to be used for producing text. The author discusses three common criticisms of AES (construct representations, measurement methods, and technical inadequacies of AES) and responds to the concerns by suggesting a socio-cognitive approach to AES in large-scale settings.

Myford, C. M., & Wolfe, E. W. (2003). Detecting and measuring rater effects using many-facet Rasch measurement: Part I. *Journal of Applied Measurement,* *4*(4), 386–422.

And

Myford, C. M., & Wolfe, E. W. (2004). Detecting and measuring rater effects using many-facet Rasch measurement: Part II. *Journal of Applied Measurement,* *5*(2), 189–227.

Myford and Wolfe (2003, 2004) is a two-part paper that describes measuring rater effects using the many-facet Rasch measurement (MFRM). In Part I, the authors provide a historical review, focusing on how previous measurement literature conceptualized and measured rater effects, theorized the relationships between rater effects and rating quality, and make various efforts to keep rating effects under control for rating quality. The authors also introduce Andrich's (1978) rating scale model modified within the MFRM frame and three hybrid MFRM models based on mathematical and conceptual backgrounds of MFRM, and make thorough comparisons of the models. In Part II, the authors offer a practical guidance on using the Facets (Linacre, 2001) computer program to measure five rater effects, namely, leniency/severity, central tendency, randomness, halo, and differential leniency/severity, as well as interpret the results. The authors emphasize the importance of embracing diverse psychometric perspective in researching rater effects.

Yan, X. (2014). An examination of rater performance on a local oral English proficiency test: A mixed-methods approach. *Language Testing, 31*(4), 501–527.

Yan (2014) examines rater performance and behavior on a local speaking test for prospectus international teaching assistants (ITAs). The rater performance was evaluated by investigating inter-rater reliability estimates (consistency, consensus, and measurement statistics) of 6,338 ratings. The author also qualitatively analyzed 506 sets of rater comments for listener effort, fluency, pronunciation, grammar, and language sophistication. The results revealed that overall reliability was high ($r=0.73$) but exact agreement rate was relatively low, which was associated with examinee oral English proficiency levels: higher agreement was found on passing scores across different language groups. Many-facet Rasch measurement results indicated that rating scales were used consistently, but severity varied among raters with small effect size. Chinese raters were more lenient towards Chinese examinees and more severe towards Indian examinees than native speaker raters. Qualitative analysis indicated that Chinese and native speaker raters had different perceptions towards intelligibility of Indian and low-proficient Chinese examinees. The author suggested considering various interactions among linguistic features in understanding rater disagreement and addressing intelligibility by representing construct of ITA English proficiency in real-world communication.

References

Andrich, D. (1978). A rating formulation for ordered response categories. Psychometrika, 43, 561–573.

Ballard, L. (2017). *The effects of primacy on rater cognition: An eye-tracking study*. Doctoral dissertation. Michigan State University.

Cronbach, L. J. (1990). *Essentials of psychological testing* (5th ed.). New York: Harper & Row.

Davies, A. (2008). Textbook trends in teaching language testing. *Language Testing, 25*(3), 327–347.

Elder, C., Barkhuizen, G., Knoch, U., & Von Randow, J. (2007). Evaluating rater responses to an online training program for L2 writing assessment. *Language Testing, 24*(1), 37–64.

Fulcher, G. (2012). Assessment literacy for the language classroom. *Language Assessment Quarterly, 9*(2), 113–132.

Hamp-Lyons, L. (1995). Rating nonnative writing: The trouble with holistic scoring. *Tesol Quarterly, 29*(4), 759–762.

Inbar-Lourie, O. (2008). Constructing a language assessment knowledge base: A focus on language assessment courses. *Language Testing, 25*(3), 385–402.

Ivancevich, J. M. (1979). Longitudinal study of the effects of rater training on psychometric error in ratings. *Journal of Applied Psychology, 64*(5), 502.

Lim, G. S. (2011). The development and maintenance of rating quality in performance writing assessment: A longitudinal study of new and experienced raters. *Language Testing, 28*(4), 543–560.

Linacre, J. M. (2001). Facets Rasch measurement software. *Chicago: Winsteps.com*.

Myford, C. M., & Wolfe, E. W. (2003). Detecting and measuring rater effects using many-facet Rasch measurement: Part I. *Journal of Applied Measurement, 4*(4), 386–422.

Stemler, S. E. (2004). A comparison of consensus, consistency, and measurement approaches to estimating interrater reliability. *Practical Assessment, Research & Evaluation, 9*(4), 1–19.

Upshur, J. A., & Turner, C. E. (1999). Systematic effects in the rating of second-language speaking ability: Test method and learner discourse. *Language Testing, 16*(1), 82–111.

Vaughan, C. (1991). Holistic assessment: What goes on in the rater's mind? In L. Hamp-Lyons ((Ed.), *Assessing second language writing in academic contexts* (pp. 111–125). Norwood, NJ: Ablex.

Weigle, S. C. (1994). Effects of training on raters of ESL compositions. *Language Testing, 11* (2), 197–223.

Woehr, D. J., & Huffcutt, A. I. (1994). Rater training for performance appraisal: A quantitative review. *Journal of Occupational and Organizational Psychology, 67*(3), 189–205.

Yan, X., Zhang, C., & Fan, J. J. (2018). "Assessment knowledge is important, but … ": How contextual and experiential factors mediate assessment practice and training needs of language teachers. *System, 74*, 158–168.

8

DATA COLLECTION, MANAGEMENT, AND SCORE REPORTING

While Chapter 3, *Local test development*, and Chapter 5, *Local test delivery*, deal with the front-end of test development, this chapter discusses the back-end, i.e., data collection and management. More specifically, this chapter discusses what types of test-taker data need to be collected (e.g., background bio data), and how the data are stored, organized, and retrieved (e.g., relational databases). Database design is at the center of these discussions. We argue that appropriate data collection and management need to be explicitly incorporated into test design at the earliest stages of development because they are essential for the ongoing analyses of test reliability, validity, and research. The data collection and management systems are sometimes used not only for result storage but also for score reporting. Therefore, this chapter also discusses the relevance of information included in different score/result reports in relation to different score users and uses.

Introduction

When you design a local language test, the focus tends to rest primarily on test content and delivery, as well as the development of a rating scale in the case of performance-based tests. Of course, you are concerned about whether the tasks you design engage test-takers as expected and, therefore, elicit relevant language performances. You are also concerned about whether the test delivery platform (traditional or digital) serves the test purpose and is cost-effective and whether the rating scale allows you to discriminate among the different proficiency levels. Response collection and storage, however, tends to receive less attention during the test development stages because it may seem naturally determined by the test delivery platform you select. For example, if your L2 writing test is computer-delivered, then the responses you collect are probably in the form of saved word processing documents (e.g., Microsoft Word or text), which may be stored on the computer's hard drive, a local server, or a USB drive, or they may be sent to a specific email address. You may also have a situation (e.g., oral interviews) in which the test responses are not recorded because they are rated live, although a number of oral responses may be recorded for examiner- and rater-training or task analysis. Even though the test delivery may influence the data collection to some extent, hybrid approaches to delivery and response collection facilitate quality control and reporting. For instance, test responses or other test-related data (e.g., test-takers' bio data) may be collected on paper and subsequently digitized and stored in a database. Scores and raters' notes from oral interviews may also be stored in a digital database where they are linked with test-taker data. The widespread use of computers and the use of digital databases for test data storage and retrieval have become commonplace, especially because task responses are distributed to raters for scoring procedures, and together with other test data, they are used for test analysis, program evaluation, and research.

The test data are also used to process score reports for test-takers and score users. A well-structured database facilitates the preparation and distribution of test results to different stakeholders, and the production of result reports can be automatized if the report parameters are well-defined. The automatic production of reports is efficient and minimizes human data processing errors.

Given that appropriate data collection and management is central for the ongoing test analyses and research, the test database needs to be explicitly incorporated into the test design in the earliest stages of test development. In this chapter, we first introduce the flow, storage, and management of data, and then focus on test data uses for result reporting, item analysis, program evaluation, and long-term research.

Data flow

In order to highlight the importance of planning test data storage and maintenance as part of the test design, we outline the test data flow at all stages of test administration. As Figure 8.1 shows, data collection and storage occur mainly during registration, testing, and rating. When the test-takers register to take the test, their demographic information (e.g., name, L1, age) is gathered. Then, the collected test responses are accessed by the raters during the rating session. The scores, feedback, and, sometimes, rater notes are recorded and linked to test-takers' background data and test responses for the purpose of producing scores/result reports. Test data can also be used for analysis of the test's reliability and validity, as well as research and program evaluation.

The basic data we collect during registration are related to test-taker identification information, such as name, age (date of birth), gender, personal identification number, contact information (email, phone, address), and test session (place date, and time when the test-taker is registered to take the test). When tests are administered to test-takers with different language backgrounds and nationalities, information regarding the languages they speak (mother tongue and other languages), country of residence, and nationality may also be collected. In university contexts,

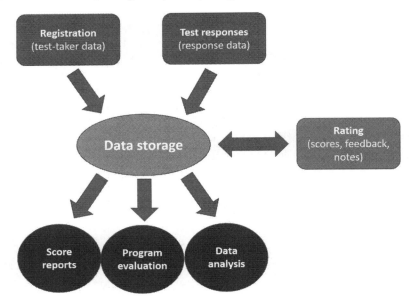

FIGURE 8.1 Flow of test data

test-taker data could also contain information about test-taker's department, study program, degree (BA, MA, PhD), and student advisor or program liaison. If the test is administered across several schools, school branches, or language centers, information about test-taker's school/center may also be needed. All of these data are usually associated with a test-taker ID, which is used to protect personal information through anonymous data handling.

Test-taker IDs are essential when there is a need to connect different data associated with the same test-taker. For example, if test-takers are tested several times over a certain period (e.g., pre- and post-test), then the IDs help to connect the results from each test so that the individual test-taker's growth can be measured. Test-taker IDs are also useful to identify the test-taker correctly when several test-takers in the database have the same first and last names. They can be automatically generated by the database software, or they can be designed with a particular structure (see the role of IDs in section *Research, digitization of test data, and corpus development* below). The test-taker IDs in the OEPT 1.0 contained information about the semester and year when the test was administered, along with the test-taker number. For example, SP20020039 meant that the test-taker was the 39th person who took the test in the spring semester of 2002.

Which type of data you need to collect and store depends on the needs of your local context. Personal data protection laws and regulations require that personal data collection is limited only to the most necessary information needed for the purpose, and so you have to carefully consider what personal data are relevant for your test, i.e., what data you need to report the results and to perform test analyses for quality purposes. For example, collecting information about the visa or residency status of international students at your university may provide interesting information, but it may not be directly related to the purpose of the test, and thus the data should not be collected. Collecting irrelevant personal data may also breach research and testing ethics.

Personal data protection regulations tend to be enacted at the institutional, national, or international levels. For example, the General Data Protection Regulation (GDPR) (Regulation (EU) 2016/679) of the European Parliament and the Council is enacted at the international level in the European Union and the European Economic Area (European Commission, 2019). GDPR stipulates that institutions involved in personal data handling must employ a data protection officer whose responsibility is to manage organizational data protection and oversee GDPR compliance. The GDPR has led to development of similar international privacy protection acts in the Asia-Pacific (APAC) region, like the APEC Privacy Framework, although these countries have also implemented national privacy acts (Asia-Pacific Cooperation, n.d.). For example, the national Australian Notifiable Data Breach (NDB) scheme, which is an addendum to the Privacy Act of 1988, shares many similarities with GDPR, especially in relation to management of electronic data (Australian Government, n.d.). In the US, however, personal data management is regulated by the Family Educational Rights and Privacy Act of 1974 (FERPA), which is a Federal law that applies only to personal data management in the educational sector (US Department of Education, 2018).

If your institution has a data protection officer, a research review board (e.g., IRB), or a research ethics committee, then you may need to obtain their approval regarding the type and use of the test data that you collect and the type, place, and length of data storage. Such a board or committee would be cognizant of the personal data protection laws relevant for your context. Example 8.1 discusses the procedures used to ensure that the TOEPAS data collection complies with GDPR.

EXAMPLE 8.1 IMPLEMENTING PERSONAL DATA PROTECTION GUIDELINES REGARDING TOEPAS DATA COLLECTION AND USE

TOEPAS data collection procedures

The TOEPAS administration requires collection of test-taker personal information, such as name, date of birth, contact information, language(s), job, and department, as well as video recording of the test performance. The data are stored on a secure server owned by the CIP.

In order to ensure compliance with GDPR, we implemented the following measures:

1. Approval was requested from the data protection officer at UCPH regarding the acceptability of data collection and storage.

2. A written document was prepared for the test-takers in which we explain the TOEPAS procedure and the type of data collection, and inform them that these comply with GDPR guidelines.
3. Using a consent form, permission is requested to use anonymous test data for research by CIP researchers, research by researchers outside CIP, and rater training.
4. Using a consent form, permission is requested to use anonymous sound file, blurred photos, or blurred videos in conference presentations related to TOEPAS research.
5. Test-takers are allowed to withdraw their consent at any time.

Test responses are collected during the testing session and can be in the form of correct/incorrect (0/1) answers, text, audio files, or video files, depending on whether the test contains multiple-choice or performance-based items (see Chapter 4 for task descriptions). Test response data are collected to facilitate the scoring or rating process, but they are also used for subsequent item and test analyses, as well as research. Digital language tests allow for the collection of other types of test-related data that could be used for further item/test development and an improved understanding of the language ability. For example, you could record response-preparation time, time spent on prompts, or response time.

In terms of rating data, however, we usually refer to scores assigned to each item, as well as overall test scores. Additionally, rating data can include rater comments and notes, which could be used to support score decisions, as well as feedback reports. Rating data also include rater information, i.e., provides a record of the scores that each rater assigns, rater background data (e.g., mother tongue, gender, rater certification date), or task information if multiple tasks are involved. Table 8.1 summarizes the types of test data commonly collected.

TABLE 8.1 Type of test data

test data	type of information
registration data	• test–taker ID
	• name
	• origin
	• age
	• mother tongue
	• educational background
response data	• answers (text, audio files, correct/incorrect)
	• preparation time
	• response time
	• notes
rating data	• rater information (mother tongue, gender, rater certification date)
	• rater comments, notes, feedback reports
	• scores

EXAMPLE 8.2 DEVELOPMENT OF ADMINISTRATIVE APPLICATIONS

The OEPT administrative application

The OEPT App is an administrative application that allows registration of examinees, creation of test sessions, assignment of raters to exams, computer-based rating, score reporting, and assignment of departmental liaisons. The app can be used to generate score reports for individual examinees, departments, and colleges. The app score database now includes data for more than 8,000 examinees. Starting from 2016, all test recordings are accessible through the app, with recordings from 2005–2015 stored on the software developer's server and available upon request. The development of the app again increased our efficiency, reducing the time to administer and rate the test by an additional 20%. The databases and reports are used for score reporting, annual reports, and research.

App functions and users

Using a web interface, OEPT Program administrators enter user information and designate roles for each user: Administrator, Facilitator, Liaison, Rater, or Examinee. User roles determine which parts of the app the user can access. All parts of the secure app, with the exception of the practice tests and orientation videos, require a username and password.

Administrators create test sessions and register examinees for these sessions. Facilitators administer the test and test survey. Administrators assign test responses to raters, score tests, and access score reports and other reports. Liaisons in academic departments access student scores and certification status. Raters train using the RITA rater training program and rate tests.

Anyone can access the OEPT practice tests and orientation videos on the platform without being entered into the application with a user role. No password is required for these functions.

App reports

The OEPT App has a number of report functions. Some reports allow testers to view exam and survey data; others serve as quality assurance measures; still other reports are used in the analysis of test, examinee, and rater data.

The OEPT Survey Report allows administrators to view OEPT Survey responses and statistics. The OEPT Practice Test Report creates an entry for each use, showing the date accessed, which tests were accessed, and user comments. The RITA Report (for rater training) is organized by user; it shows the user's name, progress, and practice rating scores.

The SAS Report contains all rater item and overall scores, as well as final scores, along with rater IDs and rater types. When raters are assigned to rate a test, each one is designated as either "Scoring" (meaning they are up to date on training and their scores will contribute to the final test score) or "Apprentice" (meaning they are still training and their scores do not contribute to final score determination). Raters can also be designated as "Training" when the test is assigned only for training purposes.

The Examinee Score report includes exam IDs, dates, and final scores, along with examinee department, college, country, language, sex, and year of birth. The SAS and Examinee reports are used to create data sets for use with SAS, FACETS, and other statistical software.

In Chapters 5 and 7, we discussed response collection and rating in detail, pointing out the advantages and disadvantages of different test delivery and response collection methods (paper or digital). In order to ensure appropriate data flow (i.e., collection, storage, and retrieval), you need to consider adequate data storage and management systems. What storage and maintenance systems are adequate depends both on how you want to use the data and what types of data were collected (paper, audio, video, text). The storage system allows you to keep the data in an organized and secure environment, while the management system enables you to find relevant data, to specify the type of data access different users have, and to group data into categories (e.g., individual test-taker data, test session data). In order to handle the stored data, the data management system has to be compatible with the type of data storage you use. For example, when we designed the data management system for the TOEPAS, we experienced difficulties connecting the web-based interface for data retrieval with the database for demographic data and the stored test responses in the form of video recordings. The database developer failed to find the relevant plug-ins that would allow the database to communicate with the server where the videos were stored. Therefore, we could store data from registration and test responses, but we could not access them for report processing and data analysis.

Data storage

The storage of test data has evolved from the storage of physical data (e.g., paper booklets, tapes) to digital data storage on internal and external hard drives and, more recently, to client-server technology and cloud computing services. Despite the evolution of digital data storage, physical data, or parallel systems of physical and digital data, still exist in local settings because the volume of local test data is relatively small when compared to data collected with large-scale tests.

In the past, the storage and management of test data required large cabinets and storage rooms, as well as efficient indexing systems. Boxes with test booklets and audiotapes and file cabinets with rating sheets and forms with test-taker data were commonly found in institutions where local tests were administered. Locating data was time-consuming because it required a physical search through boxes and cabinets, and retrieval was only possible if an efficient filing and labeling system was in place. Due to limited storage space and search capacity, the data could easily become unusable and had to be destroyed after a certain period of time. Figure 8.2 is an example of how the testing data (including exam sheets, essays, and score reports) for the EPT at the University of Illinois at Urbana-Champaign was stored before the online platform and database were developed.

With the increased accessibility to computers in local institutional contexts and the development of digitally-delivered tests, the storage of directories with test responses and other test data on institutional or program internal hard drives became standard practice. Due to the limited size of computers' hard drives in the 1990s and early 2000s, CDs, DVDs and, later, external hard drives were used for data storage. For example, when the OEPT became operational in 2001, the database with test-taker information and scores was stored on the program's computer hard drive, and backed up on CDs. Many institutions continue to store test data on internal and external hard drives, especially because the hard drives that are commercially available today have much larger storage capacity than they did 20 or 30 years ago. The drawback is that, if the hard drive is damaged, then the stored test data may be rendered irretrievable. All data storage systems require at least one viable back-up system.

In order to secure safe storage and retrieval of test data, IT specialists recommend the application of network storage through client-server technology or cloud computing. In addition to safe storage, client-server and cloud applications allow for data to be accessed from different devices. Furthermore, since client-server and the

FIGURE 8.2   EPT data storage

cloud applications are independent from the local device (computer, tablet, smartphone), any damage to the local device's hardware or software will not result in data loss (Figure 8.3).

The client-server model allows local devices (e.g., computer, tablet, smartphone), which are called "clients", to obtain resources or services from other devices (usually computers), which are called "servers", through a computer network or the internet. In other words, you can use local devices to collect response or other test data, which are then exported to and stored on the server. The internet allows for the communication between the client and the server. In fact, the server has the same functionality as an external drive. The only difference is that the external drive is local, while the server is remote and can be accessed through the internet. To give an example, simulated lectures, which are the test response data from TOEPAS, are recorded as video files. Through a file transfer protocol (FTP), the recorded video files are immediately transferred to and stored on a server instead of a local internal or external hard drive. To access the video files after storage, we need the unique URL address associated with those files.

The newest type of network storage is offered through cloud storage services. In many ways, cloud services are similar to client-server models because they both allow for the remote storage of data. The cloud is different, however, in that you use the services of cloud providers who provide you with storage space for a fee. Therefore, the advantage of cloud services is that the cloud provider maintains the storage space, and so you do not need to invest in server updates and maintenance as you do with client-server technologies. Moreover, the data on the cloud are regularly synced automatically, and your data are safe and sound despite any potential damage to your local hardware and software. You may be familiar with the cloud services of Dropbox and OneDrive, which are used primarily for storage of personal data files. For institutional use, Amazon Web Services is a more robust provider, offering a range of cloud computing services (Amazon, n.d.).

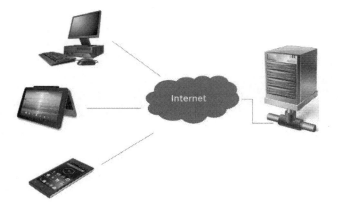

FIGURE 8.3 Client-server network model

Although cloud computing has great potential and seems to represent the future of data storage solutions, concerns are often raised regarding data security and privacy. Many institutions do not allow storage of sensitive data, like test scores and personal information, on cloud servers because they do not trust a storage security system over which they do not have control. When we tried to use ACE-In at the University of Copenhagen, we were required to buy the Amazon cloud services for Europe, instead of Amazon United States, which provided the cloud services for the ACE-In administration at Purdue. Moreover, no personal test-taker identifiers (e.g., names, national ID numbers) were stored on the cloud server. All personal identifiers were associated with test-takers' IDs and stored on a local computer hard drive. Therefore, checking the local policies and requirements for personal data management before designing the data storage system is essential.

The technical information about different storage alternatives may seem overwhelming for some, but we hope it provides a starting point for discussions with your local IT specialists or programmers when you are deciding on storage options.

Data management

Although you may find a storage system where you can keep the test data in an organized and secure environment, this system will be of little use if exporting, reorganizing, and recovering data from the storage is difficult. Just as boxes filled with tests on the shelves of a storage room need to be labeled and indexed, digital data also need consistent naming and organization to facilitate retrieval. You need a data management system that will enable you to send the data to the correct place and to find what you want to use. In other words, the data management system can consist of interfaces that allow (1) test administrators to input registration data, (2) raters to access test responses and to submit their scores, (3) test administrators to process score reports, and (4) researchers/analysts to access data for analysis.

The learning platform(s) used at your institution can serve as data management systems that do not require much maintenance, or the institutions already have staff who manage the learning platform. Example 8.3 illustrates how the English Placement Test (EPT) at the University of Illinois at Urbana-Champaign (UIUC) utilizes the Moodle learning platform for test delivery, scoring, and data management.

EXAMPLE 8.3 MOODLE FOR EPT DATA MANAGEMENT

Using Moodle for test administration and data management for the EPT

The EPT utilizes Moodle as its test delivery platform. Each EPT administration is created as a Moodle course site and set up to be affiliated with students' university ID. Once students register for the test, they can directly log into the Moodle site to take the test during the available window. The learning platform is set up such that it saves both examinees' spoken and written responses into downloadable files. After each test window, the examinees' responses are automatically downloaded and saved in the EPT database, using Python scripts.

The rating interface is also available on the Moodle site, which randomly assigns each exam to two raters. Raters also need to log in to each EPT site to access the exams and to submit their scores and comments. There are several advantages of using learning platforms like Moodle. First, UIUC and other universities use these learning platforms to host their regular course sites so that the learning site is available at no additional cost. Furthermore, when the test is delivered on the same learning platform, students' test scores can be easily linked to their course grades. This allows teaching and testing to be better connected, thereby enhancing the effectiveness of instructional programs (see Chapter 2 on linking testing to instruction). In addition, there is a technical team on campus that provides technical support for the Moodle site and makes recommendations for test site setup in order to allow for/optimize different task design features.

Databases are typically utilized for the management of test-taker demographic data, rater data, and scores. Databases allow for systematic collection of data that are organized in database tables. Each column of the table represents a data category (e.g., name, age, L1, scores, test date), while each row shows a database record, i.e., all data associated with one test-taker. Spreadsheets (e.g., Microsoft Excel) can be used as simple databases in which data are structured in a linear way, i.e., each row represents one record. Spreadsheets allow for limited data searching and restructuring, using functionalities like "find", "sort", or "transpose". For example, in order to find out the number of test-takers who obtained a particular score, you can sort the records by score (lowest to highest or vice versa).

Although spreadsheets can be easily set up and maintained, the linearity of records limits their functionality. Therefore, more complex relational databases, such as Microsoft (MS) Access, SQL, or MySQL are frequently employed. Instead of creating one table with data records, MS Access is a database management system that allows for the creation of multiple tables that are related through a unique ID. Each table contains categories associated with a specific type of information. For example, in a language test database, one table can contain test-takers' background data, another can contain scores, and a third can contain rater information. You can create queries to search data across tables, which helps you structure data differently for the production of different types of reports and for conducting test analyses. In other words, using specific parameters in a query, you can create a new table containing information from each of the three tables (test-taker data, scores, and raters) that shows the L1s of all test-takers who obtained a particular score when rated by Rater 1. MS Access databases also allow for viewing, entering, and changing data through pre-determined forms, a functionality that minimizes database corruption due to direct access to the tables. In the first versions of the OEPT and the TOEPAS, MS Access databases were developed for data storage and retrieval. Although these databases seemed quite functional, one of the drawbacks was linking other test data with actual test response data.

Another database solution is MySQL, which is a new version of SQL (Structured Query Language). MySQL is an open source relational database management system (RDBMS), which means that the source code is available for its users, and modifications and customizations are encouraged as a way to constantly improve the application. MySQL has a client-server network architecture, where the MySQL server handles the database commands from a MySQL client interface. Figure 8.4 shows how you can use a web interface to enter and retrieve data from the database stored on the server.

Data management systems, such as MySQL, also offer the possibility to differentiate user roles and streamline the test data flow by alerting relevant users about the current status of data processing. The differentiated user role provides an opportunity for differentiated access to data based on user roles (e.g., administrator, rater, test-taker). Differentiated access means that the users obtain access only to the type of data that is relevant for their role in the system (see also Example 8.2). Raters access only the rating interface and test responses assigned to them, while administrators (admins) access the interface that gives them opportunity to enter and retrieve test administration data (e.g., registering test-takers, assigning raters, preparing reports) for which they are responsible. The supervisor administrator (superadmin) has access to all data with the permission to override entries from other user types, if necessary, while the admins have access only to the data for which they are responsible (see Figure 8.5).

Streamlining the data flow, on the other hand, is especially important when different types of users with different roles are involved in the data management process. (see Example 8.4) Receiving notification or an email to inform users when it is their turn to handle the data can simplify the data management process. Figures 8.6 and 8.7 provide examples of how the rating and result reporting processes can be streamlined.

FIGURE 8.4 Data management using a MySQL database system

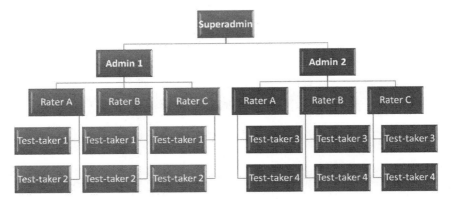

FIGURE 8.5 User roles

EXAMPLE 8.4 TOEPAS DATABASE USES

TOEPAS database evolution

In the first version of the TOEPAS, we used an MS Access database for test-taker and rater data, which had to be manually entered, while response videos and feedback reports were organized in folders on a network drive. To access specific test response videos or feedback reports, performing a database query was necessary to identify the responses and to find their storage location. Another drawback was the inability to fully specify differentiated access to data based on user roles (e.g., each rater accesses only the data related to test responses assigned only to him or her, or each test admin accesses data associated with his or her test center).

In order to overcome the difficulties related to linking the database with test responses and specifying user roles, a MySQL database was developed as part of the second version of the TOEPAS. To explain how MySQL functions in practice, the TOEPAS database can be accessed through a website, which serves as a client interface. By selecting different fields on the web interface, MySQL commands are sent to the database so that relevant data are stored or retrieved. For example, you can enter test-taker background data in relevant fields on the website, which are transformed into MySQL commands handled by the server on which the database is stored.

The MySQL solution also enhanced the TOEPAS rating and the result reporting workflows. When Rater A and Rater B enter the post-score, if their scores agree, then Rater A receives an email directing her to enter the final score and write the feedback report. If Rater A and Rater B disagree on the post-score, the admin receives an email about the disagreement so that the test can be assigned to Rater C for rating. When all raters agree, Rater A then receives the email to enter the final score and write the feedback report (see Figure 8.7). Once Rater A submits the written feedback, Rater B receives an email that the feedback is ready to be approved. If Rater B approves the feedback, then the admin is informed that the results (final score, video, and feedback) are ready to be sent to the test-taker. When the admin sends the report, the test-taker receives an email with information that the results could be accessed through a unique link (see Figure 8.8).

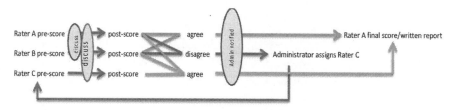

FIGURE 8.6   Example of a rating workflow (TOEPAS)

FIGURE 8.7   Example of a score reporting workflow (TOEPAS)

Although the MySQL database offers many opportunities for streamlined management of different types of data across different types of users, development of such a database requires advanced programming skills. If you do not have computer programmers on your test development team or your institution, you will probably need to outsource the design of your test database by hiring external software developers. As discussed in Chapter 3, external development of a database is a costly investment that takes time, but such development may be a viable option if the test is already established and recognized.

Finally, the type of data management system that you decide to use depends on your available resources (technology, expertise, funding), but also on the type and uses of the collected data, which will be discussed in the following sections.

Data uses

Before you read this chapter, you might have been tempted to think that your job is done after the test is administered and scored. However, the bulk of the work starts after test administration and data collection. In general, after test administration and scoring, the work on a local test involves (1) result reporting, (2) test analysis, (3) program evaluation, and (4) long-term research agenda and database management.

Result reports

In most testing contexts, after test administration, scoring, and data storage is complete, the first thing to do is to report the test results to different stakeholders. Depending on the context and purposes of your test, the stakeholders will vary (see Chapter 2). As you prepare the test score report, keep in mind that different stakeholders may have different levels of knowledge and familiarity with the assessment terminology, which is known as language assessment literacy. Thus, the language in the score report should be adjusted to the level of assessment literacy of the different users. In addition, test result reporting should be tailored towards the uses of test scores for different stakeholder groups by including different sets of test information or presenting the results from different perspectives (see also Example 8.2).

For example, an EFL end-of-semester achievement test for middle-school students will likely have the following stakeholders: students, parents, teachers, English course coordinators (loosely defined here to include head teachers or headmasters of the grade level), the school principal, and local education authorities. Therefore, the reporting system should differentiate the level of information accessible and useful for different stakeholder groups, which can effectively facilitate their use of the test results. In Table 8.2, we show a sample test result reporting system used for a municipal end-of-semester English achievement test for eighth graders in China (other test-related information can be found in Zhang & Yan, 2018). In this local testing context, the EFL teachers use the item

TABLE 8.2 A web-based test result reporting system for a municipal K-12 EFL test in China

Stakeholder	Test-related information
School principal	Ø Descriptive statistics for test and section score distributions[a]
	Ø Item difficulty, discrimination, test reliability[b]
	Ø Ranking[c] of individual classes in the school, district, and city
	Ø Ranking[c] of the school in the district and city
Teacher	Ø Descriptive statistics for test and section score distributions
	Ø Item difficulty, discrimination, test reliability
	Ø Students' mastery of target linguistic forms and functions[d]
	Ø Individual students' item and test scores
	Ø Ranking of individual students in the class, school, district, and city
	Ø Ranking[c] of the classes that they teach in the school, district, and city
Student and parents	Ø The student's item and total scores
	Ø Mastery of target linguistic forms and functions
	Ø Ranking of the student in the class, school, district, and city

Note. a. score distribution was reported for individual classes, the school, district, and city; *b.* item statistics were estimated based on item responses of all students within the city; *c.* ranking of classes and schools were based on the students' average scores on the exam; *d.* mastery of different forms and functions was estimated based on scores on items targeting that same form or function.

scores on the English exam to assess students' learning outcomes and to make instructional adjustments based on students' performance on the exams. In addition, teachers use item scores, total scores, school averages, and ranking to communicate with students and parents regarding the students' learning progress and the need for one-on-one tutoring after school or cram schools during summer and winter vacations. However, the school principal would more likely be interested in the overall score distribution on the English exam at School A, as well as the average scores on every English exam for individual classes at School A compared to the district and city averages.

If your test assesses speaking and writing skills, it is important to include a simplified version of your rating scale to explain the meanings of the scores. If the test is intended to have an impact on language teaching and learning, it might also be desirable to include comments from the raters to justify the scores and offer more fine-grained information about the test-takers' performances. This information can help language teachers (and learners) to identify the strengths and weaknesses of the test-takers' performance and to establish appropriate learning goals. For example, the TOEPAS reports include a score, a video recording of the performance, a written report, and an oral feedback session. The first version of the feedback report included descriptions of performance in terms of fluency, pronunciation, grammar, vocabulary, and interaction. The revised version of the feedback report, however, focused more on the functions of the test-taker's language in the EMI classroom so that awareness is raised about different language strategies in the classroom (Dimova, 2017). Contextualized feedback is more feasible in the local tests because the raters (often teachers in the program) are familiar with the specific language domains needed in the context of language use (see Figure 8.8).

Score reporting is also an opportunity to strengthen the connection between different test-related resources in the local context. Because local language tests tend to be constrained in terms of resources, they need the support of their stakeholders to make the test sustainable. Frequent communication with stakeholders can effectively enhance their understanding of the test purpose, item types, and score meanings. This kind of communication is also a recommended practice based on ethical considerations for language tests (see guidelines for practice EALTA, 2006; ILTA, 2007).

Item analysis

In most local testing contexts, the same test items are repeatedly used for test administration. Thus, as part of quality control, it is crucial to continue monitoring whether the items are doing a good job of placing examinees into the appropriate levels. For that purpose, item analysis is a necessary procedure that test developers perform after regular administrations. There are a range of statistical analyses that can be performed to examine the quality of the items (Bachman, 2004; Bachman & Kunnan, 2005; Brown, 2005). The more sophisticated

---

Name:
Test center: Centre for Internationalisation and
Parallel Language Use (UCPH)

Date:

[X] **No training is required.**
[ ] No training is required, but training may be
beneficial in one or more of the assessed
areas.
[ ] No training is required, but is strongly
recommended.
[ ] Training is required.

Result: 50

Feedback:

The lecture focused

You delivered your lecture effortlessly at an appropriate speech rate throughout the lesson – not too fast or too slow. You explained the content in an organized manner. You used effective transitions to provide structure, as well as communicative strategies, such as paraphrasing and illustration. In addition, you continuously recycled material and concepts using a wide variety of language for clarification, and you summarized each point before moving on to the next.

e.g. "Let's see if we can..."; "From an academic point of view..." **(guiding listener)**
e.g. "What you should probably take note of..." **(highlighting point)**
e.g. "This is the most simple"; "What is basically is saying..."; "Now it starts to become more complicated" **(clarifying and explaining)**
e.g. "This is the first one, this is the main debate they are putting on"; "That is a second layer; I don't think I will surprise you if I say the third layer..." **(signaling new concept)**
e.g. "Let's see if we can take a little bit of this one, too" **(transitioning to new topic)**
e.g. "Just like fish have to breath in water because they have gills, ordinary people have to have all ideas pulled down from top down, because they are idiots" **(using analogy for emphasis)**
e.g. "This is highly, highly problematic" **(using repetition to emphasize)**

You displayed a range of vocabulary for general, academic, and discipline-specific use for teaching. In addition, you used synonyms and varied vocabulary to convey nuances of meaning. Throughout your lecture, you emphasized important content and defined new terminology as it arose. There were issues regarding appropriate word choice, in particular your use of the words "things" and "stuff" as place fillers (these words lack nuance and sophistication), but this did not detract from your message.

FIGURE 8.8 Contextualized feedback report

analyses can provide fine-grained information regarding test items, but they also tend to be more technical and require larger sample sizes, making those analyses viable only for large-scale, high-stakes tests. Nevertheless, local test developers can gain a great deal of useful information about test items and test-takers from even the most basic type of item analysis. Here, we introduce three basic and yet vital statistics that all types of item analyses can generate: score distribution, item difficulty, and item discrimination.

- **Descriptive statistics** are the first step of most data analyses. A local language test, although much smaller in scale compared to large-scale tests, tends to have enough test-takers whose scores will show an approximately normal distribution. Therefore, the first step is to examine the score distribution in order to see if the distribution is roughly normal. When examining the score distribution, be sure to check the central tendency (i.e., mean, median, and mode), as well as the shape of the distribution (i.e., a histogram or bar chart of the scores). A normal distribution would indicate that, while some test-takers perform well on the test, there are others who did not perform as well. That also means that the test items are neither too easy or too difficult. This kind of distribution allows you to better differentiate test-takers across proficiency levels. If the test items are too easy or too difficult, then test-takers might tend to score close to the highest or lowest score point on the test, respectively. When either situation occurs, the distribution is considered to be skewed, which can make the results of the item analysis unreliable or misleading. Thus, examining the score distribution is very important.

- **Item difficulty** is the first item-level statistic that we typically look at. It is also called facility index. This statistic is computed as the percentage of test-takers who answer the item correctly. It ranges from 0 to 1, with a value closer to 1 indicating an easy item and a value close to 0 indicating a difficult item. If we assume a normal distribution of test-taker ability, then the difficulty level of a good item should be somewhere around 0.5. That is, around half of the test-takers get a particular item correct. In that case, we would say that the item targets the average proficiency level of the test-takers reasonably well. However, this is not necessarily the case, as we prefer to have items with a range of difficulty levels on a test so that we can target different proficiency levels within the test-taker population.

- **Item discrimination** is another important statistic when evaluating the quality of a test item. What this statistic tells us is the extent to which an item can differentiate between test-takers of high and low proficiency, assuming that all items are measuring the same or similar knowledge or abilities. This index can take two forms. One type of item discrimination statistics is called *discrimination index*. In order to compute the discrimination index, you need to rank the test-takers by their total score and equally divide them into three thirds. Then, you calculate the item difficulty for the top ⅓ and bottom ⅓ separately, and find the difference between the two. The other type of item discrimination statistics is a correlation coefficient between score on the item and the total score of the test, often referred to as *point-biserial correlation*. In both cases, item discrimination ranges from -1 to 1. Ideally, we prefer items that are higher than .25. If an item has close to 0 or even negative item discrimination, then it should be flagged for further scrutiny and revision. Sometimes, it could be that the answer key is wrongly specified, which is an easy fix. At other times, the problem could be more complicated, such as content that might alter the intended task responses on the item; then, it would require item writers to look further into this item or item type to see if content revision is needed. It should be noted that, when a test has different sections (e.g., reading, listening, speaking, and writing), item discrimination should be calculated within each section, as you will want to examine the quality of items in reference to other items that measure similar things.

In some cases, after a long period of testing, you might need to perform a more sophisticated analysis in order to examine more complex testing problems, such as whether a Japanese reading passage gives an unfair disadvantage to test-takers who speak Chinese as their L1, or whether all of the lexico-grammar items are measuring grammatical competence. In such situations, it might be helpful to include a statistician or data analyst on your team. Even so, having a basic understanding of the core concepts and statistics in item analysis can facilitate the communication between you and the data analysts to better address your needs.

Program evaluation

Test data are important for program evaluation. By definition, program evaluation is a systematic assessment of the effectiveness and efficiency of a particular program. The evaluation process tends to involve the collection and analysis of information from a variety of projects and activities conducted in the program. For a local language testing program, such information can include, but is not limited to, the appropriateness of test purpose, procedures of test development, quality of test items, summary of examinees and their test results, quality control procedures, research conducted on the test, and feedback from the test stakeholders. Test purpose and quality control are typically examined in a qualitative fashion, which can be done through conversations with stakeholders regarding their test score uses and documentation of the quality control procedures in place. In contrast, the other types of information are typically examined quantitatively, by analyzing the examinees' scores, performances, and feedback on various aspects of the test. While examinee scores and performances can be obtained from the test performance itself, test-taker feedback needs to be collected after the test administration through either a post-test questionnaire or semi-structured interviews. Local language tests should collect and analyze this information as part of the quality control procedures, so that the information can be regularly assessed in order to improve the effectiveness and efficiency of the test. For example, when the TOEPAS was introduced at Roskilde University, each test-taker filled out a survey after they had taken the test. The survey consisted of open-ended questions related to the dissemination of the information before the test (e.g., invitation, place/date, preparation, procedure), the actual test administration, and the usefulness of the oral and the written feedback. The survey also asked for suggestions for improvement.

A local language test can help with the evaluation of a language program, especially when the test is an entry and/or exit test embedded in the program. Language programs are asked to demonstrate the effectiveness of instruction and learning to their stakeholders. The desirable way to demonstrate learning is to assess language before and after instruction to show changes. Therefore, a local test embedded in a language program can be used to achieve this purpose.

Research, digitization of test data, and corpus development

While score reporting and program evaluation are regular procedures, local test developers should also consider data uses long-term. Unlike large-scale, inter-national tests that can generate a large amount of data in a single administration, local tests rarely have more than 500 test-takers per year. It is rather difficult to build a large database in a short period of time, but over time, it is possible to build a database sufficiently large enough to allow for analyses that require large numbers of subjects. As part of the test database, it is important to keep the demographic information about test-takers, in addition to test result records (see Table 8.1 for information about test data types). When there are multiple sources of data per examinee, it is important to create a unique ID or word string and include it in the name of all files for every examinee so that you can connect the different data sources for analysis (see section **Data flow** above for creation of test-taker IDs).

If the test performance data are not collected electronically, you will need to transcribe or convert the data into a computer readable format. The digitization of text and speech data may require different approaches. The digitization of essays into text data varies, depending on the format of the raw data. If an essay test is delivered on paper, then it is necessary to hire human transcribers to convert the handwritten essays into text files. There are also image processing technologies (e.g., the OCR) available that can automatically recognize handwriting and con-vert it to text files. However, if you are assessing a second or a foreign language (L2), it can be more challenging to use this kind of technology because it is based on natural language processing techniques and machine learning algorithms. These algorithms recognize words based on predictions from word collocations and the probability of co-occurrence of word strings. While these models can be quite accurate for first language (L1) data, their accuracy is much lower for L2 data because considerably greater variability is often present, depending on language proficiency and learner error. When used to convert L2 writing, the algorithms may either fail to recognize words or automatically correct grammatical errors. Auto-correction of errors can be detrimental to the quality of the data, as these errors constitute an important source of information for analysis in L2 research. Therefore, digitizing essay data requires time. In contrast, managing test data col-lected on a computer is much easier because the essays can be saved electronically. However, it is better to save the essays as .txt files, as this is the format that is most compatible with different text processing tools and algorithms.

Digitization of speech data is slightly different and potentially more time-consuming. First, the speech samples should be recorded and saved after each test administration. However, for the purpose of speech processing and analysis, it is recommended that you save the speech files in .wav format, as it tends to contain the most acoustic information. This procedure will allow for more kinds of speech analyses. While recording and storing the speech files is not difficult, it can be time-consuming to transcribe the speech samples. However, transcripts can reveal information about the quality of speaking performance, as well as the acoustic information of speech, and oftentimes, you need to use both sources of data in tandem to answer your research questions. That said, it is not necessary to transcribe all of the speech samples if you have a larger test-taker population. Speech corpora tend to be much smaller than text corpora because of the complexity involved in speech processing techniques and the rich information that speech provides. Thus, you may want to consider selecting a stratified sample of benchmark performances and have them transcribed. If you keep this as a regular practice, it will be possible to build a sizable speech corpus in just a few years. For example, as part of the OEPT validation research, we used test data to analyze the characteristics of speaking fluency across the different OEPT scalar levels and across speakers with different language backgrounds (for more information see Ginther, Dimova, & Yang, 2010).

Although building a test performance corpus for local language tests can be time-consuming, the kinds of data included in the corpus can be unique and high in quality. Because the test administration is standardized, the performances in a test corpus are more consistent in terms of tasks and response conditions. Therefore, it is suitable for more in-depth investigations than other natural language corpora collected from non-controlled environments. In addition, because the corpus is built upon a local language test, it can be used to address all sorts of interesting questions regarding the local context (Barker, 2012).

Summary

This chapter focused on the local test data flow, which includes (1) collection of different data types (test-taker background information, responses, scores), (2) storage and management of test data, and (3) data uses for result reporting, item analysis, program evaluation, and research. Collection of relevant data and the establishment of a well-structured database facilitates result reporting and ongoing test analysis for quality assurance. Digital technology enhances test data storage, management, and use, and so you may want to consider digitizing paper-based written responses or taped speech responses for long-term research. We would emphasize, however, the importance of ensuring that the data collection, storage, and use comply with the personal data protection laws in your context.

Further reading

Davidson, F. (2000). The language tester's statistical toolbox. *System*, *28*(4), 605–617.

Davidson (2000) discussed procedures and purposes of statistical tools that are used for common activities in developing language tests, as well as for analyzing and managing test data. The statistical methods are based mainly on Classical Test Theory and Item Response Theory. The author also introduces computer software that can perform each statistical analysis method, categorized into three tiers: computer spreadsheets (e.g., Excel); statistical packages (e.g., SPSS and SAS); and specialized software (e.g., FACETS and Bilog). The author stresses the importance of meaning interpretation of statistical analysis and warn against statistical determinism in language test development, clarifying the preference of statistical simplicity over complexity. The author recommends combined uses of statistical and non-statistical evidence (e.g., expert judgment) in evaluating and making decisions on educational quality of language testing and test tasks, reminding us that the ultimate goal is to develop and implement valid assessments.

Shin, S., & Lidster, R. (2017). Evaluating different standard-setting methods in an ESL placement testing context. *Language Testing, 34*(3), 357–381.

Shin and Lidster (2017) examine three commonly practiced standard-setting procedures of making cut-off score decisions: the Bookmark method, the Borderline group method, and cluster analysis, which are differentiated by their orientations (i.e., test-centered, examinee-centered, and statistical orientation, respectively). Motivated by the issue of frequent discrepancy among the different methods in cut-score decisions, the authors investigated validity and reliability of placement cut-offs that each method derives in the context of an intensive English program at a large US public university. The analysis revealed that each method resulted in significantly different cut-off scores, which calls for a more rigorous selection process. The authors provided strengths and weaknesses of each standard-setting approach and, in particular, noted procedural and internal issues of using cluster analysis for placement tests in programs with fixed curricula in English for academic purposes contexts. Suggestions for improving the Bookmark and the Borderline group method were also made.

Zenisky, A. L., & Hambleton, R. K. (2012). Developing test score reports that work: The process and best practices for effective communication. *Educational Measurement: Issues and Practice, 31*(2), 21–26.

Zenisky and Hambleton (2012) discuss the development of score reports and reporting practice to advance clear and meaningful communication of interpretable test scores with various stakeholders, including non-professionals. The authors begin by reviewing the recent empirical research-based effort that systemize and synthesize score reports, development methods, and scoring approaches under the influence of the passage of the No Child Left Behind Act. The focus of the review is on current and recommended best practices concerning the development process, design, format, contents, ancillary materials, and dissemination of score reports. The authors further introduce a score report development model that guides design and validation with seven principles to meet non-professionals' information and usability needs. For future directions, the authors stress the need to investigate the areas of online reporting, subscore reporting, and practitioners' understanding and use of reports.

References

Amazon Web Services (AWS) – Cloud Computing Services. (n.d.). Retrieved from https://aws.amazon.com/

Asia-Pacific Cooperation. (n.d.). APEC privacy framework. Retrieved from www.apec.org/Publications/2005/12/APEC-Privacy-Framework

Australian Government. (n.d.). Notifiable data breaches. Retrieved from www.oaic.gov.au/privacy/notifiable-data-breaches/

Bachman, L. F. (2004). *Statistical analyses for language assessment*. Cambridge: Cambridge University Press.

Bachman, L. F., & Kunnan, A. J. (2005). *Workbook and CD for statistical analysis for language. Assessment*. Cambridge: Cambridge University Press.

Barker, F. (2012)). How can corpora be used in language testing? In A. O'Keeffe & M. McCarthy (Eds.), *The Routledge handbook of corpus linguistics* (pp. 633–645). New York: Routledge.

Brown, J. D. (2005). *Testing in language programs: A comprehensive guide to English language assessment* (2nd ed.). New York: McGraw-Hill College.

Dimova, S. (2017). Life after oral English certification: The consequences of the Test of Oral English Proficiency for Academic Staff for EMI lecturers. *English for Specific Purposes, 46*, 45–58.

EALTA. (2006). EALTA Guidelines for good practice in language testing and assessment. Retrieved from www.ealta.eu.org/guidelines.htm

European Commission. (2019, July 24). EU data protection rules. Retrieved from https://ec.europa.eu/commission/priorities/justice-and-fundamental-rights/data-protection/2018-reform-eu-data-protection-rules_en

Ginther, A., Dimova, S., & Yang, R. (2010). Conceptual and empirical relationships between temporal measures of fluency and oral English proficiency with implications for automated scoring. *Language Testing, 27*(3), 379–399.

ILTA. (2007). International language testing association: Guidelines for practice. Retrieved from cdn.ymaws.com/www.iltaonline.com/resource/resmgr/docs/ilta_guidelines.pdf

US Department of Education. (2018, March 1). Family Educational Rights and Privacy Act (FERPA). Retrieved from www2.ed.gov/policy/gen/guid/fpco/ferpa/index.html

Zhang, C., & Yan, X. (2018). Assessment literacy of secondary EFL teachers: Evidence from a regional EFL test. *Chinese Journal of Applied Linguistics, 41*, 25–46.

9
REFLECTIONS

This chapter presents reflections on our experiences with test development and implementation in our individual contexts. We reflect on the challenges we have faced and the approaches that we have applied to address them. Due to the performance-based format of our tests, most of our reflections refer to scale development and revision, along with rater training. The reflections on the TOEPAS focus on issues related to designing a platform for data management, as well as the process of scale revision and the adequacy of scale descriptors, especially language norms. The EPT section continues with reflections on the scale revision process, including reflections on building a testing team, communicating with stakeholders, and considering the time needed to implement test revisions. The OEPT reflections emphasize the role of instructors in the design of scales, the rating of responses, and the embedding of the test in an instructional program.

Introduction

In the previous chapters, we discussed the essential considerations when making decisions about activities related to test planning, design, and implementation. Instead of proposing a single approach to test development, we emphasized that the type and order of activities in which you engage during the test development process will depend on the needs and the resources available in your local context. These unique characteristics of the local context may create unique dilemmas or challenges for test development, and you have to learn your lessons and find solutions from these situations. Thus, we would like to conclude this book by sharing our reflections on some of the dilemmas that we experienced while developing and revising our tests, as well as the lessons that we learned in the process.

Due to the performance-based format of our tests, most of our reflections refer to scale development and revision, along with rater training. Although we shared some experiences in the development of the three tests, we each reflect on the most salient aspects of test development, implementation, and grounding in our particular contexts. The reflections on the TOEPAS focus on issues related to designing a platform for data management, as well as the process of scale revision and the adequacy of scale descriptors, especially language norms. The EPT section continues with reflections on the scale revision process, including reflections on building a testing team, communicating with stakeholders, and considering the time needed to implement test revisions. The OEPT reflections emphasize the role of instructors in the design of scales, the rating of responses, and the embedding of the test in an instructional program. We hope that these points will provide some support, either technical or emotional, whenever you feel perplexed, frustrated, or even discouraged in your efforts to develop your own test.

Some reflections on the revision of the TOEPAS

Slobodanka Dimova, Associate Professor, Centre for Internationalisation and Parallel Language Use, University of Copenhagen

I joined the TOEPAS testing team in 2012, three years after it was first developed as part of the UCPH strategy that outlined a parallel language use strategy that stipulates the use of Danish and English in the educational programs at Master's level. To implement the strategy, the UCPH management had to ensure that the teaching staff had sufficient English language proficiency to cope with the demands of English-medium instruction at the university. Taking into consideration the marketization of higher education, UCPH also needed to show that the EMI programs at the university are comparable to programs at anglophone universities.

As mentioned in Chapter 3 (see Example 3.2), the test method for the TOEPAS, which is based on a simulated lecture, was designed using needs analysis across different university departments. The development of the TOEPAS rating scale entailed an extensive review of numerous scales that were used for assessment of speaking across a variety of academic contexts, as well as theoretical descriptions of the speaking construct. At that time, the "native speaker" norm was widely represented in level descriptors of speaking scales, and in the University's branding, the "well-educated native speaker" norm was established. We adopted that norm for the TOEPAS.

In the first version of the TOEPAS, an analytical scale with five different categories (fluency, pronunciation, grammar, vocabulary, interaction) was adopted. The level descriptors for each category were developed by the testing team relying on the expertise of individual team members. For example, the development of descriptors for pronunciation was led by a team member with expertise in phonetics. The purpose of the scalar descriptors was not only to assign scores to the observed performances, but also to write up formative feedback reports that test-takers receive alongside their scores.

An MS Access database was developed to keep the TOEPAS test data in an organized manner. The flow of data consisted of several stages. The test-takers registered to take the test via an online registration form, which the TOEPAS administrator entered in the MS Access database. The raters entered the scores they assigned in the rating form, which was available in paper version. The administrator collected the completed rating forms and entered the scores in the MS Access database. The TOEPAS coordinator accessed the database to perform queries in order to find the relevant performances for rater training and data analysis.

Five years after the implementation of TOEPAS, several issues were raised regarding the scale and data management. The following points refer to those issues and our decisions on how to address them.

Take one step at a time when developing an online test platform

One challenge we experienced was related to the development of a stable test database. The data flow system we had in place (i.e., paper forms and MS Access database) was problematic because it required a lot of administrative work. Furthermore, the database could easily be compromised, and the database management had to change. When we discussed these issues with the IT specialists at UCPH, the solution they proposed was to hire a software developer from UCPH that they recommended who would develop a relational database accessible through an online interface. In our first meeting with the software developer, we explained all the different types of test data we collect (e.g., test-taker data, scores, videos, feedback reports) and all the different uses of the database (e.g., data storage, score reporting, rater training). After a year of meetings with the software developer and huge costs, we realized that the database solution offered to us failed to serve our needs because it was not user-friendly and could not relate to the different types of data input, especially saving and retrieving videos. Therefore, we had to cancel the contract with the software developer from UCPH, and upon recommendations from the IT specialists, we hired a software developing firm.

This time, the communication with the software developers was mediated by an IT specialist because he could explain our database needs using the relevant IT terminology. Another difference in our approach was that the software development was planned in stages spread out in a period of one year. In the first stage, we only defined the user roles so that the basic architecture of the database could be established. In the second stage, decisions were made about how to relate the different types of test data (e.g., numerical, string, texts, video files) that need to be stored and retrieved from the secure server. In stage three, the fields, buttons, and dropdown menus that relate to the alphanumeric data were created and appropriately labeled. In the following stages, data reporting tools were designed, and the automatized email updates to relevant users at different stages of the testing process were set up. Then, we trialed the platform several times in order to check whether the data flow functioned as expected. The database platform was updated several times based on the bugs identified during the trials before it became operational in 2017. In the next stages, we plan to develop a rater training interface, which will relate rater training data to the existing database platform.

Identify the language norms that are appropriate for your context

The analyses that led to the development of the TOEPAS focused on identifying the appropriate tasks and the needs of the EMI teachers and programs, but they failed to take into consideration the English as a lingua franca (ELF) context of the UCPH. Given that UCPH is traditionally a non-Anglophone university and that most teachers and students are L2 speakers of English, the need to reconsider the "well-educated native-speaker" norm and the emphasis on pronunciation and grammar accuracy became apparent. However, selecting adequate norms for an ELF context was not an easy feat. The uses of English in ELF contexts appear characterized not only by structural variations of the language at morphological and phrasal levels, but also the central communicative discourses appear based on negotiation of meaning and practices of mediation (Hynninen, 2011; Mauranen, 2007, 2010, 2012; Ranta, 2006). The revision of the TOEPAS became quite challenging because we were uncertain of how to deal with the tension between the observed variation of norms in the ELF context and our need to standardize the scale (Dimova, 2019).

Based on additional interviews with EMI teachers, analysis of the video recordings with performances at different proficiency levels, and previous research findings regarding pragmatically effective speakers in the EMI classroom (Björkman, 2010; Suviniitty, 2012), we decided to remove the native speaker reference from the scale and to revise the scalar categories to reflect the pragmatic strategies lecturers use when they teach. Some of the new categories we added include descriptors related to lecturers' abilities to discuss material effectively through summaries, examples, or emphasis of important points, as well as their abilities to deliver their lectures in an organized and structured manner exploiting different types of explicit and implicit cohesive devices. Although we let some structural linguistic descriptors (e.g., grammar, syntax) remain, we made sure they were hugely deemphasized (Dimova, 2019).

Technical descriptors are not necessarily good descriptors

The analytical scale descriptors also needed revision because some of them were too technical, and some raters and test-takers had difficulties understanding them. When we asked test-takers to explain what terms like "discourse markers", "sound contrasts", "pragmatic meaning", and "hesitation" meant, they could not relate them to their own speech production (Dimova, 2017). In order to ensure consistent interpretation of descriptors by the raters, as well as improved comprehension of the formative feedback for the test-takers, we decided to either remove the technical descriptors or to use them together with explanations. For example, although "intonation" may be a more precise linguistic term, "speech melody" seems more comprehensible for test-takers.

Another issue with technicality was identified with the content of the written feedback report for test-takers. The first version focused on performance descriptions based on the five scale categories (i.e., fluency, pronunciation, grammar, vocabulary, and interaction). When we analyzed test-takers' uses of the feedback report, we realized that the test-takers, i.e., the EMI teachers, could not identify the implications of the feedback for their teaching in the classroom (Dimova, 2019). Moreover, the feedback had the negative effect of reinforcing their insecurities related to native-like pronunciation and grammar.

In order to communicate the feedback to the test-takers, we decided to contextualize the descriptions of test-takers' performance by using references to the EMI classroom. In other words, we emphasized the role of different language characteristics and strategies in teaching a linguistically diverse student body. This approach also allowed us to discuss the interaction of different aspects of the performance in relation to classroom communication. For example, instead of describing test-takers' fluency and then their pronunciation, we refer to both speech rate (fluency) and pronunciation, as well as other strategies like repetition and emphasis, in relation to intelligibility.

These reflections about the rescaling of TOEPAS have dealt with scale descriptors and norms. The following section continues with reflection on rescaling, but with a focus on building the testing team, communicating with the stakeholders, and considering local resources for test revision.

Some reflections on the EPT scale revision process

Xun Yan, Assistant Professor, Department of Linguistics, University of Illinois at Urbana-Champaign

When the EPT was launched in 2001, it was a day-long integrated writing test that asked test-takers to compose a first draft in the morning and return in the evening to revise and submit the final draft. EPT was the only university-level ESL writing placement in the US that elicited writing performance in a process-based, multiple-draft approach. The number of test-takers was somewhere between 100 and 200 students per year, and all the tests were administered within a one-week window before the start of each semester. The test-takers enjoyed this relatively stress-free testing process and having the opportunity to meet other students after they arrived on campus. The test worked well for placing students, along a 3-point scale, into different levels of writing courses. However, while the format of the test is authentic, it became less practical over the years. The number of students increased by ten times to approximately 2,000 students per year; the day-long testing model became inefficient at accommodating all the students within the allotted one-week time window. In addition, the average language proficiency of ESL students at UIUC has increased over time, and the range of proficiency has also shrunk. Over the years, the ESL program where the EPT is housed has trimmed the rating scale from five levels to two that only classify students into higher and lower levels. While trimming the scale increased the efficiency of scoring to a certain extent, since raters only have to choose between two levels, it loses the ability to provide more fine-grained information about test-taker performance. As the descriptors were all in relative terms (higher vs. lower level, more vs. fewer errors), the scale does not offer much useful information about the test-takers to the instructors. Under this backdrop, we started a three-year test rescaling project that was accomplished through tester-teacher collaboration. The rescaling process and the resultant scale have been described in different chapters throughout this book. In this section, we provide some reflections on the rescaling project, discussing what we have learned and what we wish we could have avoided.

You cannot develop a local test alone

You might not find this lesson surprising by the time you have reached this point in the book. Indeed, you should not, and we did not expect it to bear repeating in our own experience. However, one of the major challenges in the revision of the EPT was getting the personnel required to do it. When we requested additional positions for a test coordinator and research assistants to help with managing the test, the response from the different levels of administration was something to the effect of: "You are a professional language tester; you should be able to do it by yourself!" No one can develop a test single-handedly, let alone those who might have only recently found the time and courage to take on the task. We went to many meetings and repeatedly informed administrators that developing a local language test is not a solo performance. What we realized from this experience is that, while most stakeholders recognize the value of the test, they are not all familiar with the amount of work and effort involved in developing and running a test. Therefore, this needs to be communicated to them as early as possible in the planning stage of test development (see Chapter 3 for information about test development). A sufficiently-staffed test can run seamlessly, with each step latching onto the next, all the way from item development to score reporting. However, an understaffed test will likely experience backlogs, especially in scoring, with constant requests for score reports, many emotionally charged, from different stakeholders (e.g., course coordinators who need the scores to be in the system for course placement; undergraduate advisors who need the scores to provide early advising sessions to students for course registration). Thus, an effective local language test should be carefully budgeted for additional personnel from the beginning.

You do not have to change the whole test at once, even if that is the long-term goal

Besides concerns with personnel and budget, when revising the test, I was faced with the question of whether I should wait to develop a completely new test at once or make changes bit by bit. There is no absolute advantage to taking one approach over the other, and you should choose according to the assessment questions at hand and the resources available. I started with the former, even though I had very limited resources. This proved to be unproductive: I intentionally stayed away from any connection to the old test and spent a month with three core members contemplating a new test to achieve different purposes the local test could fulfill. At first, we all felt excited about the prospects of a new test for the ESL program. However, that feeling quickly wore off, as we kept adding design features to the test at every meeting, until it soon became an impossible task. Eventually, we compromised (which helped us to keep our sanity) by only changing the scale and examining the need for further changes after the new scale was in use for a while. Incremental change is possible for local language tests as the stakes are relatively lower and tolerate ongoing test development. If you have a similar dilemma in your own context, then you should consider developing the test bit by bit rather than all at once, even if that is the long-term goal.

All tests have a shelf life; do not be pressured to develop a "perfect" test that will last forever

Another challenge during the rescaling process, which was more of an emotional one, was that I was reluctant to change a test with unique features and a long history. For a while, after I took on the rescaling project, I was struck by the fear that the new test may not be as effective as the old version once was, and that it might not last long and need revision within a few years. What's worse, at the early stages of the rescaling project, this pressure to make a "perfect" test made me afraid of – and resistant to – any negative feedback from the stakeholders, and even some core members of the development team. As I look back on the rescaling process, I could have avoided a couple of rounds of scale descriptor refinement had I lowered my "affective filter" and accepted the feedback from other members. To some extent, this feeling is inevitable; you might have the urge to impress stakeholders with your new design or product as a way of demonstrating your expertise, or you might look anxiously for consensus within the development team to hasten the development process in order to save time or money (or both). This feeling only started to fade after I saw how well the new test worked and received positive feedback from the stakeholders a couple of years later. You might feel similarly when developing your own test. If this is indeed the case, do not feel guilty, as it is human nature to compare the effectiveness of what came before with whatever immediately follows; however, be assured that your test, if designed to address the local assessment needs, will eventually bring positive results, even if you need to tweak it here and there along the way. In contrast, an old test is bound to have trouble addressing new assessment needs, even if it worked well in the past. Your goal should not be to develop a test that will last forever; instead, you should aim to design a test that addresses the current assessment needs of the local context.

The feelings of uncertainty will weaken and eventually disappear after you see the positive changes that the new test brings.

When introducing the new test, expect pushback and give it some time to settle in

After the new scale was drafted and piloted within the development team, we introduced the scale to the rater community within the ESL program. While we anticipated questions and concerns about the differences between the old and new scale, we underestimated the pushback we would receive from the rater community, despite general excitement about the improvement that the new scale would bring. Many raters felt reluctant to use the new scale, even those who had suggested changes to the old scale during the planning stage. The pushback was so strong that some raters remained quiet throughout the entire semester of rater training. The raters' pushback was also reflected in their rating performance during the initial rounds of training. Although rater performance improved substantially over the course of the semester, the raters maintained a rather negative feeling about the introduction of the new scale.

While it was a disheartening experience for the scale development team, in the ensuing semesters, the amount of negative energy surrounding the new scale gradually decreased. Instead, we started to hear comments and conversations from the raters about how the new scale matches the range of writing performance on the test better and how it also made them view student performance in class differently. This shift in the raters' reaction took time, but it brought about a stronger sense of achievement and comfort than if it had occurred during the first semester. Now that three years have passed since the introduction of the new scale, rater performance has increased substantially from the first semester, and rater training has become a less fraught process. Looking back at this experience, we feel that the initial pushback was perhaps inevitable, as we were introducing changes that required time and commitment from the raters. These changes had an impact not only on their rating practice but also on the courses they teach. However, as the test settled in and the positive changes became more apparent, the raters eventually embraced the new scale. Just remember, you need to give your new test a bit of time to settle in to your local assessment context, and expect some emotional turbulence from the raters or other stakeholders during the transition stage.

There is nothing in assessment development and use that is completely new from teaching, although it takes a different perspective

As we collaborated with teachers to develop and refine the scale descriptors, we frequently heard from them (and non-testing colleagues in other contexts) that assessment is not relevant to their daily job responsibilities. This statement can result from the impression that language testing and assessment requires a strong background in statistics, coupled with the fear that they do not have the ability to model large sets of quantitative data. Such attitudes are reflective of a rather narrow view of what language testing involves. In fact, teachers' or local members' assessment literacy should not be underestimated. There are many elements of language testing that are inseparable from teaching and learning. We might even argue that teachers assess all the time when they teach. In the context of the EPT, the new scale is impossible without feedback from the teachers, who helped refine the scale in such a way that the descriptors became more user-friendly and interpretable to other stakeholders. Moreover, inspired by the changes to the rating scale, a committee of teachers in the ESL program was formed and tasked to redesign the rubric used for classroom assessment and to develop a norming session for the rubric. At first, one of the committee members joined our development meeting and the language testing reading group at our institution to brush up her assessment knowledge so that she could develop the rubric in an informed way. During meetings and conversations, she realized that there is nothing in assessment development and use that is completely new for language teachers. It is just that, when thinking about tests, the principles for assessment practice and the quality of the test are prioritized.

Some reflections on the development of the OEPT

April Ginther, Professor, Oral English Proficiency Program, Department of English, Purdue University

I began as the director of the OEPP in 2001. My work as a program administrator has been rewarding and interesting because I have been able to contribute to the development of a language test within a local instructional program. We have often been under pressure to produce impressive results quickly. Some efforts work well and can be completed quickly; others do not. Managing development efforts becomes easier when all involved have obtainable objectives linked to specific time periods (e.g., one-, three-, and five-year goals). Having a variety of goals and time periods for short- and long-term accomplishments relieves some of the pressure and invites more realistic planning.

Back in 2001, our first task was to build a new test. We wanted to make something totally new – a computer-based, semi-direct test of oral English proficiency for prospective international teaching assistants. The task presented challenges, but we were optimistic. First of all, we knew that we would need to develop a computer-based platform, test content, item and screen designs, and multiple forms. We concentrated on those tasks first. We then turned towards the scale, practice tests, test specifications, and rater training materials. The list of tasks grew and grew! We had to seriously attend to the database. Later, we realized that we needed a rater training platform and a volunteer application. Tucked into all these activities were two complete revisions of the platform and complementary/opportunistic revisions of the content of the OEPT.

Overall, our original optimism has been rewarded, but our confidence has been tempered. What we thought would proceed smoothly and quickly, with a clear end in sight, was revealed as an ongoing process. Once started, test development never ends (consider the different versions of the TOEFL). Revising an existing test or developing a new one is like inheriting or building a house. After a while, you realize that the house owns you as much as you own it, and that there's always something that needs attention.

We (grad student instructors and staff) began conducting research early on. OEPT data has been used by student researchers in Second Language Studies, Linguistics, Speech and Audiology, and Education. Other studies have taken a while to complete and have been dependent on the continued interest of graduate student researchers (e.g., Ginther, Dimova, & Yang, 2010). In the past twenty years, the OEPP has produced a prodigious amount of instructional materials and test data, most of which remains underutilized. There is never enough time.

Despite the fact that there's always too much work, the rewards can be great. As stated in previous chapters, the OEPT was developed to replace the SPEAK, retired versions of the Test of Spoken English (Educational Testing Service, 1980a, 1980b). SPEAK items represented generic contexts, and we had the opportunity to represent our local context in our development of its replacement. OEPT items/tasks are always introduced with the local context in mind (e.g., *In teaching and research contexts at Purdue, you will have many opportunities to introduce yourself … provide a brief introduction*). The test's orientation to the local contexts of use provide test-takers with a short but meaningful introduction to instructional research contexts at the university. For many, this is the only introduction that they will receive before they start teaching. Because many will be assigned teaching duties in the following week, and because those who pass have limited options for support, we have always rated conservatively. We argue that, all things considered, the best outcome is for test-takers to fail and then receive support. So far and for the most part (there's always some noise), both students and graduate advisors agree. However, the extent to which test-takers, graduate advisors, and program administrators support instruction remains an area of ongoing scrutiny and negotiation. Winning that argument means that the test and program must stand on their merits and be seen as enhancing student opportunities.

Shelter as structure

Like local language tests, local language programs occupy an in-between, intermediate space where instructors introduce and guide students from sheltered into increasingly unsheltered contexts of language. Most of us welcome shelter, especially hard-pressed international students, but perhaps their international and domestic instructors welcome it even more; the metaphor of *program as shelter* works best when the program provides shelter for everyone.

Because we spend so many hours at work, the importance of having a comfortable, productive, engaging work environment cannot be underestimated. We reside in a field that is associated, for better or worse, with teaching and service, where incentives and rewards are limited. Instructors are the central players. When they are convinced that they are adding value for their students, the students tend to agree. Providing common structures for instructors goes a long way for creating an environment that feels like a shelter for both instructors and students. Instructors want to experiment and come up with creative interventions for classroom challenges; at the same time, being excellent students, they want to come up with the right answers.

We have found that the 50/50 rule works well for providing a foundation, allowing experimentation, and encouraging adaptability. Assigned, common activities (conversations, presentations) occur on half of the days that students are in class, and teachers are free to develop or select activities for the remainder. Instructors may select from a library of tried-and-true teaching activities, organized by week and theme, that we have collected over the years and are available in the OEPP Course Reader and Instructor's Manual (Haugen, Kauper, & Ginther, 2019).

Instructors are usually fairly busy, many are overworked, and all are underpaid. The development of a local test requires realignment and reassignment of work duties; program instructors, staff, and administrators must accept additional responsibilities and contribute to test development and administration for a local test to function. OEPP instructors, who had experience training teaching assistants, were central to the development of OEPT tasks and the OEPT scale (actually, graduate instructors were the only labor available). Fortunately, we have been able to adjust workloads along with instructors' changing roles and responsibilities. For example, we were able to reduce instructors' class hours to make room for the hours they would be needed to rate exams. Instructors appreciated their lighter instructional loads and the value of their dual instructor/rater roles because of the training involved (they may serve as program administrators and may need to develop tests and assessments) and because of the greater instructional coherence that can occur when testing is embedded. Instructors often accept rater responsibilities if/when they see that their involvement in rating tests improves practice, but adaptations and adjustments must be made.

Even with half of the schedule fixed, we still have a lot going on. One of the best ways we found to manage all activities seems obvious: providing a semester schedule for instruction and testing/rating (see appendix A). I used to think that schedules were about managing time, but now I think that they are primarily an expression of values: what merits space and time in the schedule indicates where the values of the program lie. Regularly scheduled activities provide the basis for technical reports (regular statistical analyses), annual reports for administrators (testing volumes, pass rates, class enrollments by department and college), and program newsletters (look what we've done for you lately).

Conduct rater training on a regular basis

Instructor/raters meet regularly in mentoring meetings and in rater training meetings. We have found that, when incorporated on a regular basis into instructors' duties, rater training can be highly effective. What is important is that training is less effective if conducted only as an introduction and/or a one-time fix. Raters have been found to perform well after initial training, and then diverge, but recalibrate and increase their effectiveness over multiple training/rating sessions. Large-scale tests usually require raters to calibrate to the scale by rating a previously rated set of exams before beginning a rating session.

Local programs can institute similar calibration practices by assigning sets of previously rated sets of exams as part of the regular rater training process. There are many ways to train raters. After experimenting with some, we now emphasize benchmark performances – those responses that will be most likely to elicit agreement. In our experience with OEPT rater training, we have also found it useful to ask raters to focus on why a performance was assigned a score rather than why an individual rater may disagree with a score assignment; this is another way to enhance agreement. Rater training can be tricky, especially in tight-knit communities. So, finding ways to enhance agreement is worth the effort.

Nevertheless, it is always tempting to focus on those performances that result in split scores to determine, *once and for all*, whether the performance is best identified as representing a higher or lower score. These conversations are always interesting, some of the best, but seldom resolve the underlying issues. Some performances will always produce split scores because they capture aspects of performance that lie between score points. Perfect rater agreement is impossible and undesirable. Some examinees will always fall on the margins, and raters will focus on different aspects of performance. Discussion of similarities and differences across examinee performance at the same and different levels of the scale are fascinating, sometimes problematic, always interesting, and never fully resolvable. Regular rater training can be something instructor/raters look forward to, but it may take a while to get there.

Extend the local scale from the test to classroom assessments and self- and peer-evaluations

Test developers and instructors may be tempted to create unique scales, rubrics, and guidelines for each test task or assessment activity; however, we have found that extending a single scale across assessment opportunities can produce great benefits. Herman (1992) argues that effective classroom assessment practices benefit when the use of scales and tasks can be extended and she recommends that instructors:

- design comparable, parallel tasks, based on pre-specified design characteristics (the same scheme can be used to assess, for example, Civil War history, immigration history);
- use uniform scoring schemes across disciplines;
- use the same assessment to derive holistic information for large-scale assessment and diagnostic information for improving classroom practice. (p. 77)

Translated to language programs, these guidelines mean that the same scale can be applied across items and classroom assessments. For example, the holistic OEPT scale is used to evaluate performance across different item types within the test (e.g., express an opinion, compare and contrast, or respond to a complaint), and also as the basis for the evaluation of classroom presentations. Evaluation and instruction overlap.

I am fortunate to be in a position where I direct both the test and the program, which has made it much easier to embed the OEPT in the OEPP. Coordinating across program directors and programs requires negotiation and makes the aligning of a test with a program more complicated. Despite complications and setbacks, however, when considering all aspects of my academic career, my experience as a program director is what I value most.

Conclusions

In the test development and analysis literature, most discussions focus on the principles of developing large-scale tests or classroom-based assessments, while the development of local language tests tends to be overlooked. Local language tests can be positioned at different points in the continuum between large-scale tests and classroom assessment and, hence, they may share characteristics with both; while local language tests undergo a certain degree of standardization, they are also used to inform classroom instruction. The central characteristic of local tests is their embeddedness in context, as they represent local language uses and local educational, professional, or cultural values.

Given the close ties of local language tests with the local context, language test developers may experience constraints related to a lack of material, spatial, and human resources, or unrealistic stakeholder expectations. On the other hand, local stakeholders may be interested and supportive when they are involved in the test development process and when they see that the subsequent use of the test benefits the community.

The primary aim of this book has been to raise awareness about the opportunities and challenges of local test development, but more importantly, to present the opportunities that language testers have for an improved representation of the characteristics of the local context. Our reflections highlight our individual contexts and our preoccupations and ongoing concerns. All things considered, we are confident that the potential benefits of local test development are well worth the effort.

References

Björkman, B. (2010). So you think you can ELF: English as a lingua franca as the medium of instruction. *Hermes–Journal of Language and Communication Studies, 45*, 77–96.

Dimova, S. (2017). Life after oral English certification: The consequences of the Test of Oral English Proficiency for Academic Staff for EMI lecturers. *English for Specific Purposes, 46*, 45–58.

Dimova, S. (2020). Language assessment of EMI content teachers: What norms. In M. Kuteeva, K. Kaufhold, & N. Hynninen (Eds.), *Language perceptions and practices in multilingual universities*. London: Palgrave Macmillan and Springer.

Educational Testing Service. (1980a). *Guide to SPEAK*. Princeton, NJ: Educational Testing Service.

Educational Testing Service. (1980b). *Test of Spoken English*. Princeton, NJ: Educational Testing Service.

Ginther, A., Dimova, S. and Yang, R. (2010). Conceptual and empirical relationships between temporal measures of fluency and oral English proficiency with implications for automated scoring. *Language Testing*, 27: 379–399.

Haugen, M., Kauper, N., & Ginther, A. (2019). *English 620: Classroom communication for international teaching assistants. Course reader and instructor's manual*. Cincinatti, OH: Van-Griner.

Herman, J. (1992). What research tells us about good assessment. *Educational Leadership*, *49* (8), 74–78.

Hynninen, N. (2011). The practice of 'mediation' in English as a lingua franca interaction. *Journal of Pragmatics*, *43*(4), 965–977. Doi:10.1016/j.pragma.2010.07.034.

Mauranen, A. (2007). Hybrid voices: English as the lingua franca of academics. In K. Flottum, T. Dahl, & T. Kinn (Eds.), *Language and discipline perspectives on academic discourse* (pp. 244–259). Cambridge: Cambridge Scholars Press.

Mauranen, A. (2010). Features of English as a lingua franca in academia. *Helsinki English Studies*, *6*, 6–28.

Mauranen, A. (2012). *Exploring ELF: Academic English shaped by non-native speakers*. Cambridge: Cambridge University Press.

Ranta, E. (2006). The 'attractive' progressive – Why use the -ing form in English as a lingua franca? *Nordic Journal of English Studies*, 5(2), 95–116.

Suviniitty, J. (2012). *Lectures in English as a lingua franca: Interactional features. Doctoral dissertation (monograph)*. University of Helsinki. HELDA E-thesis: http://urn.fi/URN:ISBN: 978–952–10–8540–6.

APPENDIX A

OEPT Review

Listen to each OEPT item response and provide descriptions of and comments about the student's performance. Complete the item, synthesis, and formative section prior to meeting with the student. Work on the goal section with the student in the first few weeks of the semester. Think about strengths as well as areas that need improvement and <u>describe these to your student during your first conference or tutoring session</u>. It is important that students understand why they did not pass the test and were recommended to take ENGL 620. You will also use this information while preparing goals and the Mid-term Evaluation.

Item Section

Item	Descriptions/Comments
1 News Headline NEWS	
2 Pros & Cons PROS	
3 Give Advice ADV	
4 Line Graph LG	
5 Voicemail VM	
6 Conversation CONV	
7 Short Lecture LECT	
8 Oral Reading READ	

Synthesis Section

Rate elements of oral proficiency using OEPT scale

Language Skills	Developing			Sufficient		Descriptions/ Comments
Intelligibility	35	40	45	50	55	
Overall Intelligibility						
Pronunciation						
Fluency/Pausing						
Stress/Intonation/ Rhythm						
Volume/Projection						
Speed						
Vocabulary						
Range						
Usage						
Idiomaticity						
Discourse Markers						
Grammar						
Word Order/ Syntax						
Verb Use						
Bound Morphology						
Article Use						
Other						
Listening Comprehension						

Formative Section: Based on the OEPT Review, indicate what seems most in need of improvement this semester. Be specific and indicate what resources will be used and how language skills will be worked on at the beginning of the semester. Expand and elaborate as necessary during the first weeks of the semester.

What specific language skills does the student want to improve?

Goal Section: By the end of September, finalize the three selected language skills for improvement and formalize weekly and/or daily task based goals for homework and Performance Goals for what is expected in PRs, ICs, and class/conference.

At Final Evaluation, rate achievement of goals by +, ★, or -.
  + = Has met the performance goal.
  ★ = Showing improvement and making good progress towards
      the performance goal.
  - = Showing little or no progress in meeting the goal.

	Language Skill	Task Based Goals (Practice Strategies for Homework)	Performance Goals (Outcomes)	Final Evaluation
1				
2				
3				

Core Language Skills	Mid-term Evaluation				Final Evaluation			
	35–40	45	50–55	Description of skills	35–40	45	50–55	Description of skills
Intelligibility								
Overall intelligibility								
Pronunciation								
Fluency/Pausing								
Stress/Intonation/Rhythm								
Volume/Projection								
Speed								
Vocabulary								
Range								
Usage								
Idiomaticity								
Grammar								
Word order/syntax								
Verb use								
Bound morphology								
Core Interactive Skills								
Indicating Comp.								
Seeking Clarification								
Providing Clarification								

Mid-term: Given the characteristics of the mid-term evaluation above, at this time, we believe this student:

___ is progressing satisfactorily. Continued progress at current level or above will increase the probability of certification at the end of this semester.

___ may benefit from additional semesters(s) of ENGL 620. (Students may take ENGL 620 up to three times in an effort to become certified)

PROSE SUMMARY COMMENTS (REQUIRED):

FINAL PROSE EVALUATION: Explain why you think this student should or should not be certified. If you believe the student should repeat 620, or if the student is borderline, please be explicit in your explanation.

English 620 PR 2 Self Assessment Name/date _____ Page 1: Rubric

time	TASK	35	40/45	50 Satisfactory	55 Superior
	Self Introduction	States name only.	States name and place of origin.	Some extra info about name, self, place of origin (see superior).	Pronunciation clues for name; what people call you. Native language. Something personal.
	English/ Communication statement	No mention of how to avoid miscommunication; no encouragement to ask questions.	States that English is 2nd language and tells audience to ask Qs if problems arise.	Tells audience to ask for clarification, repetition, examples, Qs of any kind related to language or to the presentation content.	Encourages and tells why, how, when audience and presenter can ask Qs and ask for clarification about language and the presentation content.

(Continued)

	Objective/ Purpose statements	No statements.	Ineffective statement(s) does not tell audience what they can expect to learn; vague.	Statements tell audience clearly what they can expect to learn.	Effective purpose and objective statements tell audience what they can expect to learn and observable outcomes.
	Preview outline	Doesn't preview outline.	States main points on the handout.	Uses discourse markers effectively and states main points of the outline.	Paraphrases main points of outline; consistent use of idiomatic discourse markers and inclusive language (we, let's).
XX	**Comprehension checks**	Doesn't stop for comprehension checks.	Any questions? Are you following? OK so far?	Do you have any questions about (*something specific you just talked about*)?	Asks specific questions that require audience to think and demonstrate understanding.
	Intro to topic	States topic and begins covering main points on outline.	Signals intro with discourse markers; simple intro but no "big picture" or background info.	Gives "big picture" and background information. Tries to relate topic to undergrad audience.	Gives "big picture"; links topic to audience's prior knowledge; makes topic interesting, appropriate to undergrads.
	Support (examples, illustrations, word origin etc.)	Insufficient quantity of support to aid audience in understanding.	Sufficient quantity of support but use and explanations are ineffective in aiding understanding.	Sufficient quantity of support; use and explanations are effective in helping audience understand concepts.	Good quantity and quality of support; variety of different types of support give audience a clear and broad understanding of concepts.

(*Continued*)

XX	**Q&A procedures**	Very little or no use of Q&A procedures.	Little or inconsistent use of Q&A procedures; unsuccessful clarifications.	Follows most procedures; mostly successful clarifications.	Follows all procedures all the time; successful clarifications.
XX	**Organizing language**	No use of organizing language.	Little or inconsistent use; unidiomatic language.	Adequate amount but occasionally unidiomatic or ineffective use of organizing language.	Consistent, effective and idiomatic use for intro, conclusion, all transitions between parts and topics; inclusive language (we, let's).
XX	**Eye contact**	Avoids eye contact (looks at board, computer, wall, notes).	Inadequate amount of eye contact; avoids part of audience; doesn't look at individuals.	Makes eye contact with each individual in audience, but not consistently throughout.	Makes EC with everyone throughout; maintains EC long enough to make personal connection but not too long as to make individuals uncomfortable.
XX	**Handout, Blackboard, Use of Visual aids**	Provides handout but missing some info; no use of board or screen.	Handout has outline, key terms, definitions; rarely or never refers to handout; little use of visuals.	Handout has all required info; refers to handout; writes and draws on board to aid audience comprehension or uses screen.	Uses board or screen to complement and enhance oral communication; effective use of handout to aid comprehension. Handout is well done.
XX	**Nonverbal communication: Use of space, gestures, facial expr.**	Stays in one spot; no gestures; blank or unpleasant facial expression.	Unnatural, confusing, or distracting movements or gestures; some facial expression.	Uses different parts of the room; gestures reinforce spoken points; pleasant or	Gestures complement and enhance spoken language; uses space and facial expression effectively to maintain

(Cont.)

				interested facial expression.	audience attention and to communicate directly to audience.
	Conclusion and Closing	No conclusion to outline; no closing to presentation.	Simple expressions to conclude or close (e.g. That's all).	Summarizes/ reviews main points to conclude. Closes presentation and thanks audience.	Concludes outline with interesting/ new info; closes presentation with idiomatic language and thanks audience.

Engl 620 **PR2 Self Assessment** Name/date _____ page 2

All pages are to be completed and handed in to your classroom instructor within one week of your PR 1. Type or write by hand. If writing by hand, use the back of the pages if necessary.

Page 1 Rubric: watch your presentation recording and highlight or underline descriptions of what you did.

Core skills: While watching your recording, evaluate your use of the following core skills by making an X to indicate a score for each item. Write comments about specific skills in the column to the right. (Read descriptions of the skills in the document: Evaluation Criteria/Language Skills found on Blackboard.)

Core skills	35	40	45	50	55	comments
Pronunciation						
Fluency/Pausing						
Rhythm/Stress/Intonation						
Volume/Projection						
Speed						
Grammar						
Vocabulary						
Seeking clarification						

Written comments about your overall PR1 performance and your ability to communicate successfully with the audience:

1. Strengths:

2. Weaknesses:

3. Plans for improvement for Presentation 3:

Engl 620 PR 2 Self Assessment Name/date _____ page 3

1. How did you **encourage** your audience to ask questions? Transcribe what you said.

2. How many **comprehension checks** did you make? _____ Transcribe two of your best comprehension checks (write the exact words you said):

3. **Q&A procedures**: for one of the questions you answered, transcribe a) the audience question, b) your restatement/clarification of that question, c)how you checked to see if you answered the question::

Question:

Your restatement:

Your check to see if you answered the question:

4. Transcribe one or two questions you asked (other than rhetorical questions):

5. How many times did you **rehearse** your presentation, actually speaking your sentences? _____

6. Did you rehearse your presentation before an audience?_____ If so, who were they?

Engl 620 PR 2 Self Assessment Name/date _____ page 4

7. **Transcribe 2 minutes of your presentation.**

INDEX